African American Religion
and the
Civil Rights Movement
in Arkansas

African American Religion and the Civil Rights Movement in Arkansas

Johnny E. Williams

University Press of Mississippi
Jackson

www.upress.state.ms.us

The University Press of Mississippi is a member of the Association of American University Presses.

11 10 09 08 07 06 05 04 03 4 3 2 1

∞

Library of Congress Cataloging-in-Publication Data
Williams, Johnny E.
African American religion and the civil rights movement in
Arkansas/Johnny E. Williams.
p. cm.
Includes bibliographical references and index.
ISBN 1-57806-545-3
1. African Americans—Civil rights—Arkansas—History. 2. Civil
rights movements—Arkansas—History. 3. African American civil
rights workers—Religious life—Arkansas. 4. African
Americans—Arkansas—Religion. 5. African American
churches—Arkansas—History. 6. Religion and
politics—Arkansas—History. 7. Arkansas—Race relations.
8. Arkansas—Church history. I. Title.
E185.93.A8 W55 2003
261.7'089'960730767—dc21   2002151813

British Library Cataloging-in-Publication Data available

Contents

PREFACE

Jesus Christ allows us to do things through his grace. All the things you may do in life, the dissertation that you're doing for your PhD., you're depending on God's grace to give you the strength to make the proper contacts, . . . to be able to bring all your stuff together to put it in proper form so that you can say to those persons . . . judging you or sitting in judgment of you in regards to the degree, here's the situation. Grace, grace. You [accomplish your goal] despite . . . those people who say you can't do it, the doubters. . . . I like grace because everything is possible through him. Even when you do wrong it's because he allows you to do it. . . . Whatever you accomplish, whatever goal you might have, whatever you fail to do, he allows us to determine our progress. . . . However far you go is dependent upon his grace.

—Arkansas Civil Rights Participant, 1991

The *grace* that this respondent spoke of was an integral part of my life growing up in Little Rock, Arkansas. My father, mother, and grandmother were very active members in the Baptist church, and had strong religious identities that helped our poor family of nine survive tough emotional and financial times. My parents and grandmother believed that it would be by the grace of God that we would overcome our situation. Eventually, we did. My two mothers (I include my grandmother as my mother since we called her Big Momma and she basically raised my five brothers and me while my mother and father each worked two jobs to keep our family afloat) and father, who was a Baptist deacon, instilled in me the desire for social justice and an inquisitiveness to understand why religion affected them in the way that it did. On numerous Sundays, Big Momma would "get happy" or "shout" after an inspiring spiritual song or sermon. She would run up and down the church aisles shouting, "Yes, Lord," or "Thank you Jesus." One day, as an eight-year-old, I mustered enough courage to inform my grandmother that her antics were embarrassing and asked her why she behaved this way during a song or sermon. Her response: "Honey, you can't control yourself when the

Holy Spirit is upon you. You just got to move." Somewhat older and wiser I am now starting to understand Big Momma's point that religious beliefs affect human behavior in ways beyond rational comprehension.

My grandmother's actions and explanations provided me with a nascent understanding of cultural meanings' sway over human behavior. The insight I gained from the beliefs and behaviors exhibited by my grandmother and parents in the Baptist church would later make me keenly aware of the inability of the prevailing social movement theory to explain culture's role in motivating and sustaining political participation. When I took a graduate social movements course in 1988, the predominant theoretical analyses of social movements acknowledged the importance of culture in the emergence of collective action, but maintained that the availability of resources (e.g., money, leaders, and facilities) were more important determinants in the launching and likely success of collective action. This perspective was called the resource mobilization approach. A variant of this approach, the political process theory, particularly piqued my interest. Although the political process theory acknowledged the importance of culture in facilitating social movements, it, too, like its parent theory, argued that culture is not sufficient in and of itself for initiating collective action. The theory claimed that movements are less the product of culture than beneficiaries of shifting political conditions that open up political and economic systems for change. I considered this approach overly rationalistic because it argued that since discontent is always present among aggrieved groups, the crucial constituent for translating grievance into action is the perception that instability within institutions creates vulnerability for change. By relying on shifting political conditions to explain variations in interpretation of social situations, this approach insufficiently focuses on the role of cultural meanings in directly and independently precipitating social protest. As a result, political process theory could not sufficiently explain why some people initiated social protest when political conditions and the availability of resources were limited. Given my experiences in the African-American church, it was apparent that it was a mistake for the political process model to downplay culture's (relationships, deeply felt commitments, aspirations, and hopes) impact on political participation. Consequently, I began thinking about the origins, development, and maintenance of the Civil Rights Movement in cultural terms. This interest, together with my belief that culture can be a powerful resource in defeating racial and social oppression, culminated in the writing of my dissertation, which was an important but preliminary starting point for my investigation of the relationship between culture and collective action, and in the more intricate and nuanced writing on cultural processes and social action embodied in this book.

In the course of writing this book, I frequently felt I had "bitten off more than I could chew." Trying to extrapolate from mounds of data the "nuts and bolts" of cultural processes that encourage or discourage people's involvement in political participation is tedious but rewarding work. While gathering the data for this book, I interviewed many interesting and thoughtful people who thought nothing of their contributions to the Civil Rights Movement. They viewed their activism not in terms of individual interests but as an obligation to better society for everyone, in particular future generations. Writing this book was cathartic because it allowed me to introspectively examine my self-conception as an African-American Arkansan whose understanding of reality was profoundly shaped by a devout family who required me to attend church four to five days a week. Regular church attendance as a kid led to religious service burn out. Nowadays I attend church when the spirit moves me or my mother coerces me into going. My mother and some of my religiously oriented brothers perceive my lack of religious engagement as a "backsliding" problem I need to resolve. Consequently, I am constantly engaged in a sort of battle of wits with my mother, brothers, and sisters-in-law over what they perceive as my chaotic but, I believe, logical thoughts on religion and society. My folks often ask me: how can you research and write on the effects of religion but shun the church and Jesus Christ? I always provide them with a succinct answer: "As a scientist and trained skeptic, it is hard for me to grasp that there is only one way to encounter God. The diversity found on this planet in terms of peoples, cultures, and living things, and in the universe with its infinite number of galaxies, planets, and stars suggests to me that there is an immeasurable number of ways of experiencing religion. The existence of this diversity suggests that my systematic examination of religion may be just another ritual for reaching God. So, it is problematic to imply that my research and writing about religion's effect on everyday life doesn't contribute something to our understanding of faith simply because I don't regularly attend church and profess my allegiance to Jesus." Despite our disagreement, my family frequently lets me know how excited and happy they are to have a family member who examines African-Americans' experiences in Arkansas.

This book was inspired by childhood memories of the Civil Rights Movement, especially its Black Power variant. As a child growing up in Little Rock after the Little Rock Central High school integration crisis, I attended elementary schools in the late 1960s and early 1970s that were exclusively black due to the slow pace of integration. Within this context, I became even more aware of the struggle for social equality and still recall the delight I felt when watching and listening to Daisy Bates or Martin Luther King, Jr., discuss civil rights on television. In the education arena, I also experienced black teachers who further buttressed my desire to learn. They instilled in me a sense of pride. These influences led me to believe, often to an absurd extent, that I could be an accomplished citizen in an illogical racist society. I discovered quickly that many people deemed my blackness an irreparable handicap.

My grandmother and parents, who had long endured racism, taught me to assess individuals on the basis of their actions rather than their words. My grandmother had encountered the repulsive manifestations of racism early in life. She and my grandfather, whom I never knew due to his early death, were raising their family of two boys and two girls in Carlisle, Arkansas, when my grandfather had an unfortunate run in with a white man. While he was playing the piano in a backwoods juke joint, a white woman became enamored with him and initiated flirtatious conversation. A white man confronted my grandfather and proceeded to punch him; in defense my grandfather picked up a nearby pitchfork and fatally wounded the man. After my grandfather delivered the fatal blow, other whites in the juke joint banded together to pummel my grandfather, leaving him for dead. Though my grandfather was near death, he survived but was subsequently run out of town. This experience left Big Momma with permanent emotional scars that she hid from my brothers and me. Her desire to protect us from racism's ugly effects led her to conceal her angst about whites and her family's experience in Carlisle until my brothers and I were teenagers. She believed that we could handle her confrontation with racism somewhat better as teenagers. When she told me of the family's encounter with racism's vulgarity, she suggested that the incident unnerved her so much that she decided to "forgive but never forget what whites did to her husband." Big Momma's commendable effort to forgive but not forget made such an indelible impression upon me that I made it one of my pillar principles. My interest in combating oppression through social movements is, therefore, both personal and intellectual.

Encouraged early on by my family's experiences with racism and by my civic and history teachers in secondary school to explore why and how black people are defined as "other" and excluded from participating in various institutions, I developed an interest in the role of history, politics, and religion in perpetuating oppression. Consequently I developed a ferocious appetite for political, historical, and religious information that blossomed during my higher education career. This quest for deeper knowledge and understanding of the oppression that African-Americans experience as well as their reaction to it inspired this book.

I argue that Christian beliefs are a fundamental factor in African American sociopolitical struggles. I in no way imply that religious beliefs are the only factor but that they are an important direct and independent element in mobilizing political participation. I have chosen to interrogate religion's effect on political participation because I believe that it can shed some light on some crucial sociopolitical issues confronting twenty-first-century social movement scholars. This analysis seeks to contribute to movement literature by studying how cultural sources of distinct meanings and patterns of interaction in religious institutions influenced African-American civil rights protest in Arkansas. Since a great deal of my argument revolves around the historical development of black religious ideas, I locate Civil Rights Movement activity in the broad sweep of the twentieth century in order to ascertain how events in Arkansas arose from a historical/cultural legacy. This book in some respects is an intellectual history of black religious ideas that culminated in the Civil Rights Movement in Arkansas.

It is my hope that this book will be a useful tool of clarification and illumination in the church and academy alike for all of those who are interested in understanding religion's effect on civil rights action. My book is but one person's attempt to explain how people who lacked political clout and economic leverage engaged in protest when the odds of their action succeeding were minuscule. In no way do I claim that my book's insights on religion and actions are definitive. It will not end all debate regarding culture's role in the initiation and maintenance of social protest. I do believe, however, that my findings will raise important questions about how social protest is generated and sustained in oppressive contexts.

ACKNOWLEDGMENTS

There are many people without whom I could have never completed this book. Singled out first for thanks are the civil rights activists who so graciously sat with me for hours recalling their activism. To all of you, I am forever indebted for providing me with remarkable insights into the dynamics of social protest. Also, I want to thank you for trusting me with your experiences and encouraging me to pursue my research with the same tenacity you demonstrated as activists.

I owe thanks to six people who were most essential in helping me shape the content of this work. Stephen Valocchi was a tremendous resource for substantive and theoretical insight throughout the course of this project. Jerry G. Watts (aka Biscuit) offered thorough analytical critique of my work, encouragement, mentoring, humor, skepticism, energy, and emotional support that no reasonable colleague except a friend would do. For helping to shape my intellectual approach about the book's thesis while a graduate student at Brandeis University, I thank Egon Bittner, George Ross, and Carmen Sirianni. These professors allowed me the freedom to think about the interrelatedness of politics, religion, and social movements in ways that challenged prevailing theories in sociology. The same can be said of Robert Hall (Northeastern University), who, as the outside reader of my dissertation on social movements, made me very much aware of African-American intellectual engagement with my topic.

In addition to these six, many other colleagues read and listened to partially developed ideas, read earlier drafts of chapters, and offered encouragement and intellectual stimulation that challenged me to think more critically about my work and to persevere. I offer my gratitude to former graduate but now professional colleagues Claire Reinelt and Hock Guan Lee, and to Aldon D. Morris, Cedric Herring, Richard Alba, Donald Cunnigen, Bernice McNair Barnett, Thomas Calhoun, and Dan Clawson. I am also deeply indebted to my supportive Trinity colleagues: Vijay Prashad, Raymond Baker, Noreen Channels, Donald Galbraith, Joan Hedrick, Stefanie Chambers, Maurice Wade, Barbara Sicherman, Dina Anselmi, and former Trinity colleagues Alondra Nelson, Willam "Hank" Lewis, and Salim Washington. Calm and even keeled, Margo Perkins added humor, focus, and adroitness to my writing sojourn.

In the course of writing both the dissertation and its book derivative, there were many moments I felt I had taken on more than I could handle. But I consistently received encouragement from my mother who provided me with the extra gentle coaxing I needed to continue my work. The memories of my grandmother's elation when my mother and father loaded the Ford station wagon to take the first member of her family to college gave me even more impetus to finish this book. To my immediate family I owe my deepest thanks and heartfelt gratitude for supporting me throughout my intellectual career.

Last but not least, I am grateful for the love and support of my life partner Elisabeth Ann Neiterman. Her emotional support, tenderness, and enthusiasm sustained me throughout the process of writing this book. Her copyediting skills were invaluable to an orthographically and grammatically challenged person like me. Elisabeth's faith in and support of my career has been steadfast. No words exist to adequately express my gratitude for her helping me to construct and articulate my thoughts and ideas in a coherent fashion.

INTRODUCTION

Since the repressive powers of segregation during the 1950s and 1960s made Civil Rights Movement participation a dangerous proposition, most African-Americans in Arkansas were afraid to involve themselves in any form of political activity. However, despite the certainty that they would be harassed by police, lose their jobs, and suffer from a host of other hardships, a small cadre of African-Americans found the courage to join the civil rights struggle to create and sustain a vigorous movement in Arkansas. A unique concern of social movement research involves understanding how dominated social actors mobilize, coordinate, and sustain protest against more powerful elites, authorities, or opponents. This study examines how culture found in indigenous social organizations like the church from the period of slavery through segregation provided repositories of meanings that motivated African-Americans to mobilize for civil rights action in Arkansas.

Most social science research conducted on the relationship between religion and political action suggests that religion is a pacifying agent that inhibits political mobilization (Myrdal 1944; Frazier 1964; Marx 1967; Chafe 1980; Reed 1986). Myrdal, a chief theorist of the "opiate perspective," noted that despite the occasional appearance of activist ministers, African-American churches "remain conservative and accommodating" in the context of political activism and protest (1944:877). Likewise, Frazier (1964) characterized religion as an accommodating agent that channeled African-American dissatisfaction with restrictions on their participation in the political process into surrogate church political activities. Thus he concluded, religion and the church have "left [their] imprint upon practically every aspect of Negro life . . . and [are] responsible for the so called backwardness of American Negroes" (Frazier 1964:90).

Marx (1967) conducted the first significant study on the influence of religion on African-American protest during the civil rights era. He found that African-American religion has a general pacifying quality that mitigates militant political action. Marx's survey data suggested that religious involvement "serve[d] as an accommodative opiate, producing a highly otherworldly focus and little concern with social change" (Hunt and Hunt 1977:3). Though Marx acknowledged that African-American religion motivated some religious people to participate in civil rights actions, he concluded that religion generally directs attention away from efforts at collective social change.

In his analysis of Jesse Jackson's 1984 presidential campaign, Reed (1986) suggests that churches encourage African- American acquiescence to existing social and political relations rather than provide foundations for African-American political activism. He argues that the antidemocratic orientation of the African-American church acclimates African-Americans to the "inexorable context of subordination and dispossession" (1986:59). Reed succinctly states that "it is clear that the church's functionality as an integrative institution, as well as its vaunted success as a source for hope in a temporal situation apparently hopeless, has been predicated on acceptance of the essential structure of the world of material social and political relations as given" (1986:59–60).

Nelsen, Maldron, and Yokley (1975) suggest that religion "is not simply a conservative, otherworldly institution inculcating quietism and rationalizing inequality," but is also an agent of social change (Hunt and Hunt 1977:1). Specifically, their study of the relationship between religion and civil rights militancy suggests that religiosity—commitment to religion—among African-Americans can stimulate militancy and protest. Hunt and Hunt (1977) further corroborated these findings in their reanalysis of Marx's (1967) data, indicating that his failure to differentiate otherworldly and "thisworldly" religious orientations led to a unitary view of African-American religion that neglects the diversity of religion as a set of beliefs and expressions, and the multiple ways various religious forms can effect political participation. Thus they concluded that religion could simultaneously be an opiate *and* inspiration for protest, depending on the religious orientation of African-Americans.

Though religion's influence on African-American political behavior is widely debated in the scholarly literature, relatively few studies explicitly examine the effects of religious culture on African-American collective action. We know little, for instance, about how religiosity promotes a sense of political empowerment. The few studies that have explored the link between religion and political action suggest that there is positive connection between certain forms of religious culture and political mobilization. For example, in their study of religion and politics, Allen, Dawson, and Brown (1989) recognized the importance of religious culture in cultivating a collective orientation (that is, group identity and consciousness) among African-Americans that fosters political mobilization. Similarly, in a more recent analysis of Chicago's African-American political-religious scene, Harris concludes that, far from subverting political activism, the cultural elements of divine and moral imperatives, sermons, self-sacrificial orientation of religion, and social interaction that inhere in African-American churches stimulate African-American protest activity (1999:177). Like Payne (1995), Harris recognizes the importance of "internal religiosity [in] promot[ing] one's feelings of effectiveness in politics, as well as one's interest in political matters. It might be that internal religiosity fosters political efficaciousness through a belief in divine inspiration, while the relationship of internal religiosity to interest in politics might be associated with interest in morally defined political issues . . . that promote political involvement" (1994:62).

Similar to Hunt and Hunt (1977), Harris argues that the effects of religion's various manifestations on activism are multifaceted. He notes that though a strong attachment to religion may undermine some forms of political activism, it may also empower individuals who are actively involved in church life, to participate in collective action (1994:35). Harris's contention is that involvement in church life beyond regular services can help an individual cultivate and nurture organizational skills that engender political efficacy.

Though these studies suggest that there is a correlation between religion and African-American political mobilization, they neglect to analyze fully the actual processes by which multivalent religious culture is constructed to legitimate and promote political action. They also fail to explore adequately how religion's historical/cultural legacy contributed to the development of an African-American protest tradition. This is an especially troublesome oversight considering religion is a product of social relations that is reproduced in specific social arrangements in specific societies under historically specific conditions (Cox 2000). By examining religion's cultural antecedents from a historical perspective, it is possible to analyze how religious culture shaped African-Americans' moral and political views and behavior regarding the kinds of social relationships and society that should exist. It is impossible to understand the interrelationship between the African-American church and black oppression without examining the historical context in which it exists. In this sense a great deal of the argument in this book is concerned with the historical development of African-American religious ideas that culminate in the Civil Rights Movement in Arkansas.

Despite their explanatory shortcomings, the above studies suggest that scholars can obtain a fuller comprehension of social movements if serious consideration is given to broadening the formulation of organizational resources to include culture. For example, Harris's inclusion of culture in his definition of resources revealed that public and private commitment to religion is often expressed through "intensive and extensive organizational participation in church life," which provides people with organizational skills and social networks that can serve to promote collective action (1994:51, 53). This delineation fits well with the resource mobilization theory, a theoretical perspective that maintains that the ability of oppressed groups to mobilize resources is the most important determinant in the emergence of political action. However, resource mobilization theory's emphasis on material acquisition leads it to neglect examining how church-based resources as "qualities possessed by religiously motivated people" encourage political activism (Harris 1994:48). Thus viewing culture as a resource may help further our understanding of religious culture's effect on African-American political participation during the civil rights era.

I argue, like Hunt and Hunt (1977), Lincoln and Mamiya (1990) and Harris (1994), for the importance of analyzing religion as a multivalent force representing a diversity of beliefs and expressions that have different impacts on political participation. The multidimensionality of individual religious beliefs and behavior is evident in Mills's (1993) biography of civil rights activist Fannie Lou Hamer, which documents how Hamer consistently engaged in active processes of social/cultural appropriation and interpretation of religious meaning to strengthen her commitment to activism. "Mrs. Hamer knew the Bible well and regularly attended small black churches near her home. . . . Christianity should be 'being concerned about your fellow man, not building a million-dollar church while people are starving right around the corner,' Mrs. Hamer said. 'Christ was a revolutionary person, out there where it was happening. That's what God is all about, and that's where I get my strength'" (Mills 1993:18).

Hamer clearly understood that multiple religious meanings inherent in the church could be construed to impede political mobilization as well. In a speech at Harvard University, Hamer asserted that many churches in Mississippi were not involved in the movement because "chicken-eating preachers" were "selling out for the big Cadillacs" instead of moving their congregations to support civil rights activities (Mills 1993:238). She continued: " 'The most disgusting hour in the country is 11:00 A.M. Sunday morning when hypocrites from all walks of life converge on our churches for the sake of paying the minister's way to hell and theirs, too. . . . If Jesus were here now, he'd be called a militant because he was where it was at, right down with the grass root'" (1993:238). These comments suggest that religious organizations are confronted with the problem of members' uneven ideological development and irregular commitments to the

church and its dogma, an unevenness that is itself a direct product of dialectical processes within and without the church. As Marable argues

> The black Church is divided, because its *rasion d'être* is divided . . .
> black churchmen have almost always set a series of priorities, either
> consciously or unconsciously. Those ministers who have emphasized
> material, day-to-day challenges of being black in a racist/capitalist
> state, and those who have not hesitated to leave the cloistered halls
> of God to enter the turbulent gritty reality of the streets are part of
> what I have called the tradition of Blackwater. Those ministers who
> emphasize prayer over politics, salvation over suffrage, the study of
> Ecclesiastes over the construction of economic cooperatives, represent
> the Other-Worldly position of black faith. Both are legitimate and his-
> torically grounded within the black Church, and are often expressed in
> contradictory ways by single individuals. (2000:213)

This intimates that placing the Civil Rights Movement within a religious
cultural context of dialectical tensions and constant interactions may illuminate how the plurality of views that exist in black churches provided African-
Americans with identities, group consciousness, and meanings crucial for
promoting movement participation.

The Approach of the Study

In this book, I investigate how religious culture helped to sustain the civil rights
protest of African-American Arkansans with few resources and little permanent power. I argue that inherent cultural elements (that is, language, practices, values, relations, and so forth) in the church can independently mobilize
political action. In churches people came together to construct enduring interpersonal relations and meanings that motivated some to mobilize for political
action even when social conditions were not ripe for such actions. Consider
the example of the local and national women's club movement, which emerged
from small auxiliary church societies. Women activists in this movement did
not allow segregation constraints of the late nineteenth and early twentieth
century to impede their efforts to secure African-American political and economic equality. Instead through their church and club organizations women
interacted to create social bonds, fostering the creation of social support,
commitment, and activist identities that sustained their movement during the

height of segregation. Tarrow calls these small insurgent groups "early risers' who culturally construct political opportunities that are crucial for mobilizing larger protest (1994:189). Despite the fact that most African-American churches were established to foster political control of and exploitation of blacks, my research will show that the church's emergence in this unique historical context necessitated the creation of enduring meanings, beliefs, relationships, and cultural practices that served as resources for survival and motivating protest against racial oppression.

Though scholars have recently begun evaluating the significance of culture in the emergence of social movements, adequate attention is not given to understanding how culture links organizations and political action. Culture's undervaluation as a catalyst for mobilization is a direct result of social movement literature's emphasis on material resources as the central factor in mobilizing collective action. In movement literature, culture is presented mainly as a mediating variable between organization and collective action (McAdam 1982). Culture is assumed to have little or no independent influence on people's decisions to participate in social protest. At the broadest level, this book challenges long-standing contentions that organizational resources and individual cost-benefit arrangements are more important in mobilizing protest than culture. I define culture as both content (shared meanings, beliefs, values, symbols, and norms) and the interactive processes that change this content to construct various identities, behaviors, and perceptions of the world. Unlike previous research in movement literature that defines culture in fixed terms, my conception of culture provides a more fluid understanding of how structure (content) and social processes interact to initiate social action.

This book examines the significance of church culture in the mobilization of civil rights protest in Arkansas from 1954 to 1964. This state and period were chosen for study because 1) though much is known about the Little Rock Central High School integration action, considerably less is known about the overall development and maintenance of civil rights struggles in Arkansas; and 2) the 1954–64 decade in Arkansas, like elsewhere in the South, marked intensive civil rights struggles. Drawing on archival, secondary historical, and personal interview data on the Civil Rights Movement in Arkansas, this book examines the role of religious culture in promoting civil rights participation. I retrieved archival data for my analysis from several locations including the Arkansas History Commission, *Arkansas State Press* and *Arkansas Democrat-Gazette* newspaper archival libraries, and the University of Arkansas at Little Rock Library's Special Collections Department.

In addition, data are drawn from personal interviews that I and other researchers conducted with individuals who were involved as participants, supporters, leaders, organizers, and fundraisers in Arkansas's Civil Rights Movement during the 1950s and 1960s. Through my archival analysis and with the help of clergy and scholars in Arkansas, I compiled a list of activists to interview. I also used a modified snowball sampling technique to gather more potential respondents, particularly less well-known activists. Thirty-two semistructured in-depth interviews were conducted from 1991 to 1999. The average interview lasted one hour, though some lasted as long as two and a half hours. Since most African-Americans in Arkansas before and during the civil rights era were members of churches, virtually all of the individuals who participated in the movement were religiously affiliated. Most were affiliated with either the Methodist or Baptist church; nineteen were male, thirteen were female. The socioeconomic backgrounds of respondents ranged from working to middle class; ages ranged at the time of their involvement from twelve to forty years old. Interviews were conducted in homes, churches, medical offices, and other workplaces.

The interview questions focused on understanding the motivation of these individuals to become and remain involved in the Civil Rights Movement. To uncover their motivation I asked a series of questions to help determine their degree of activism prior to the emergence of the Civil Rights Movement such as their involvement in political activities and their membership in any organizations that actively sought to change African-American social conditions. I also asked a series of questions to determine how respondents became involved in the Civil Rights Movement and their level of religiosity and embeddedness in the church before and during the civil rights era. Questions included why they got involved in the Civil Rights Movement; if they were a member of any movement organizations during the civil rights era, and if so, which ones; their role in the movement; church affiliation, their involvement in church activities; and how their religious faith inhibited or inspired their involvement in the Civil Rights Movement.[1]

Open-ended questions gave respondents sufficient latitude to explain their activism. I tried to reduce error in memory of events that took place three or more decades ago by using landmark events as memory anchors; reinstating the context of the event or attribute being recalled; "bounding" the recall period by making explicit reference to periods and information provided in previous interviews; and asking respondents to date events after providing them with contextualized information to assist their recall (Pearson et al.

1992:88). (Later, I systematically analyzed previously published works and archival data to verify the accuracy of respondents' memories about movement events and developments). Using these techniques I was able to assist respondents in recalling their experiences and beliefs during the civil rights era.

Outline of the Book

Chapter 1 presents a succinct but comprehensive critique of social movement theory's discussion of the relationship between culture and collective action. I examine movement theory's tendency to assign culture a mediating rather than substantive role in encouraging activism. I establish that the relegation of culture to the periphery of movement research leads to a narrow formulation of culture that prevents us from ascertaining its influence on movement mobilization. Furthermore, I highlight the importance of viewing social organizations as multivalent cultural places, where social relations and meanings emerge to encourage movement participation.

Chapter 2 begins my examination of how religion historically fostered African-American political activism. Rather than theorizing how movements arise spontaneously and/or from political opportunities emerging from external sources, I argue that the roots of African-American sociopolitical movements are found in enduring cultural elements in the African-American church. More precisely, I consider how African and African-American religious cosmology as a historical/cultural source influenced enslaved and free Africans' resistance during the antebellum period, making specific references to its operation in Arkansas. I show how the organizational setting of the church enabled African-Americans to develop and sustain multiple cultural frameworks, identities, and language that assisted in mobilizing their resistance against racial oppression.

Chapter 3 examines the interaction between church culture and African-American sociopolitical movement during Reconstruction and Post-Reconstruction in Arkansas. It considers how during these periods religious culture gave people the strength and courage to participate in life-threatening activities that challenged societal oppression. Through specific protest campaigns I demonstrate church culture's role in engendering an internal sense of personal efficacy in protestors that enabled them to overcome fears of retribution for their political activism.

In chapter 4, I investigate how enduring religious cultural elements embodied in African-Americans and their indigenous organizations helped to facilitate the construction of meanings, identities, and relationships that encouraged social activism decades preceding the desegregation of Little Rock's Central High School in 1957.

Chapter 5 considers how enduring faith and religious practices helped African-Americans construct meanings and interpersonal relations to provide them with the social strength and confidence to mobilize for civil rights activities in Arkansas. Moreover, this chapter analyzes how the multivalent character of church culture made it possible for African-Americans to interpret religious beliefs in divergent ways and to draw various behavioral directives from the same religious message. In this dialectical religious context a cadre of African-Americans in Arkansas constructed religious action frames that encouraged collective action.

In addition to examining how the church's organizational setting inspired civil rights protest, chapter 6 considers how cultural processes endemic to church auxiliaries and other quasi-religious organizations (that is, women's clubs and teacher associations) contributed to women's involvement in the civil rights struggle in Arkansas. Since gender frequently defines power relations in organizations, I consider how the organizational separation of women contributed to the construct of a gendered culture and social network that promoted their participation in the Civil Rights Movement in Arkansas. This chapter examines how culturally mediated interpretive and interactive processes within social organizations led some women to join the movement out of a sense of religious efficacy and of commitment and responsibility to those in their social networks.

In the final chapter, I specify how my approach to the study of the Civil Rights Movement moves beyond most collective action scholars' view of culture as a mere framer of people's perceptions of opportunity, to a broader view that sees cultural processes as resources for promoting social action. I suggest that serious consideration be given to understanding culture's direct effect on moving people to act.

African American Religion
and the
Civil Rights Movement
in Arkansas

CHAPTER 1

Cultural Dimensions of Collective Action

R esearch has established that religious institutions during the Civil
Rights Movement provided African-Americans vital organizational
resources for sociopolitical mobilization (McAdam 1982; Morris
1984). As Aldon Morris's (1984) sociological study of the southern Civil
Rights Movement noted, the organizational centrality of the churches in
African-American life provided the movement a network of leaders as well as
places to meet to develop commitment and to "facilitate mass participation,
tactical innovations, and rapid decision-making" (Morris 1984:285).

I wish to move beyond movement research's predominant concern with
organizational resources to discuss the relationship between culture and collective action by arguing that there is a tendency in the literature to assign culture a mediating rather than a substantive role in mobilizing and sustaining
collective activism. Though researchers (Morris 1984; Snow, Rochford,
Worden, and Benford 1986; Snow and Benford 1988, 1992; McAdam 1994)
have gone some distance incorporating cultural dimensions in their studies of
movement emergence, the organizational bias of early resource mobilization
accounts continues to impede scholars' ability to investigate the link between
ideas and movement mobilization. I contend that organizational settings,
unlike resource mobilization accounts, not only generate the networks, skills,
and strategies necessary for political organizing and action but also produce
compelling cultural narratives, identities, and commitment that can directly
mobilize and sustain movement participation. In other words my study of the
Civil Rights Movement examines how churches served as both organizational
resources and transformative sites of culture and consciousness that facilitated
movement mobilization. Within churches, people are embedded in a cultural

3

context that provides them with meanings to construct their actions either to impede or facilitate movement mobilization. As Lincoln and Mamiya (1990) noted, multiple and conflicting meanings within churches create a plurality of beliefs that both challenge and affirm the legitimacy of those in power. The primary focus of this book is to explore the effects of the liberating aspect of religious culture on desegregation movement participation in Arkansas. In the theoretical overview below we will see that movement scholars' suppositions about culture's effect on movement participation are analytically problematic but can be circumscribed in part by linking culture and organization.

Though sociologists have recently focused on the significance of culture in the emergence of social movements, its importance is still undervalued (Polletta 1999). As I mentioned earlier, movement literature describes culture mainly as a mediating variable between structural opportunity and collective action (McAdam 1982). Culture is assumed to have little independent influence on people's decision to participate in social protest. In my analysis, culture is defined as both content (shared meanings, beliefs, values, symbols, and norms) and the interpretive process that changes this content to construct various identities, behaviors, and perceptions of the world. My study moves beyond previous research on culture's effect on movement mobilization in two important ways. First, while most prior research defines culture in fixed terms (McCarthy 1973; McCarthy and Zald 1977; Morris 1984; McAdam 1982), my study's conception of culture provides a more fluid and complex understanding of how structure (content) and social processes interact to initiate movement mobilization. Second, while most research contends that movement participation is driven by narrow self-interests (Olson 1968; Chong 1991) and access to resources (Oberschall 1973; Tilly 1978), my study suggests that culture engenders deeply felt commitment, aspiration, and hope to mobilize movement participation.

Theorizing on Culture and Protest

Jo Freeman contends that any examination of movement emergence must begin with microsociological questions: Whence do the people come who make up the initial organizing cadre of a movement? How do they come together and how do they come to share a similar view of the world in circumstances that compel them into social action (1975:47)? Answers to these questions are key for understanding how the Civil Rights Movement was mobilized and sustained in the South's oppressive sociopolitical environment.

Early theories on social movements concluded that movements were irrational, unstructured, spontaneous events that emerged from cultural breakdown that elicited shared grievances and collective frustration. Three theories emerged from this model: collective behavior (Le Bon 1960; Smesler 1962; Turner and Killian 1972), mass society (Arendt 1951; Kornhauser 1959), and relative deprivation (Davies 1962, 1969; Gurr 1970). Although their central premises are similar, these theories differ in their conceptualizations of segments of the model. That is, a variety of antecedent institutional weaknesses in society are causally linked to social movement emergence through an equally wide range of disturbed "states of mind" (McAdam 1982:7).

A chief theorist of collective behavior is Gustav Le Bon (1960) who envisioned collective action as non-institutionalized public gatherings of anomic, mentally unstable, and irrational individuals acting in concert. He posited rational action dictated that people argue over their differences in a reasoned and orderly fashion; if people aired their complaints outside of established channels, they lacked reason. Current research on public gatherings challenges Le Bon's contention that event participants are mentally disturbed. Clark McPhail's (1991) examinations of public gatherings like crowds and marches found that such assemblies of people behave in very disciplined and orderly fashion. For example, McPhail (1991) discerned that people generally assemble in clusters of friends and associates in crowds he termed *milling behavior*, a kind of activity that occurs when there is a pause in event action. He also found that people marched and walked in a very orderly fashion in most crowds contrary to Le Bon's contention that they engage in loose and random activity (McPhail 1991). These findings suggest it is more fruitful to examine social movements not as disorganized reactionary events but as rationally planned activities arising from social interaction.

A variant of the collective behavior model, the mass society theory, contends disruptions in the normal functioning of society lead to the disintegration of established institutions through which people are integrated into society, creating socially isolated, *abnormal* individuals who act collectively to reconstitute these organizations. Though the mass society model identifies group processes as important mechanisms in movement emergence, it focuses far more on disturbed "states of mind" mobilizing movement participation. Chief mass society theorist William Kornhauser (1959) asserts that social isolation gives rise to feelings of alienation and anxiety that are prerequisites for social protest. That is, Kornhauser argues "social atomization engenders strong feelings of alienation and anxiety, and therefore the disposition to engage in extreme behavior to escape from these tensions" (1959:39). Since mass society theorists view movement participants' substantive demands as an epiphenomenona of interpsychic conflict, their approach is neither theoretically nor empirically convincing because they ignore the fact that movements are important impetuses for social change (McAdam 1982:18). It was, as we will see, through African-American collective protest efforts in the 1950s and 60s that legalized segregation was dismantled. Institutional challenges that moved people to act rationally in concert with one another for societal justice and equality characterized this era, not structural breakdown. As McAdam (1982) argues, one cannot assume that movements are simply the unintended by-products of collective attempts at tension management. The mass society perspective circuitously directs movement scholars to examine group processes' effect on protest participation since it views feelings of alienation and anxiety that give rise to collective action as political phenomena.

Another variant of the collective behavior model, which is similar to mass society theory, relative deprivation theory, suggests that social movements are outcomes of psychological states "induced by social processes of wide variety of types whose full impact can only be understood by examining the perceptions and experiences of individuals" (Jenkins 1981:98). However, unlike mass society theorists, relative deprivation proponents (Davies 1962; Huntington 1968; Gurr 1970) suggest that socioeconomic changes stimulate social processual transformations critical for the emergence of movements. That is, relative deprivation theorists move collective behavior theory a step closer to evaluating how institutional processes and beliefs influence decisions to engage in movement participation. Samuel Huntington's (1968) formulation of relative deprivation theory, for example, postulates movements are products of the failure of political institutions to develop as quickly as socioeconomic institutions (Jenkins 1981:95). In other words, the exclusion of an increasingly materially affluent group from the electoral system fuels state challenges. According to Jenkins, Huntington's (1968) analysis is considerably more useful than other collective behavior theoretical variants because it places central emphasis on the emergence of new groups from economic development making rational demands on government (1981:96). Relative deprivation theorists claim that heightened aspirations created by improving economic conditions create a perceptual gap between "value expectations" and "value capabilities." Value expectations are the resources and social situations to which the individual feels entitled; value capabilities are the resources and social situations that the individual feels he or she is likely to obtain (Jenkins

1981:99). Incongruencies between what people expect and what they can get create frustrations that eventually find expression in collective action. The problem with relative deprivation theorizing and the collective behavior model in general is that they offer no explanation for how individual discontent is transformed into organized collective action (McAdam 1982:15). In addition relative deprivation theory does not adequately explain why protest occurs when societal institutions are relatively stable and why protest does not always occur when institutions are in flux (Morris and Herring 1986). Despite these theoretical shortcomings, relative deprivation theorizing suggests that additional insights about the intricacies of movement mobilization can be gained from examining how social interactions within organizations shape dispositions for movement participation.

Resource Mobilization

The collective behavior model has increasingly lost favor, as scholars turn their attention to analyzing movements as rational phenomena. The principal theoretical perspective to emerge from this new focus is resource mobilization theory. This theory maintains that though discontent or ideas play a role in initiating collective action, resources such as facilities, money, and potential participants are most critical for shaping those grievances into a viable social movement (Robnett 1997:12). In other words, theories aligned with the resource mobilization paradigm downplay the significance of culture, arguing instead that the availability of resources (McCarthy 1973; McCarthy and Zald 1976) is a more important determinant in the emergence and likely success of collective action (Buechler 1993:221).

The political process variant of the resource mobilization model acknowledges the importance of culture in the facilitation of social movements but maintains that culture is not sufficient in and of itself for initiating collective action. This perspective contends that movements are less the products of culture than the beneficiaries of shifting political conditions that open up political and economic systems for change. Political process theorists argue that structural opportunities do not automatically translate into protest; rather political opportunities and organizations offer insurgents only a certain objective "structural potential" for collective action. Mediating between opportunity and action are the shared meanings people attach to their situation (McAdam 1982:48).[1]

Culture's mediating role is evident in Morris's (1984) and McAdam's (1982) examination of the Civil Rights Movement and suggests that there was always a potential pool of participants available in the church who shared general ideational affinity with the movement but lacked the organizational base for expressing their discontent. Aldon Morris's (1984) study of the Civil Rights Movement identifies the church's ideational repository, or what he terms the "culture content," as an important ingredient in the emergence of the movement, although his work focuses far more on the organizational functions that churches fulfilled during the movement. Morris's analysis of the Montgomery Bus Boycott, for example, revealed that rather than the movement unfolding as an unstructured, spontaneous event, it was facilitated and sustained through church-based organizations and culture. Morris found that churches facilitated support for the bus boycott through collective giving of economic assistance and other contributions, sharing of communal experiences through mass meetings, and the generation of a shared consciousness promoting self-worth and group pride (1984:85). More precisely, Morris established that preexisting organizations like the church and "movement halfway houses," such as the Highlander School and the Fellowship of Reconciliation, operated as free spaces/alternative institutions (Gamson 1992:62) supplying African-American movement participants with extant social relationships, meanings, beliefs, and cultural practices (for example, language, stories, songs, ceremonies) that served to eradicate their sense of isolation and to define their struggle as just and right (Billings 1990).[2] Organizational culture connected African-Americans to one another via cognitive frames, dense interactions, and emotional and affective exchanges to empower them to resist societal oppression in spite of the personal sacrifice.

Polletta suggests that although scholars like Morris generally recognize that free spaces are not entirely immune from cultural codes that legitimate oppression or subordination, they have not gone beyond this acknowledgment to show how movements are advanced or impeded by broader meanings and patterned relations (1997:435). Morris, however, does specify that shifting political conditions may influence how "culture content" is interpreted. He maintains that when political opportunities are limited, the church's interpretations of "culture content" serve to channel resistance into otherworldliness or pacifism and, when structural opportunities are abundant, the interpretations help alter people's cultural perceptions and lead them to challenge dominant arrangements. Though Morris recognizes that social conditions influence how people interpret culture content in the church's free space, his reliance on structural conditions to explain interpretive variance leads him to focus far less on how culture independently mobilizes movement participation[3]—a deficiency Morris tried to address in later work (Morris 1993), arguing for the historical significance of religious institutions as social spaces in which social protest was discussed, mobilized, and organized. He does not claim, nor does my analysis, that everyone, or even a majority of church attendees, became social protesters. What Morris does argue is that the historical record clearly suggests that some African-Americans used churches as an arena in which to carve out free spaces necessary for sustaining a "black tradition of protest." My analysis demonstrates this tradition fostered the development of a collective action consciousness among African-Americans producing a nucleus of early activists whose religious interpretations encouraged them constantly to probe the social system for weaknesses they could exploit to create social change. These probes continued even when social conditions were not ripe for such actions. These small insurgent groups or "early risers" (Tarrow 1994) constructed political opportunities that were later exploited by larger African-American movement groups.

Wyatt T. Walker (1982) maintains that these "early risers" were aroused in part by an oppositional consciousness rooted in the *religious protest culture of hope*. This component of church culture content supplied civil rights participants with a range of meanings in which they found solace and empowerment in giving hope of abolishing oppression to succeeding generations. The shared spiritual and psychological satisfaction derived from feelings of efficacy, empowerment, and righteousness gained from contributing to the long and continuous struggle for African-American communal uplift sustained a "collective memory" (Polletta 1999) of protest among participants that often strengthened their resolve and encouraged future activism even when the odds of movement success were small. In this study I examine the nuts and bolts of religious culture to determine how people use it to construct and sustain ideologies and relationships within churches that give rise to a social consciousness, making African-Americans not merely respondents to political opportunity but also creators of it. Because the African-American church is a creation of a people whose daily existence forced them to confront an oppressive reality, it imbues African-Americans with oppositional ideas "about the reconstruction of a new humanity wherein people are no longer defined by oppression but by freedom" (Cone 1978:150). These ideational or ideological frames are products of complex past and present social interactions as well as constant internal dialogue and negotiation within churches (Ortiz 2000).

While political process theorists like Morris emphasize the role of structure, strategies, and institutions to advance scholars' understanding of the complexity of collective action emergence, they do not adequately take into account the mediating processes through which people attribute meanings to events and interpret situations (Klandermans 1992:77). By not considering these processes, they cannot sufficiently answer such questions as: Why do some movements emerge when resources are not sufficient? Why do some movements materialize when the sociopolitical environment is not conducive to protest? Though political process theorists make the case for the importance of preexisting social ties within organizations for movement mobilization, they do not explain how these social relations and networks transform people into political actors.

The New Social Movement Model

New social movement theory stresses the importance of movement culture or shared attitudes about society and movement identities for transforming potential participants with plural orientations and meanings into movement followers. For new social movement theorists then, political organizing around a common identity is central for understanding how movements mobilize. Alberto Melucci is the best exemplar of those writing in this tradition. Melucci describes social movements as action *systems* that have structures: "the unity and continuity of the action would not be possible without integration and interdependence of individuals and groups, in spite of the apparent looseness of this kind of social phenomena. But movements are *action* systems in that their structures are built by aims beliefs, decisions and exchanges operating in a systemic field. A collective identity is nothing else than a shared definition of the field of opportunities and constraints offered to collective action: 'shared' means constructed and negotiated through a repeated process of 'activation' of social relationships connecting actors" (1985:793).

Therefore, he argues collective action cannot be fully explained without examining how *internal* resources are mobilized. That is, Melucci contends alternative meanings or oppositional ideas about everyday life are creations of social relations submerged in small groups until they are mobilized to confront political authorities (Melucci 1985:800). Rather than a consequence of crises or dysfunctions, movements are social constructions that mobilize individuals for action through extant relationships and the allocation of meanings and values. Scholars who emphasize the new social movement approach suggest that developing a common identity for political organizing was less necessary in past movements since participants possessed similar social backgrounds and experiences (Robnett 1997:13). Contrary to this view, I contend that based on existing research (Fantasia 1988; Taylor and Whittier 1992, 1995; Robnett 1997; Pattillo-McCoy 1998; Polletta 1997, 1999) identity construction processes are crucial in past as well as in new forms of collective action. Individuals and small groups within African-American indigenous organizations like the church interpreted and appropriated religious cultural meanings about everyday life that were central in promoting Civil Rights Movement participation (Ortiz 2000). Despite the important role of the collective identity processing in new social movement theory, no social movement theorist has dissected how individuals and small groups develop politicized group identities (Taylor and Whittier 1992:105).

Recent Theorizing

Recently, social movement scholars such as Myra Ferree and Frederick Miller (1985) and Bert Klandermans (1997), among others, have evaluated how culture operates as a force in the emergence and development of social movements.[4] This literature contends that meaning systems embedded in interpersonal and organizational social networks are pivotal for both the mobilization of resources and the formation of ideational traditions that politicize movement participants. Ferree and Miller (1985), Gamson (1992), and Morris (1992) all argue effectively that social and cultural factors play an important role in the "translation of objective social relationships into subjectively experienced group interests" that are critical in the development of social movements. Specifically, they suggest that since people are embedded within both a cultural context that provides them with belief systems to help guide their actions and infuse them with meaning and a structural context that shapes and limits their actions, scholars should focus more on the intersection between the two contexts to understand the processes that make it possible for individuals and groups to act collectively (Morris 1992:351).

Other scholars like Snow et al. (1986), Buechler (1990), McAdam (1994), and Staggenborg (1998) have begun to examine how culture transforms individually held beliefs into collective beliefs. For example, Klandermans (1997) argues that individuals' beliefs are products of group or organizational socialization where people engage in a shared discourse in which beliefs are contested, refuted, reformulated, and defended. Since no two people experience socialization and discourse in exactly the same way, one can typically find beliefs within the same group or organization that vary from individual to individual (Klandermans 1997:4). Klandermans contends that "collective beliefs are like the language shared by the members of a language community. Although no individual member of a language community speaks exactly the same language, we would certainly be able to recognize single speakers as members of that community" (Klandermans 1997:4–5).

Given the multiplicity of organizational discourses, individuals draw from a variety of meanings to help them maneuver through their social milieu. However, these meanings are not randomly distributed but can be found in systems of collective beliefs such as religions and ideologies that function as "toolkits" (Swidler 1986) from which individuals "rent" meaning to construct their version of a collective action frame (Klandermans 1997:63). Once these cultural frames are internalized they can stimulate greater commitment and tenacity among movement participants faced with resistance and campaign reversals, and sustain a membership that derives greater satisfaction from movement participation (Lofland 1995:215). For example, Pattillo-McCoy's (1998) analysis of civic life in an African-American community in Chicago revealed that cultural practices within the African-American church, such as holding hands during prayer, call-and-response interaction, singing, clapping, and swaying to music, invoke collective orientations (that is, group identity and consciousness) among African-Americans that serve as resources in political organizing and activism. Pattillo-McCoy's (1998) finding suggests that a broader formulation of culture as an interpretive resource for movement mobilization may provide a more comprehensive understanding of Civil Rights Movement mobilization that reveals how churches contributed to the continuity of civil rights protest by supplying the social support, identity, and meaning needed to predispose people for social action (Nepstad 1996).

The forgoing discussion of the relationship between ideas and social movements is part of a larger trend by movement scholars to critically analyze the "structural bias" of resource mobilization theory, a bias, discussed earlier, that privileges structural explanations over subjectivist and cultural interpretations (Taylor and Whittier 1995). That is, resource mobilization and its variants do not adequately consider how organizational cultural processes persuade people to join a movement. As discussed briefly in the introduction, Harris (1994, 1999) broadens the resource mobilization perspective to include culture as a resource for political participation. Harris maintains that at the fundamental level of organizing, social movements are expressions of cultural symbols and practices that provide meaning for social action. Therefore, he argues that "the religious culture of African Americans not only stimulates mobilization by serving as a guide for interpreting political goals but, just as important, it also provides sacredly ordained legitimacy to political action" (Harris 1999:135). Moreover, Harris contends that church involvement cultivates organizational skills that engender political efficacy.

This study focuses attention on the significance of church culture in the mobilization of desegregation protest in Arkansas. Little is known about the overall development and maintenance of this movement, which emerged in part, like elsewhere in the South, from church structures. Research in this book shows that religiously affiliated local movement centers like the Arkansas Teachers Association (ATA), the Arkansas Christian Movement (ACM), and the Little Rock Eastend Civic League were all organizationally and culturally pivotal for sustaining civil rights struggle, especially after passage of the 1958 Bennett law outlawing state chapters of national movement organizations like the National Association for the Advancement of Colored People (NAACP) and Urban League from operating in Arkansas.[5] These local movement centers frequently used churches as meeting places to rejuvenate the struggle, plan actions, fundraise, and recruit participants. They functioned in this manner well into the 1960s and recruited participants from other existing community organizations like colleges and high schools to work for integration in every aspect of life.

My research in this book has led me to conclude that insurgent ideational strands are an enduring aspect of church culture that consistently persuaded adherents and potential constituents to engage in social action independent of structural conditions. As I mentioned earlier, African-Americans like those who participated in the local and national women's club movement did not allow the structurally oppressive environment of late nineteenth and early twentieth century to impede their efforts to mobilize against racial oppression. Rather, in their church and club organizations African-American women bonded in relationships that fostered the creation of strong social support and self-conceptions that sustained their movement commitment in the face of tremendous opposition. Likewise, Payne (1995) suggests in his research on African-Americans' involvement in the Civil Rights Movement that institutions like the church provided African-Americans with cultural assets (for example, religiosity and social ties) that were crucial in mobilizing their protest. These data all suggest that to obtain a more integrated understanding of religion as generative of social protest, scholars need to ask how immersion in church culture content shapes actions. This includes examining how relations between individuals in churches and individuals in society affect how persons interpret and act on religious beliefs.

The present study considers these issues by concentrating on three salient areas of research that have received scant attention in Civil Rights Movement literature: the historical role of church culture content in generating protest identities in the United States; the process by which the dialectical tensions and interactions in churches facilitate movement participation; and how class and gender experiences influence movement mobilization.

As the preceding theoretical overview suggests, movement literature has not given adequate attention to explaining how culture directly mobilizes and sustains movement participation. Although new social movement theorists stress the importance of movement identity formation, they do not provide us with an explanation of how political consciousness and relational networks politicized people for collective action. My research develops a clearer understanding of how culture is translated to encourage movement participation.

Theological Insights on Religion as a Generator of Activism

One field that can provide us some insight into how culture, especially religious culture, politicizes people for movement participation is theology—the study of religious faith, practices, and experiences. Many African-American theologians contend that faith or belief is interwoven into and enhanced by social experiences. These theologians perceive religion as a tradition that informs one's conception of reality and shapes one's idea of social practices (West 1982:117). More precisely, they assert that African-Americans' religious worldviews on the union between sacred and secular contributed to the construction of an insurgent religious consciousness in the context of repressive sociopolitical conditions (West 1982; Washington 1986; Cone 1989, 1996; Wilmore 1994). Theologian James Cone (1974), for instance, argues that enslaved African-Americans' conception of unity between the spiritual and temporal created and sustained religious cultures that fundamentally opposed an oppressive European-American definition of their humanity. In essence, christianized enslaved African-Americans' responded to oppressive European-American

Christian ideas by creating, as Dwight Billings (1990) argues, religious ideologies and institutions that morally and physically opposed oppression. In these religious institutions systems of beliefs and practices endowed in both enslaved and freed African-Americans identities and attitudes needed to promote continuous political struggle against racial oppression (Walker 1982:26). These religious viewpoints were grounded in enslaved and freed African-Americans' experiences and in their view the Gospel stood unequivocally against racial oppression. According to Cornel West (1982), the aforementioned religious perspective was expressed in many enslaved Christian African-Americans' petitions to government for freedom. In a petition to the General Assembly of Connecticut in 1779 for freedom, enslaved African-American Christians wrote: "We perceive by our won Reflection, that we are endowed with the same Faculties with [sic] our masters, and there is nothing that leads us to a Belief or Suspicion, that we are any more Obliged to serve them, than they us, and the more we Consider this matter, the more we are Convinced of our Right (by the laws of Nature and by the whole Tenor of Christian Religion, so far as we have been taught) to be free" (West 1982:101).

As we will see in some cases, this religious outlook led to unsuccessful rebellions against slavery (that is, insurrections led by Denmark Vesey, Gabriel Prosser, and Nat Turner) organized by enslaved African-American Christians. Though participants in these actions knew the odds for movement success were low, they were willing to incur the cost of their religiously motivated fight for liberation, a sacrifice that can be linked in part to social pressure induced by movement participants in religious and social networks, who expected and encouraged other group members to participate. Though data testing this hypothesis is hard to acquire, what evidence exists suggests that some members embodied a tradition or culture of protest that arose within African-American religious institutions, giving rise to persistent collective resistance to racial oppression (Ortiz 2000).

A major codified expression of religiously inspired resistance is found in the writings of Lemuel Haynes. Haynes, a celebrated African-American New England Congregational minister, argued in his 1776 antislavery tract entitled *Liberty Further Extended* that the ideological concepts of equality and inalienable rights were God-given rights, which could not be taken away. Haynes believed that by employing this idea in the Declaration of Independence, the founders of America understood the "immutable laws of God, and indefeasible laws of nature" required for human freedom. Much to Haynes's surprise, despite their espousal of equality, the founders refused to view Africans in America as humans in possession of inalienable rights. Instead blacks were viewed as commodities and savage heathens whose subhuman and "uncivilized" nature relegated them to perpetual slavery. In response to this exclusion of African-Americans from full participation in society, Haynes constructed in *Liberty Further Extended* a politico-religious rejoinder:

> But I query, whether Liberty is so contracted a principle as to be Confin'd to any nation under Heaven; nay, I think it not hyperbolical to affirm, that Even an affrican [sic], has Equally as good a right to his Liberty in common with Englishmen. . . .
>
> It has pleased God to *make of one Blood all nations of men, for to dwell upon the face of the Earth.* ACTS 17, 26. And as all are one Species, so there are the same laws, and aspiring principles placed in all nations; and the Effect that these laws will produce, are Similar to Each other. Consequently we may suppose, that what is precious to one man, is so to another, and what is irksome [sic], or intolarable [sic] to one man, is so to another, consider'd in a Law of Nature. Therefore we may reasonably Conclude, that Liberty is Equally as pre[c]ious to a *black man*, as it is to a *white one*, and Bondage Equally as intollarable [sic] to the one as it is to the other: Seeing it Effects the Laws of nature Equally as much in the one as it Does in the other. But, as I observed Before, those privileges that are granted us by the Divine Being, none has the Least right to take them from us without our consen[t]; and there is Not the Least precept, or practise, in the Sacred Scriptures, that constitutes a black man a Slave, any more than a white one. (Bogin 1983:95–96)

The foregoing suggests that inherited religious sensibilities helped to foster an African-American protest tradition and identities that gave rise to historic African-American social movements (Morris 1993). Hence construing religious ideas to promote African-American protest has been an enduring feature of American society that influenced the attitudes of religiously motivated civil rights participants. The most prominent exemplar of activist religious constructions during the Civil Rights Movement was Martin Luther King Jr. He repeatedly used the African-American church's traditional "eschatological hope for freedom" to motivate movement participation from church participants and supporters: "I choose to identify with the underprivileged, . . . to identify with the poor . . . [and] to give my life for the hungry. I choose to give my life for those who have been left out of the sunlight of life's opportunity. I choose to live for and with those who find themselves seeing life as a long and desolate corridor with no exit sign. This is the way I'm going. If it means suffering a little bit, I'm going that way. If it means sacrificing, I'm going that way. If it means dying for them, I'm going that way because I heard a voice saying 'do something for others.' . . . Will you come to the mountain, to God's kingdom and cry out . . . 'what is mine is yours?'" (Cone 1986:13). These theological insights indicate that a more detailed examination of how organizational culture serves as an interpretive resource for political organizing is warranted.

Reconceptualizing Culture

As noted, explanations of culture's effect on movement activities are insufficient. In the case of the Civil Rights Movement, one theoretical explanation—the political process model—contends that shifting political conditions trigger changes in thinking regarding the feasibility of collective action. While this model stresses the importance of expanding political opportunities in supplying the necessary "cognitive cues" for initiating movement participation, it deemphasizes the significance of ideas, assigning greater influence to preexisting indigenous organizations, such as the African-American church. As already discussed, the political process model's conceptualization of culture's effect on movements is limiting in that it presents culture as a mediating not independent factor in mobilizing movements. Political process theorists do not acknowledge that culture has a life and logic of its own, not fully accountable in structural opportunity terms. Subsequently, culture's effect on movement participation is not reducible to mere changes in "cognitive cues" encouraged by shifting political conditions. Rather, cultural symbols and practices that provide meaning for social action are integral components of social movements.

Though political process theorist Aldon Morris's (1984, 1993) research on the Civil Rights Movement provides important insights into the inner working of organizational mobilization activities, his privileging of structural explanations over cultural accounts leads him to underexamine culture's influence on movement participation. While Morris acknowledges the importance of indigenous organizations in nurturing ideational tradition and social support for protest, he fails to examine how these social elements politicize everyday interactions to create a shared consciousness encouraging participation in insurgent movements.

My research findings are consonant with Payne's (1995) conclusion, drawn from his local study of Mississippi civil rights activism, that people became involved in the movement primarily through indigenous institutional networks (for example, familial and church relational networks). Unlike Morris (1984), who identifies social networks as crucial for Civil Rights Movement emergence but neglects to demonstrate how these networks fostered movement development, Payne examines how interpersonal networks of the rank-and-file members of indigenous organizations contributed to movement mobilization. Similar to my analysis, Payne asserts that once someone in these networks became involved in protest, they were likely to draw other members of the group into the struggle (1995:274). More often than not Payne argues that social networks, not indigenous organizations themselves, provided the basis for mobilizing movement participation. My study's evidence agrees with Payne's earlier research findings. Interview data suggest that the courage of other activists, especially those in church-affiliated club organizations, and the tradition of struggle influenced their decision to participate in Arkansas's Civil Rights Movement. That is, indigenous organizations' relational networks infused African-Americans with meanings about their oppressive experiences that helped them to understand, on one hand, the instrumentality of standing up and, on the other, the moral propriety of doing so (Fireman and Gamson 1979). Consequently, prevailing movement theory's one-dimensional understanding of culture must be reconceptualized to account for the intricacies of interpretive processes involved in mobilizing collective action.

One social movement model that has the potential to provide a more complete understanding of culture's link to movement mobilization is the processual approach of collective identity formation advanced by new social movement theorist Alberto Melucci. Melucci notes: "The study of social movements has always been divided by the dualistic legacy of structural analysis as a precondition for collective action and the analysis of individual motivations. These . . . explanations never fill the gap between behavior and meaning, between 'objective' conditions and 'subjective' motives" (1995:42). Based on Melucci's contention, an analysis should consider "the processes through which a collective becomes a collective" (Melucci 1995:43). Collective identity as a process involves examining the interactive and shared manner in which cognitive definitions about social conditions are formulated, the network of relations between actors and the larger systems of relations, and sentiments that create a group unity to motivate collective action.

I concur with Melucci but like Robnett (1997) find his dichotomous conceptualization of the collective actors in relation to society analytically limiting since it cannot account for the cognitive differences within groups of collective actors. As Robnett notes: "While collective actors as a group are constituted within a larger system of relations, individual actors are also situated relationally within the group of collective actors, the movement system, and the larger system" (1997:14). As a result it is important to analyze a movement from many different perspectives. In this book I examine how class, organizational involvement, systems of relations between individuals, and gender affect interpretations of the Gospel's call for the church to transform people's daily lives. Several interviewees, for example, maintained that churches containing individuals and social groups who were involved in secular movement organizations and interpreted "culture content" as encouraging people to see themselves as God's social activists were more likely to move some to view their role as Christians not as mere carriers of faith but as implementers of it in reality. Though some churchgoers held this disposition, many others immersed themselves in religious cultural frames that legitimated social inaction by contending, "God is going to fix it." Understanding how various religious sentiments emerge in the same church setting is crucial for ascertaining culture's complex effect on movement mobilization.

Conclusion

Rather than contend that motivation to participate in political action is driven by narrow self-interest, I have argued for the importance of religious culture and networks as independent factors in motivating movement participation. Specifically, I assert that church ministers and key congregants involved in activist networks were more likely to interpret church content in activist ways as opposed to those congregations that lacked individuals who participated in social activism. Religion's rich storehouse of rituals, symbols, and networks of relationships can motivate some people to engage in collective action out of moral obligation and commitment to the group (Smith 1996). In the following chapters I make the case for viewing indigenous organizations like churches as carriers of not simply material resources but also non-material cultural resources that can independently engender movement efficacy. More precisely, I attempt to show how religion provides people with belief systems and relationships that shape their moral and political views about the kinds of social relationships that should exist in society.

CHAPTER 2

History of Activist Religious Interpretation

—————⟫⟪⟪⟩⟫⟪—————

I n the literature there is debate regarding whether or not Africans' religious sensibilities survived the experience of slavery in the United States. Frazier (1964) argues that the effects of slavery destroyed all vestiges of African cultural heritage while Du Bois (1903, 1971), Herskovits (1941) and Holloway (1990) contend that aspects of African culture persisted throughout and beyond slavery. This study takes the latter view. When Africans were uprooted from their homeland and enslaved in colonial America many brought with them views of God's transcendence that informed their conceptions of reality (McCall 1980). Africans experienced God as an active agent in human affairs who cared for their material and spiritual well-being (Parrinder 1969; Mbiti 1982; Muzorewa 1985). Since religion permeated all areas of life it was largely responsible for shaping an African consciousness that did "not sever man from his total environment, so that in effect human history is cosmic history seen anthropocentrically and microcosmically. God is not divorced from this concept of history; it is His universe, He is active in it and apparent silence may be a feature of his divinity" (Mbiti 1990:47).

Theologian, James Cone (1974, 1989) contends that when enslaved African-Americans were converted to Euro-Christianity, which specified God's preoccupation only with spiritual concerns, they formulated ideologies and created institutions that opposed Euro-Christian teachings. These institutions and the oppositional ideologies they housed, as we will see, endowed African-Americans like escaped bondsman Anthony Burns with attitudes and philosophies that encouraged them to act on their belief that "God made me man—not a slave and gave me the same right to myself that he gave the man who stole me to himself" (Smith 1972:506).

Given religion's potential to subvert slavery, many slaveholders were reluctant to fulfill their Christian obligation to propagate their religion among "heathens." That is, slaveholders opposed converting enslaved African-Americans because they feared that the Christian principle of "inner sameness" or "equality of *all* souls" would imbue in African-Americans' "better Notions of themselves than is consistenst with their state of Slavery and their duty to their Masters" (Jordan 1968:182–83). Closely associated with this objection to conversion was the persistent notion that no Christian could hold another Christian as a slave. To negate these hypothetical objections, the Euro-Christian church proclaimed that conversion did not necessitate enslaved African-Americans' manumission. Some African-American converts were required to take the following oath affirming they sought spiritual not secular liberation: "You declare in the presence of God and before this Congregation that you do not ask for the holy baptism out of any design to free yourself from the Duty and Obedience you owe your Master while you live, but merely for the good of Your Soul and to partake of the Graces and Blessings promised to the Members of the Church of Jesus Christ" (Turner 1989:50). In addition, states reinforced debased religious interpretations of the "equality of all souls" doctrine with laws that reassured slaveholders that they were not legally obligated to manumit African-Americans after conversion. For instance, the Virginia House of Burgesses in 1667 passed legislation stating: "Baptisme doth not alter the condition of the person as to his bondage or freedom" (Mencarelli and Severin 1975:30).[1]

Missionaries appealed to slaveholders to convert African-Americans by arguing that Christianity promoted obedience among the enslaved. Their slogan was: "The deeper the piety of the slave, the more valuable he is in every respect" (Harding 1969:81). Missionaries informed slaveholders that they could construe biblical verses like those found in Paul's *Letter to the Ephesians* to instruct the enslaved to "be obedient to them that are your masters according to the flesh, with fear and trembling, in singleness of your heart, as unto Christ. Not with eyeservice, as menpleasers, but as the servants of Christ, doing the will of God from the heart" (6:5–7).[2]

Despite these instructional and legal adjustments, African-American conversion was relatively infrequent until slaveholders began searching for a cultural mechanism to socialize Blacks into accepting their slave status. According to Stampp, slaveholders understood that using force alone to control African-Americans was not viable: "A master did not take seriously the beliefs that [Africans] were natural born slaves. He knew better. He knew that

[Africans] freshly imported from Africa had to be broken into bondage; that each succeeding generation had to be carefully trained. This was not an easy task, for the [enslaved] rarely submitted willingly. Moreover, he rarely submitted completely. In most cases there was no end to the need of control" (1989:144). The slaveholders' need to reconcile Blacks to slavery ensured that the choice before them was not whether to convert African-Americans but whether they could construe the religious temperament of slaves to make them believe that their enslavement was in their best interests (Sernett 1972:98).

To facilitate among enslaved African-Americans the internalization of pacifying religious elements, slaveholders integrated their churches and established black churches under their supervision. Within these churches European-American ministers regularly emphasized African-Americans' religious obligation to obey their masters, as illustrated in the words of this former Arkansas bondsman: "the preacher made one sermon do for both races. A big long shed served as meeting-house. Into it the white people went to hear the preacher in his powerful exhortations. . . . 'Us servn's stayed outside, an' set down on de logs close by. . . . When de preacher git all warm' up . . . he stick his haid out de window now an' den ter exhort us servan's: You cullud people out dar—lissen at me! De way to make good slaves, is ter obey yo' Massa an' Missis! Obey em' constant—' " (Taylor 1979:203–4).

Many enslaved African-American Arkansans vigorously resisted being subjected to such preaching. One teen-aged girl described how she "would be locked up in the seed bind and she would cuss the preacher out. . . . She would say 'master, let us out.' And he would say, 'You want to go to church?' And she would say 'No, I don't want hear that same old sermon: ". . . don't steal your missis' and masters' chickens. . . . Don't steal your missis' and master's hams." I don't steal nothin'. Don't need to tell me not to' " (Taylor 1979:221). However, many enslaved African-Americans employed less confrontational means to convey their dissatisfaction with plantation ministers' disengaged sermons. Plantation missionary Charles Colcock James recalled the reaction of a large enslaved congregation to his 1831 sermon which "insisted upon the fidelity and obedience as Christian virtues in servants upon the authority of Paul, condemned the practice of running away, one half of [the] audience rose and walked off with themselves, and those that remained looked anything but satisfied, either with the preacher or the doctrine. After dismission, there was no small stir among them: some solemnly declared 'that there was no such Epistle in the Bible'; others, 'that I preached to please the masters'; others, 'that it was not in the Gospel'; others, 'that they did not care if they ever heard me preach again!'" (Raboteau 1978:294). Rather than being passive recipients of slaveholders' Christianity, some enslaved African-Americans constructed alternative Chrsistian frameworks "which lightened their burden of oppression, promoted group solidarity, . . . sustain[ed] hope, [and] buil[t] self-esteem" (Blassingame 1979:105). These religious frameworks regularly provided enslaved African-Americans with meanings that subverted slaveholders' disengaged and oppressive legitimating Christian interpretations. For example, Blassingame found in his study of enslaved African-American religious culture that:

> Most slaves, repelled by the brand of religion their masters taught, the racial inequalities in white churches, and the limitations on bondsmen's autonomy, formulated new ideas and practices in their quarters. The true shepherd of the black flock was the slave preacher. Often one of few slaves who could read, the black preacher was usually highly intelligent, resourceful, and noted for his powerful imagination and memory. Because of his traits of character and remarkable personality, he was able to unify the blacks, console the sick, weak, and fearful, uplift and inspire them. Suffering with his flock, he understood their tribulations and was accepted as a counsellor and arbiter in the quarters. In his sermons the slaves often saw the invisible hand of God working for their earthly freedom and retribution against whites. Whatever the content of the sermons, the slaves preferred a black preacher. (1979:130–31)

Raboteau's research on enslaved African-American religion also found that many African-Americans resisted slaveholders' debased Christianity by insisting that there existed a real Bible from God—not the "Bible now used [by] master"—which did not mandate "Servants, obey your masters" (1978:295).

Slaveholders tried to prevent the emergence of oppositional religious culture among the enslaved through mixed church worshiping where religious messages were, as we have seen, carefully construed by European-American ministers to legitimate slavery. However, mixed churches presented a number of challenges: masters hesitated to enter into intimate religious fellowship with the enslaved; preaching suited for masters was often considered wrong for the enslaved; and, masters were hesitant to vent their emotions before the enslaved

(Richardson 1947:10). In essence slaveholders found it problematic to worship with people whom they considered inferior. As a rule whenever African-Americans attended church with slaveholders, they were assigned segregated seating, usually in church balconies (McDonald 1974:29). Enslaved African-Americans were members, though in an inferior status, of slaveholders' churches.

The difficulties of mixed worship were eventually resolved through the establishment of separate churches under the supervision of a European-American minister. This arrangement avoided social mixing, permitted special preaching to the enslaved, and provided white supervision of enslaved African Americans' gatherings (Richardson 1947:10). Some church association leaders like Dr. P. S. G. Watson, one of Arkansas's notable Baptist ministers, supported separate church service by contending, "That the . . . plan of having the colored people attend religious worship with the whites is very defective and inefficient is evident, without argument by the very small number of them that are professors of religion" (Taylor 1979:217). His solutions for increasing African-American religious participation involved "competent white ministers" preaching regularly to enslaved congregations (Taylor 1979). Watson's support for "white" preachers over enslaved African-American itinerants reflected his concern not only about the spiritual welfare of the slaves but also with European-American Baptists' "official" attitude toward slavery, which "was one of full, unqualified, unapologetic, and unchanging support for the institution of slavery" (Taylor 1979:218). Hence, though some church leaders and associations were genuinely concerned about enslaved African-Americans' spiritual welfare, many used their ministers as social control agents who counseled: "slaves [s]hould anticipate the spiritual joys of eternal life, but while waiting must live in a state of eternal temporal bondage" (Taylor 1979:218).

Official church views about entrusting African-American religious functionaries with the task of preaching obedience to fellow African-Americans gradually changed when it became too burdensome for European-American clergy to supervise both European-American and slave services. Though African-American functionaries generally fulfilled their obligation to teach obedience, some, as P. S. G. Watson foresaw, quietly used their ministry to delegitimize slavery. To prevent slaveholders and European-American missionaries who supervised their church services from detecting how their sermons engendered political efficacy, enslaved ministers frequently used obscure symbols and figures to conceal activist messages in their homilies (Hatcher 1908). Genovese (1972), for example, found that some enslaved African-American ministers used code words in their sermons such as "goat" to represent slaveholders and "sheep" to represent Africans, to prevent slaveholders and European-American clergy from discerning how their exhortations conveyed oppositional religious meanings.

"Invisible" Church Culture

Enslaved African-Americans' disgust with slaveholders' debased Christianity moved many to assemble in secret meetings to worship. In these unauthorized gatherings in Arkansas, enslaved African-Americans found enough autonomy to worship God as they desired. A former bondsman commented: "My father (a preacher) would have church in dwelling houses and they had to whisper. My mother was dead and I would go with him. Sometimes they would want a real meeting with some *real preach'* (italics mine). It would have to be durin' the weeknights. You couldn't tell the difference between Baptists and Methodist then. They was all Christians (They used to sing their songs in a whisper. [There] was a prayer meeting from house to house) once or twice a week" (Hinson 1979:53).

According to Peter Randolph, a slave in Prince George County, Virginia, until he was freed in 1847, secret religious gatherings helped to sustain life in the enslaved community: "The slave forgets all his sufferings, except to remind others of the trials during the past week, exclaiming: 'Thank God, I shall not live here always!' Then they pass from one to another, shaking hands, and bidding each other farewell. . . . As they separate, they sing a parting hymn of praise" (Raboteau 1978:217). Prayer, singing, and fellowship refreshed enslaved African-Americans by affirming their personal autonomy, instilling in them positive self-conceptions and courage to confront collectively the reality of their earthly oppression. Such affirmations and unsupervised preaching concerned slaveholders like South Carolina planter, Charles Cotesworth Pinkney: "We look upon the habit of Negro preaching as wide spreading evil: not because a black man cannot be a good one, but . . . because they acquire an influence independent of the owner, and not subject to his control. . . . [W]hen they have possessed this power they have been known to make improper use of it" (Raboteau 1982:56). "Improper" in the sense that independent African-American functionaries frequently used their ministries to engender identities, meanings, order, and purpose that nursed a collective faith for temporal freedom that frequently translated into practical action.

When slaves assembled in the "invisible" church, they interacted to develop multiple Christian understandings of their circumstances that constructed their actions to either encourage or discourage involvement in transforming their social status. In this dynamic religious context, multiple forms of an important constituent of enslaved African-Americans collective faith called *hope* emerged to offer slaves a means to transcend and challenge prevailing reality. Hope imbued slaves with religious meanings that enabled them to hold onto the belief that with divine guidance they could defeat slavery. While some slaves constructed pacifying interpretations of hope that suggested that God would mete out justice in the afterlife for moral transgressions against them on earth, others cultivated a hope that saw salvation not as an objective act of God in which God washes away sin in order to prepare people for their new life in heaven but as an involved attempt by God to liberate people spiritually and materially. Enslaved African-Americans holding the latter conception usually interpreted the main thrust of Christianity as former bondsman Rev. Henry Highland Garnet did, "to use every means, both moral, intellectual and physical" to transform the world (Young 1977:93).[3] In short, the multivalent character of the "invisible" church provided slaves with multiple meanings of hope from which some constructed interpretations that obligated them, as Garnet articulated, to "tell [slaveholders] in a language which they cannot misunderstand of the exceeding sinfulness of slavery, and of a future judgment, and of the righteous retributions of an indignant God. Inform them that all you desire is FREEDOM, and that nothing else will suffice. Do this, and forever after cease to toil for the heartless tyrants, who give you no other reward but stripes and abuse. If they then commence the work of death, they, and not you will be responsible for the consequences. You had better all die—die immediately, than live slaves, and entail your wretchedness upon your posterity" (Wilmore 1994:94).

Moreover, autonomous cultural space in the "invisible" church provided the opportunity for some slaves to construct religious meanings that labeled slaveholders' "Christian" morality as hypocritical. One former bondswoman stated: "Dey allus done tell us it am wrong to lie and steal, but why did the white foks steal my mammy and her mammy? Dey lives clost to the water, somewhere ovr in Africy, and de man come in a little boat to de sho' and tell dem he got presents on dat big boat . . . and my mammy and her mammy gits took out to dat big boat and dey locks dem in a black hole what mammy says so black you can't see nothin'. Dat de sinfulles' stealing de is" (Raboteau 1978:295).

African-Americans' experience with slavery was a central factor in shaping their religious views and actions. Additional support for this perspective is evident in Stampp's (1989) research, which found that African-Americans' experiences with slavery led them to develop a different moral definition of stealing in relation to slaveholder's property. "For appropriating their master's goods they might be punished and denounced by him, but they were not likely to be disgraced among their associates in the slave quarters, who made a distinction between 'stealing' and 'taking.' Appropriating things from the master meant simply taking part of his property for the benefit of another part or as Frederick Douglass phrased it, 'taking his meat out of one tub, and putting it in another.' . . . Stealing, on the other hand, meant appropriating something that belonged to another slave, and this was an offense which slaves did not condone" (Stampp 1989:126–27).

Cultural constructs of this sort within the invisible church were instrumental in helping the enslaved develop identities, meanings, and language that empowered them to mobilize against slavery. Organized rebellions against slavery, such as Gabriel's revolt in Henrico County, Virginia, in 1800 often used the "invisible" church's culture to invoke a collective orientation among enslaved African-Americans that promoted movement participation. Like most other insurrectionists who preceded him, Gabriel used stories in the *Old Testament* to appeal to enslaved African-Americans' deep religious convictions (regarding God's transcendence) to persuade some six thousand people to join him in an attempt to liberate African-Americans from slavery (West 1982:102).[4] Specifically, Gabriel convinced his small group of followers, through *Old Testament* stories, that God was on the side of the oppressed; thus "God would stretch forth his arm to save, and . . . strength a hundred to overthrow" slavery (Harding 1969:182). Interpretations and appropriation of church culture content, as we will see, continued unabated in "independent" churches whose cultural resources were used by some African-Americans to encourage mobilization against slavery and racial oppression.

"Independent" Church Culture as a Mobilizing Resource

The independent church movement emerged mainly from slaveholders' desire not to worship in mixed churches with African-Americans whom they considered "subhuman" and African-Americans' dissatisfaction with discriminatory and segregationist practices imposed on them in integrated churches.

Some slave attendees of mixed churches believed that that since God created *all* humans equal and free, European-American churches' support for slavery and oppressive practices toward them were contrary to God's will; they, therefore, withdrew to form independent churches that engendered values, meanings, and purpose that motivated some congregants to mobilize against slavery and oppression.

Baptist

Independent African-American Baptist churches appeared in the South more than a hundred years before the Civil War. The Harrison Street Baptist Church was organized in Petersburg, Virginia, in 1776; the African Baptist Church in Yama Craw, South Carolina, in 1777; the First African Baptist Church in Savannah, Georgia, in 1779; the African Baptist Church in Williamsburg, Virginia, in 1785; and the African Baptist Church in Lexington, Kentucky, in 1790 (Woodson 1972).[5] Freed African-American ministers, some of whom had gained their freedom by virtue of their exceptional preaching abilities, were the principal leaders of early independent Baptist churches (McKinney 1971:458). Though these churches were under the auspices of European-American churches, they were relatively autonomous spaces in which enslaved African-Americans reaffirmed their belief "that spiritual bondage was a greater affliction than material bondage, and that freedom from one might lead to freedom from the other. They knew their churches were chattel arrangements, but they stubbornly trusted in the promises of the Bible that God is a liberator" (Washington 1986:8). In these relatively free religious spaces, African-Americans responded to slaveholders' debased Christian ideas by constructing and articulating Christian views in oppositions to slaveholders'. For example, African-Americans concluded like this enslaved woman that "she once thought it was her duty to serve her Master and Mistress but since the Lord converted her, she had never believed that any Christian kept Negroes or Slaves . . . [and that] believed there was Thousands of white people Wallowing in Hell for their treatment of the Negroes" (Posey 1956:119).

Slaveholders were always conscious of Christianity's ability to ignite enslaved African-Americans' uprisings. Christianity's efficacious power was evident in the bloodiest slave uprising in U.S. history, led by Nat Turner in Southampton, Virginia, in 1831.[6] Upon capture, Nat Turner, a Baptist preacher, was asked about his motives. He answered, "that in 1826 . . . he had been directed to act by an omen from God," which led him to believe that the biblical passage "Seek ye first the kingdom of God . . . and these things shall be added unto you" (Matthew 6:33) should be interpreted as directing him to apply Gospel teachings to life (Raboteau 1978:164). In other words, Turner believed that God, who took an active interest in both people's spiritual and material well-being, commanded him and his followers to engage in social actions designed to rid the United States of slavery. He never wavered from this position even when asked, as he faced execution, whether or not he thought shedding blood was necessary. Turner replied: "Was not Christ Crucified?" He felt that just as "Christ ha[d] laid down the yoke he borne for the sins of men," he and other Christians were charged to struggle against sin (read: slavery) (Aptheker 1966:137).

To inhibit enslaved African-Americans' development of political efficaciousness through religion, southern states passed laws restricting religious activities among the slaves (Genovese 1979). Virginia, for example, enacted a law stating that "no slave, free Negro or mulatto, whether he shall be ordained or licensed, or otherwise, shall hereafter undertake to preach, exhort, or conduct, or hold any assembly or meeting for religious or other purposes, either the day time or at night," under penalty of not over thirty-nine lashes (Aptheker 1966:81). Consequently in Virginia, African-Americans, freed and enslaved, were prohibited from worshiping without European-American supervision. This attempt at control, as mentioned earlier, was never completely effective at preventing Africans from eking out some degree of religious autonomy in Baptist churches because "Baptist polity required that each congregation govern itself.[7] In some churches, committees of black members were constituted to oversee their own conduct. These committees listened to black applicants, related their religious experiences and heard the replies of members charged with moral laxity. Meeting once a month, committees of 'brethren in black' conducted business, reported their recommendations to the general meetings and gave to black church members experience in governance" (Raboteau 1982:57).[8]

These meetings provided the enslaved with venues for nurturing organizational skills and relations with others that encouraged escapees who fled north to organize independent Baptist churches and associations when predominantly European-American churches refused to support antislavery agitation (Washington 1986). Lincoln and Mamiya (1990) found that the Northern European American Baptists' contention that slavery was a political question that had nothing to do with the church's mission led formerly enslaved African-American abolitionist ministers like Sampson White to urge all free African-American churches at the American Baptist Missionary Convention in 1858 to sever all connections to European-American Baptist associations.[9] The Convention agreed, "in view of the wicked prejudice and proscription which exists among our white brethren, we, the churches composing this Convention, withdraw our connexion with the different associations, and form one among ourselves" (Washington 1986:41). A year later, White presented three resolutions to the Convention that clearly specified that Baptists translate their religious beliefs into deeds. "*Resolved,* That slavery is against the progress of the gospel at home and abroad. *Resolved,* That we use all laudable means to abrogate it. *Resolved,* That no slaveholding minister be invited into the pulpits of any of our churches" (Washington 1986:41).

In general, African-American Baptist associations, unlike their European-American counterparts, were more concerned with people's temporal needs; thus they actively pushed for the eradication of slavery. Formed in 1834, Meigs County, Ohio, Providence Baptist Association was so committed to the abolition of slavery that it publicly supported a free African-American man who defied the Fugitive Slave Law of 1850 by aiding a runaway bondsperson.[10] According to Washington, the association maintained "that this man's 'Good Samaritan' act was 'a practical illustration of Christianity.' They chided the sort of Christianity 'which expends itself in distributing tracts, in making long prayers, in erecting splendid church edifices, and reclining upon richly cushioned seats, listening to invectives against crinoline, chewing tobacco and dancing, while it opens not its ears to the piteous groans of the bleeding slaves, as they issue from the hell of slavery'" (1986:29).

This indicates that some Baptists identified themselves not only as hearers but also doers of God's words. That is, as prominent Baptist minister Samuel Davis articulated before the National Colored Convention in Buffalo, the Baptist church is God's instrument for bettering life in the world. Consequently, "Shall, we, then, longer submit in silence to our accumulated wrongs? Forbid it, heaven! that we should longer stand in silence, 'hugging the delusive phantom of hope,' when every gale that sweeps from the South, bears on its wings, to our ears, the dismal sound of slavery's clanking chains, now riveted on three millions of our brethren, and we ourselves are aliens and outcasts in our native land" (Washington 1986:37). Davis concluded that "no other hope is left us, but in our own exertions, and an 'appeal to the God of armies!'" (Washington 1986:38)

Like their invisible church predecessor, independent Baptist churches embraced a plurality of meanings that some African-Americans drew from to construct liberating beliefs that promoted engagement in the world. Those individuals and groups who interpreted church culture in an activist manner maintained that religion unrelated to African-American liberation was irrelevant. That is, these individuals insisted that since the Gospel is contextual, it must be understood in the light of African-Americans' lives and servitude (Cone 1986). Consequently, the Gospel had to address both spiritual and material concerns or cease being an important part of African-Americans' lives.

Methodist

African-American members of the Methodist Episcopal (M.E.) church, like their Baptist counterparts, inferred that the Gospel obligated the church to offer practical solutions to social and political injustice or risk becoming meaningless. Moreover, they inferred that since the Gospel obligated the church to liberate the oppressed and downtrodden both spiritually and materially, it was unacceptable for regional M.E. conferences to maintain that the subject of slavery was "not one proper for the action of the church" (Blassingame 1979:48). This stance, when coupled with freed African-American Methodists' unwillingness to be subjected continuously to insults and indignities associated with segregation and discrimination in the M.E. church, fueled their desire to establish their own Methodist churches (Kennicott 1970). The failure of European-American Methodists to accede to and practice the belief that all persons are equal before God and endowed with equal value moved a group of freed African-American Methodists to mobilize a protest in Philadelphia's Saint George's church in 1787 to push for equal treatment by challenging the practice of segregated seating. Led by Richard Allen, one of the founders and future bishop of the African Methodist Episcopal (A.M.E.) church, their attempt to integrate church seating failed. Though their efforts failed, their translation of their religious belief that God is "no respecter of person" into practical action encouraged them to move beyond requesting equal treatment to seceding from the M.E. church. In essence, the independent A.M.E. church evolved from freed Africans' attempts to implement the Gospel in the world, particularly in the M.E. church.

Rather than form their own church immediately, Allen and cosecessionists used the Free African Society, a nonsectarian mutual aid organization founded by some secessionist group members prior to their departure from the M.E. church, as a sanctuary and base in which to plan their future as a religious group. With the Free African Society, Allen and his cosecessionists began a public subscription campaign to solicit funds to construct a church under the auspices of the M.E. church. Although secessionists did not like oppressive M.E. church practices and policies, they still sought to sustain a connection with the church. Allen wrote that he "was confident that there was no religious sect or denomination which would suit the capacity of the colored people as well as the Methodist; for this plain and simple gospel suits best for any people; for the unlearned can understand; and the reason that Methodists [are] so successful [in] the awakening and conversion of the colored people, [is their] plain doctrine and . . . good discipline" (Walker 1982:5).

The solicitation for building funds for a new church faltered somewhat when a split developed within the Free African Society after its membership voted to adopt a religious program oriented more towards Episcopalism than Methodism.[11] Consequently, Allen and a small band of the original seceders left the society and moved into an old blacksmith shop he owned to worship and continue their solicitation for building funds.

Saint George's Methodist officials refused to endorse Allen's efforts to build a church, though he assured them that his group sought its own edifice not because they found fault with the doctrines, form of government, and evangelistic and soul-saving orientation of Methodism but because they could no longer endure the constant humiliation and restrictions imposed on them at Saint George (Richardson 1976). Little credence was given to Allen's reassurances. Methodist officials refused to support any church that was not under their supervision. Consequently, Allen was ordered to desist soliciting funds or risk being thrown out of the church. Despite this threat, Allen and his group continued raising funds and dedicated their own building on June 29, 1794, as Bethel church in a ceremony presided over by M.E. bishop Francis Asbury.[12] Though the bishop blessed the building, the M.E. church still refused to support Bethel's petition to be recognized as a Methodist Episcopal church. Since M.E. church support was not forthcoming, Allen and his group moved to legally separate from the M.E. church through Pennsylvania's judiciary system. In 1816, the court declared Bethel an independent church (Walker 1982:8). Shortly after this legal victory, independent African Methodist churches throughout the north met in Philadelphia on April 9, 1816, to establish a national organization and elect a bishop. Initially the body voted Daniel Coker as Bishop, but he resigned the next day in favor of Richard Allen, whom the general conference later elected Bishop.[13] After his installation on April 10, Allen presided over the conference's adoption of the

Discipline of the Methodist Episcopal church with some minor changes such as discarding its proslavery provisions and limiting office holding in the new A.M.E. church to Africans and their descendants (George 1973:111).

From its inception, the A.M.E. church expressed a religious mission to engage the world by promoting the self-development and self-respect of freed and enslaved African-American communities. Keenly aware they were cut off from most social services in the North, African-American Methodists created a church to service both their spiritual and temporal needs (Walker 1982). Moreover, they acted on their obligation to uplift the downtrodden and liberate the oppressed through the establishment of church-sponsored mutual aid societies that worked to meet communal spiritual and social needs. Members of the A.M.E. church believed that spiritual and secular concerns were intertwined. Thus, if people were enslaved temporally this condition affected their spiritual development and vice versa. They also believed that their church was an instrument of God's providence. That is, God established the A.M.E. church to fulfill the divine promise of equality on earth by freeing Africans both mentally and physically from oppression.

This religious belief, which was initially cultivated in the "invisible" church, was interpreted by many African Episcopal Methodists to mean that the best way to achieve God's goal was through active participation in sociopolitical social change efforts. For instance, from the late 1820s through the early 1830s the A.M.E. church used its pulpit to urge free Africans to express their opposition to slavery by boycotting slave-produced goods (George 1973:132). Though the boycott eventually failed, African Methodists learned how to organize their church's material and cultural resources to seek liberation for enslaved African-Americans. After the A.M.E. church made inroads into the South during the antebellum period, some found themselves deeply entangled in local abolitionist struggles. For example, Morris Brown, who later became bishop of the A.M.E. church, used his church in Charleston, South Carolina, to raise funds to purchase enslaved persons' freedom. He coordinated these purchases several years before the Denmark Vesey insurrection conspiracy. For his effort, Brown was incarcerated for a year (Walker 1982:20). Furthermore, Denmark Vesey used the A.M.E. church, which he, Brown, and others had founded some years earlier in Charleston to facilitate the mobilization of a slave revolt in 1822. Levine (1977) contends that the importance of religious culture in mobilizing the uprising was evident in the testimonies of captured coconspirators. They testified at Vesey's trial that he appealed for their help by "saying all men had equal rights, blacks as well as whites" (Levine 1977:75).

Moreover, they asserted that Vesey, at meetings in the A.M.E. church and at his home, justified insurrection on religious grounds by contending that enslaved African-Americans "like the Israelites, could throw off the yoke of slavery and that God would come to their aid" (Kennicott 1970:7). Their effort, he declared, was "pleasing to the Almighty"; therefore, their success was guaranteed (Harding 1969). Shortly after the conspiracy was discovered and thwarted, it became apparent to "white" American "authorities" that independent churches provided the enslaved with a forum in which to express and imbue a sense of integrity, dignity, and identity at odds with a toleration of their enslaved status. In response to the Vesey conspiracy, the A.M.E. church was prohibited from operating in South Carolina (Woodson 1972).

African Methodist Episcopal Zion

Another African-American Methodist church, the African Methodist Episcopal Zion church emerged in New York City in 1796. African-American Methodists were dissatisfied with John Street Methodist Episcopal Church and especially its treatment of them. Bishop James W. Hood later described: "[The Negro] was wanted in the church for the support he gave it, for the numbers he enabled sectarians to claim in exhibiting their strength, and with the minority, who were truly pious, he was wanted there for the good of his soul. For these and other reasons he was not kept entirely out of the church. But in the church he was hampered and regulated. His privileges were proscribed and limited; every possible effort was made to impress him with a sense of inferiority. Preachers were selected who delighted in discoursing to him upon such texts as 'Servants, obey your masters,' and who were adept at impressing the Negro with inferiority in the most ingenious and least offensive way" (Walls 1974:44).

As a result of these conditions, blacks began holding meetings among themselves at John Street. However, as the number of African-American worshipers increased, African-American Methodists desired a separate building, which they erected in 1800 (Woodson 1972:68). Though they worshiped in their own building, African-American Methodists remained under the jurisdiction of John Street M.E. church until they decided to sever all connections with it in 1820. They established the African Methodist Episcopal church of New York. In 1821, the new church adopted the charter of the A.M.E. church of America, elected a number of elders, and organized the church as a national body.

Although the new church was doctrinally similar to the A.M.E. church, it chose not to unite with the A.M.E. church. Instead, it added the word "Zion" to its incorporation name in 1848 to differentiate itself from its sister institution in Philadelphia (Woodson 1972).[14] The A.M.E. Zion church, like its A.M.E. counterpart, was heavily involved in the uplift of the downtrodden and liberation of the oppressed. Though founded in the North, the church's mission, Bishop Hood contends, placed it in the forefront of struggles against slavery. "In the days of slavery the Zion ministers were generally leaders of the antislavery movement and their pulpits were always open to antislavery lectures. If no other house could be obtained for an antislavery meeting it was known that the Zion church could be had. The doors of [the] church [were] never closed against one who wanted to plead for the oppressed" (Walls 1974:38).

Moreover, A.M.E. Zion church doctrine encouraged members to believe that since all humans derived from "one blood one nation came to dwell on the face of the earth," oppression, especially slavery, was immoral and sinful. This view is summarized best by an excerpt from a statement issued by the A.M.E. Zion church's General Conference of 1856 in New York City:

> Whereas, the whole nation is now agitated upon the great sin of American slavery, which is regarded as the "sum of all villainies," it is time for every honest hearted man to define his position before the world either for or against the great moral evil. Upon this subject no neutral ground can be taken, for Christ says, "He that is not with me is against me." Therefore, the minister who evades or does not come on the side of liberty and the Gospel is not on the side of God. Therefore,
>
> Resolved, that it is the duty of the members of this General Conference to take a Gospel stand against the sin of slavery, as against all other sins, in teaching, preaching, praying, voting; and let the world know that so long as this sin remains, and we live, we will through God's help, be found on the side of the slaves, whether they be white or black; and, that our motto is and ever shall be, "Freedom forever." (Walls 1974:171)

The A.M.E. Zion church's formal stance against slavery played a central role in helping congregants create identities, meanings, solidarity, and commitment that encouraged them to participate in African-African liberation activities by way of African-American religious, benevolent, and freedom organizations. For instance, William Hamilton, an original trustee of the

A.M.E. Zion church, and James Varick, one of its founders, took the lead in organizing groups such as the New York Clarkson Association, the Wilberforce Benevolent Society, and the New York African Mutual Aid Society to aid in the fight for freedom. Moreover, A.M.E. Zion church culture contained multiple meanings, which those who wished to make use of them could interpret to promote mobilization against slavery. For example, Zionites' belief that Jesus' proclamation in the Gospel of Luke that he was sent by God to preach deliverance to the captives and to liberate those who are bruised convinced many that the Gospel required that they translate its words into deeds. Since the Gospel was interpreted in this activist manner, many congregations along the Mason and Dixon line became way stations in the Underground Railroad for escaped bondspersons fleeing northward to freedom (Wilmore 1994:87).

Frederick Douglass's testimonial on the church's influence on his commitment to social justice also suggests the importance of Zion church culture in facilitating congregants' activism:

> My connection with the African Methodist Episcopal Zion church began in 1838. This was soon after my escape from slavery and my arrival in New Bedford. Before leaving Maryland I was a member of the Methodist Church in Dallas Street, Baltimore, and should have joined a branch of that Church in New Bedford, Mass., had I not discovered the spirit of prejudice and the unholy connection of that Church with slavery. Hence I joined a little branch of Zion, of which Rev. William Serrington was the minister. I found him a man of deep piety, and of high intelligence. His character attracted me, and I received from him much advice and brotherly sympathy. When he was removed to another station Bishop Rush sent us a very different man, in the person of Peter Ross, a man of high character, but of very little education. After him came Rev. Thomas James. I was deeply interested in not only these ministers, but also in [others] . . .
>
> It is impossible for me to tell how far my connection with these devoted men influenced my career. As early as 1839 I obtained a license from the Quarterly Conference as a local preacher, and often occupied the pulpit by request of the preacher in charge. No doubt that the exercise of my gifts in this vocation, and my association with the excellent men to whom I have referred, helped to prepare me for the wider sphere of usefulness which I have since occupied. It was from this

Zion church that I went forth to the work of delivering my brethren from bondage, and this new vocation, which separated me from New Bedford and finally enlarged my views of duty, separated me also from the calling of a local preacher. (Wilmore 1984:89)

Douglass's remarks clearly identify relational networks within the church as crucial mechanisms in transforming religious cultural meanings into concrete collective actions. Ministers, like those referred to by Douglass, played an important role in helping people interpret and act on the link between the church's mission and the cause of freedom. Given this linkage, the A.M.E. Zion church cultivated religious interpretations and social consciousness among members that predisposed some to mobilize against slavery.

Since both the A.M.E. and A.M.E. Zion church cultures invoked anti-slavery zeal among freed and enslaved African-Americans, many southern states outlawed their establishment in their region (Harding 1969; Richardson 1976). White southerners feared that the withdrawal of enslaved African-Americans from their congregations implied an act of defiance that subverted slavery. In response, white southerners created a climate so repressive for independent African-American churches that their establishment in the antebellum South ceased.

Multivalent Church Culture

Like any social organization, independent African-American churches were dialectical cultural units in which multiple and conflicting religious meanings were produced regarding the best strategy of action for achieving African-American liberation in the United States. Church people, for example, varied in their response to the American Colonization Society's (ACS) attempt to aid in the improvement of free African-Americans by removing them to West Africa. The ACS was organized in 1817 by slaveholders, after early efforts by private individuals to reduce problems associated with increasing numbers of free African-Americans in the United States (Brown 1979). The ACS evolved from white American fears that if free African-Americans remained in the United States, they would demand equality of treatment and fuel rebellion among enslaved African-Americans. When blacks became aware of the ACS's ulterior motives, they organized a meeting at Bethel A.M.E. church in Philadelphia to express their opposition to emigration. Shortly after this meeting free African-Americans Christians initiated annual National Negro Conventions to determine the feasibility of emigration to Canada, to develop and implement plans for improving African-Americans condition in the United States, and to issue a statement against the American Colonization Society. The various objectives suggest that there were conflicting thoughts on how best to accomplish black liberation in the United States.

The Negro Conventions were organized and attended primarily by clergypersons whose interpretation of the Gospel predisposed them to translate their religious beliefs about injustice into political action. Many conventioneers concurred with A.M.E. minister Daniel Payne's perspective: "I am opposed to slavery, not because it enslaves the black man, but because it enslaves man. And were all the slaveholders in this land men of color, and the slaves white men I would be as thorough and uncompromising an abolitionist as I now am; for whatever and whenever I may see a being in form of a man, to plead his cause, against all the claims of his proud oppressor; and I shall do it not merely from the sympathy which man feels towards suffering man, but because God, the living God, whom I dare not disobey, had commanded me . . . to plead the cause of the oppressed" (Young 1977:70–71).

Though conventioneers agreed with Payne's perspective, they differed on which political strategy the Gospel deemed appropriate for resisting the ACS and achieving African-American liberation: moral suasion, self-help, or active resistance. Bishop Richard Allen, the first president of the Convention, advocated a strategy as conflictual as those articulated at the conference. Allen believed that moral suasion was the first method the Gospel called for African-American abolitionists to use to convince slaveholders that it was their Christian duty to free blacks. "If you love your children, if you love your country, if you love the God of love, clear your hands from slaves; burden not your country with them. My heart has been sorry for the blood shed of the oppressors, as well as the sight of him who hath said 'He that sheddeth man's blood, by man shall his blood be shed'" (Young 1977:35).

In short, Allen's liberation strategy afforded slaveholders a chance to repent their sins and free African-Americans without further bloodshed. However, if slaveholders refused to free slaves, Allen suggested that, as a last resort, God sanctioned the use of insurrection to secure the freedom of the enslaved. Though reluctant to articulate this view, Allen stated: "The dreadful insurrection [enslaved African-Americans] have made when opportunity has offered, is enough to convince a reasonable man that great uneasiness and not contentment is the inhabitant of their hearts. God himself hath pleaded their cause; He hath from time to time raised up instruments for that purpose, sometimes mean and contemptible in your sight, at other times he hath unseen such as it hath pleased him, with whom you have not thought it beneath your dignity to contend" (Young 1977:36).

The death of Bishop Allen prior to the second Negro Convention intensified discord over which strategy of action to use to achieve African-American liberation. At the 1843 Negro Convention, Rev. Henry Highland Garnet's speech entitled *An Address to the Slaves of the United States* poignantly made the case for God's active support for insurrection. He asserted: "The diabolical injustices by which your liberties are cloven down, NEITHER GOD, NOR ANGELS, OR JUST MEN, COMMAND YOU TO SUFFER FOR A SINGLE MOMENT. THEREFORE, IT IS YOUR SOLEMN AND IMPERATIVE DUTY TO USE EVERY MEANS, BOTH MORAL, INTELLECTUAL, AND PHYSICAL THAT PROMISES SUCCESS" (Young 1977:93).

The prominence of Garnet's position and interpretation of the Gospel in later conventions is evident in the fact that his ideas nearly garnered enough votes at one Negro Convention in the 1840s to pass a symbolic resolution expressing support for overthrowing the U.S. government if it did not grant African-Americans their liberation immediately (Bell 1969:80).

Due in large part to the moderating influence of moral suasionists like Bishop Allen and Frederick Douglass, who interpreted the Gospel as commanding Christian abolitionists to be prophets not avengers, active resistance was never completely endorsed by the conventions. Rather than support active resistance, the convention designed and implemented a blueprint for action called *The Constitution of the American Society of Free Persons of Colour* to raise African-Americans' status through self-help. Conventioneers felt comfortable with this strategy of action because their churches pioneered the use of self-help, and it required no monumental sacrifice of life.

The above account suggests that though conventioneers disagreed on which strategy the Gospel endorsed for achieving African-American liberation, they were united in their belief that Christianity obligated them to render some form of aid to the oppressed. Therefore, the convention organized the "American Society of Free Persons of Colour, for improving their Condition in the United States; for Purchasing Lands; and for the Establishing of a Settlement in Upper Canada," with local auxiliaries to ensure that local churches and congregants had access to organizational mechanisms through which they could mobilize whatever resources and social action they deemed necessary (Gross 1946:435).

Conclusion

This chapter suggests that enslaved African-Americans and their descendants' sociopolitical movement mobilization is best understood as part of a continuous history of struggle that was driven in part by religious cultural elements that were interpreted to encourage social activism. Specifically, black religion and churches during the antebellum period provided African-Americans with a reservoir of enduring religious meanings that some interpreted and appropriated to resist oppression and promote political activism. For many Blacks, religious ideas were inextricably linked to and shaped by a longing for freedom and equality.

CHAPTER 3

Church Culture and Sociopolitical Movements during Reconstruction and Post-Reconstruction

——◦((◦))◦——

onvinced that economic advancement was crucial for their future as a free people, northern delegates at the 1864 National Negro Convention in Syracuse, New York, created a new organization called the National Equal Rights League whose purpose was twofold: "To encourage [among black people] sound morality, education, temperance, frugality, industry, and promote everything that pertains to well-ordered and dignified life: to obtain by appeals to the minds and conscience of the American people, or by legal process when possible, a recognition of the rights of the colored people of the nation as American citizens" (Harding 1981:247). Numerous local League branches were formed in the South and North that emphasized both African-American self-help and political action for citizenship rights (Harding 1981). These organizational objectives facilitated the development of many post-Civil War politico-religious societies, programs, and associations in Little Rock, Arkansas, through which African-American men and women insisted that the nation and its leaders develop policies to help define and create the free, new time (Harding 1981:290).

Since most of these local organizations were established independent of the League, there was virtually no coordination between them. Consequently, African-American religious groups who traditionally linked religion to political action, like the Baptists, moved to unite their churches, religious associations, and politico-religious organizations under one statewide convention to better coordinate their efforts. By 1867, African-American Baptists in Arkansas had organized their state convention, which provided them with a social forum where they regularly interacted with others of their faith who maintained that the duty of the ministry was to elevate the laity and fulfill their Christian obligation to transform society by getting involved in socio-political work (Woodson 1972:177).

Though one of the primary goals of the state Baptist convention in Arkansas was to coordinate organizational efforts to improve conditions among African-Americans, there was disagreement over whether ministering to people's material needs required clergy to participate in political action and propagate political opinions (Washington 1986:115). The disagreement between Rev. James T. White, an educated African-American carpetbagger, and Rev. George Robinson, an illiterate popular antebellum African-American preacher in Arkansas, is a case in point.

> The primary issue between Robinson and White seemed to involve conflicts over clerical style and evangelistic territory rather than any ostensible political differences ... ideological differences actually exacerbated the split within the Arkansas state convention once it was organized. ... It was a fundamental split between the old guard and the slightly "uppity" black Northern missionary in the postwar South. White became the pastor of the First Colored Baptist Church of Helena, and won a seat in the Arkansas Senate in 1868. During that year, the political struggle in Arkansas was so intense between Democrats and Republicans that several local [religious] associations were unable to hold their meetings. Radical black Republicans were especially susceptible to the harassment of popular white Democrats. Wilson Brown, pastor of the First Colored Baptist Church of Little Rock "before the slaves were freed," refused to permit the black Arkansas River Union Baptist Association to meet in his edifice as previously agreed.[1] Brown refused because "there was so much political excitement that he thought it unsafe for us to meet there then— especially as some of our ministers were taking an active part in politics." (Washington 1986:114)

Though it is not clear whether Brown was for or against political evangelism, his refusal suggests that there was strong disagreement among Arkansas Baptists on political questions.

This dispute did not rage among the northern-based leadership of the Consolidated American Baptist Missionary Convention (CABMC), which was established in 1866 for the specific purpose of uniting Baptist associations in the east and west into one national body (Washington 1986:115). After the formation of CABMC, convention missionaries filtered into the South to provide both ecclesiastical and social leadership for formerly enslaved African-Americans. Once on the scene, missionaries helped southern African-Americans to establish their own churches and urged them to promote their interests pro-actively in the sociopolitical arena. However, many native southern African-American Baptists, especially ministers, refused to accede to CABMC missionary calls for political evangelism. Instead they "admonished their people to live righteously, to pray their situation might be different, and to wait patiently upon God" (Cunningham 1985:270). Though this theological approach tended to buttress passivity it also contained a message of hope that encouraged some Baptists to engage in actions in the "here and now" to make life tolerable for African-Americans. Religious messages intended to mollify contained a range of meanings that African-Americans readily interpreted in light of their own experiences as oppressed people. From these multiplicities of religious mean-ings, some African-Americans constructed religious frames that emphasized internal action through economic self-reliance while others developed frames that encouraged engagement in political activism to improve conditions in their communities. The writings of Rufus Perry, one of the CABMC's most influential leaders and editor of its periodical, the *American Baptist*, demon-strate how activist religious frames were constructed during Reconstruction. In the *American Baptist*, Perry tried to allay African-Americans' reluctance to mobi-lize for social change by constructing religious frames that specified "God [was] on the side oppressed" in the struggle against oppression; hence, "the God of justice will lead [us] to victory" (Washington 1986:116). Since God is a revo-lutionary and the Gospel mandates engagement with the world, Perry argued that clergy and churches were obligated to teach their congregants how to par-ticipate in the political process. He wrote: "We learn from observation that the only way to make the ballot a blessing is to educate and Christianize the voter. Education and piety are the only influences to which the ballots of the masses will yield and be governed for the general good of the people, the strength of gov-ernment and the development of national resources" (Washington 1986:116).

Moreover, Perry constructed religious frames in his writings that sug-gested African-Americans were divine instruments in God's effort to trans-form the United States into the Gospel's beloved community. Though this process was slow, Perry wrote in his 1868 CABMC Annual Report: "To know that God is working for any good object, is to regard it as accomplished and rejoice over the result. Although the work of our hands be slow and doubtful, yet there is a power behind the throne whose will cannot be resisted" (Washington 1986:116).

African-Americans constructed religious meanings that deemed it impractical for them to abstain from sociopolitical efforts to advance their community. For instance, during Reconstruction in Arkansas, many churches, especially Baptist, maintained that God obligated them to be directly involved in building the divine kingdom on earth. Consequently, churches deemed it necessary to care for people's material as well as spiritual needs. In attempting to fulfill this obligation, churches transformed their edifices into schools and encouraged people to secure a basic education to ensure they sustained their newly won freedom. My analysis of church culture's influence on black sociopolitical movements during the Reconstruction and Post-Reconstruction era in the South, particularly in Arkansas, is presented in six sections. Sections one through two examine how religious education stimulates political activism. In sections three through six I explore politicized religious beliefs' effect on African-Americans' actions in Arkansas during the protest against the 1891 election bill and de jure segregation, the African migration movement, and the organization of the Progressive Farmers and Household Union and the Southern Tenant Farmers Union.

Reconstruction Era

Secular engagement through religious education

To ensure African-Americans viability as a free people in Arkansas, African-American churches with the help of some European-American Christians organized secondary schools to teach young and old African-Americans to read and write. Missionaries from the American Baptist Home Mission Society spearheaded this endeavor through their Sunday school movement. Sunday school missionary Joanna P. Moore, who taught young and old to read and write during her mission work in Arkansas, noted: "Through the Sabbath school we led the young people into the churches, for even as early as this many of them were losing their interest in preaching. Through the Sabbath school many also learned how to read. In 1879 myself and others helped to reorganize seventy-five new Sabbath Schools. They would run for a month or six weeks and then die. We started them off again the next time we visited them and so kept on until they were strong enough to run the year through" (Tyms 1965:143).

The assistants to whom Moore alludes were typically African-American Baptist laypersons and clergy the American Baptist Home Mission Society trained to organize and implement religious education among African-Americans. Keeping with European-American Baptist Home Mission Society's policy of developing African-Americans' abilities to help themselves educate their communities, European-American Baptist missionaries usually apprenticed African-Americans in the techniques of organizing and carrying on Sunday school work in the field for a period of time before leaving them alone to extend religious and secular instruction to African-Americans. Indigenous religious instruction played a significant role in cultivating efficacy among African-Americans whose experiences with slavery had socialized them to see themselves as having little right and capacity to exercise self-determination. Participation in Sunday school usually exposed these individuals to African-American teachers and preachers, who exuded confidence in their own moral, intellectual, and social abilities to effect change in society through their teaching. These Sunday school interactions and instructions were so effective at producing African-Americans with ways of knowing and visions of the future important for advancing the community that a resolution was passed by the Freedmen Baptist Association of New Orleans in 1879: "Resolv[ing], that our pastors and deacons shall start and keep alive during the whole year, a Sabbath school in every church" (Tyms 1965:143–44).

Since black American and European-American Sunday school missionaries believed that communal advancement hinged on how well African-Americans acquired moral, intellectual, and social skills, they initiated efforts to increase instruction time for Sunday schools from one hour on Sunday to several days of the week. Two new educational systems were created to fill this need: the Fireside School and the Sunshine Band movement. Joanna Moore established the Fireside School system in 1884 to ensure that children received moral and religious training seven days a week. This school system required that "[t]hose parents who willingly accepted the plan of the school pledged themselves to pray with and for their children daily, to teach them God's word, and to expect their daily conversion; they agreed to be good parents for their children in daily life, in temper, words, and dress; and to train their 'children to live for the glory of God in body, mind, and spirit'" (Tyms 1965:145). The establishment of this new school was followed in 1892 with the initiation of the Sunshine Band movement in Little Rock, which extended the Fireside exercise a step further by establishing systematic Bible study among neighbors (Tyms 1965). Within these study groups, individuals interacted with like-minded individuals from whom they gained further strength, celebrated a shared culture, and acquired skills that facilitated self-confidence and efficacy.

Moreover, participation in the Baptist Home Mission's Sunday school movement exposed African-Americans to religious educational principles that mandated:

(1) The freedmen were to be educated as *men*, for education that fails to recognize the full, absolute, equal humanity of black men is fatally inadequate. (2) The freedmen were to be educated as *American citizens*, in recognition of the fact that the rights, powers, and duties of citizenship should be a part of their training . . . [And 3,] [t]hey were to be educated as *Missionary Christians*, indicating that each believer must be taught that he belongs to the human family and that whoever has received the gift is a minister of the same to all men. (Tyms 1965:146)

Hinson's research on European American Baptists in Arkansas found that though they concentrated primarily on educating African-American ministers, they sometimes articulated a broader need to educate African-Americans about their "rights, powers, and duties" as citizens. A proposed resolution at the Arkansas State Baptist Convention in 1888 illustrates this phenomenon.

Whereas, The colored people of our State have become citizens among us; and, whereas the good of our civil government, as these people have been enfranchised, depends to a great extent upon their mental culture; and, whereas also their qualifications for citizenship depend upon their moral and religious culture, and, whereas these colored people are dependent upon the white Christians; therefore,
Resolved, That we, the members of this Convention, advise our ministering brethren to endeavor to help the colored people, especially their ministers, by aiding them all we can in this direction. (Hinson 1979:165)

These broader concerns and principles reinforced African-American Baptists' belief in the equality of humanity and, as outlined earlier, inspired them to continued collective efforts to organize and sustain their own state and national conventions to pursue their communities' moral, intellectual, economic, and social advancement.

The effort to consolidate Baptists nationally culminated in 1896 when ten states' delegates met in St. Louis to form the National Baptist Convention. Each state sent the following numbers of delegates to the meeting: Alabama, 61; Arkansas, 3; Florida, 1; Georgia, 3; Louisiana, 2; Mississippi, 10; North Carolina, 4; Ohio, 1; Tennessee, 6; and Virginia, 5 (Tyms 1965:148). The primary concern of the meeting was "to consider the moral, intellectual, and religious growth of the denomination, to deliberate on the great questions which characterized the Baptist churches" (Tyms 1965:149). This suggests that Baptist national conventions from their start had a central objective of educating African-Americans. Like others throughout the United States, the Baptist state convention members in Arkansas came to realize that secondary school organization was only the first step in the elevation of African-Americans. Consequently, they established Arkansas Baptist College in Little Rock in 1883. In 1885, Arkansas Baptist College was officially incorporated and immediately commenced instructing students in the art of pursuing communal spiritual and secular advancement.

After the Civil War, the A.M.E. and A.M.E. Zion churches, like their Baptist counterparts, quickly began establishing their own churches and educational institutions in Arkansas. Shortly after Arkansas Baptist College opened, the A.M.E. Church's 1885 annual conference in Arkansas passed resolutions establishing a joint commission on church schools to formulate plans to organize an educational institution. Five ministerial representatives of this commission met in Little Rock in May 1886 to establish Bethel Institute. The school was sorely needed, insofar as 43 percent of African-Americans in Arkansas were illiterate (Moneyhon 1985:226).[2] Though this rate was substantially lower than the 53 percent illiteracy rate in 1880, African-American Methodists were not satisfied with the slow pace of progress. African-American Arkansans had long been deprived of educational opportunities that could substantially improve their socioeconomic status (Moneyhon 1985:226). To lower the illiteracy rate and increase educational opportunities, the A.M.E. Church established secondary schools like Bethel Institute, which held its first class sessions in September 1886 in the basement of its namesake, Bethel A.M.E. Church in Little Rock.[3]

In undertaking the task of educating African-Americans, the A.M.E. church in Arkansas "manifested faith, courage, noble regard for the education process, and an insatiable desire on the part of [African-Americans] themselves, to help themselves" (Smith 1975:6). Some Methodist ministers in Arkansas used their church culture to invoke a collective politico-religious identity and consciousness that some African-Americans use to interpret and act on Jesus' proclamation in the *Gospel of Luke*: "The spirit of the Lord is upon me; therefore he has anointed me. He has sent me to bring glad tidings to the poor, to proclaim liberty to captives, recovery of sight to the blind and release to prisoners." This interpretation of the *Gospel of Luke* had long been a part of A.M.E. Church culture and is best exemplified by the remarks of abolitionist Martin R. Delaney, who asserted in his writings:

> The time has now fully arrived, when the colored race is called upon by all ties of common humanity, and all the claims of consummate justice, to go forward and take their position, and do battle in the struggle now being made for the redemption of the world. Our cause is a just one: the greatest at present that elicits that attention of the world. For if there is a remedy; that remedy is now at hand. God himself as assuredly as he rules the destinies of nations, and entereth measures into the "hearts of men," has presented these measures to us. Our race is to be redeemed; it is a great and glorious work, and we are the instrumentalities by which it is to be done. (Wilmore 1994:112)

To take on their redemptive role, African-American Methodists understood that they had to create institutions to direct and educate ministers and teachers who could emancipate the minds of Blacks from the slavery and their hands from the bondage of menial labor (Smith 1975:5). This educational imperative in combination with the realization that pooling various African-American denominations' resources improved the quality of the education offered encouraged the A.M.E. church to open its schools to nondenominational members (McSwain 1982).

Like the A.M.E. church, the A.M.E. Zion church's educational project cultivated organizational skills and religious culture that provided African-Americans with the impetus for social action. Sensing the importance of an educational social setting for instilling organizational skills and encouraging and legitimating socio-political engagement, the A.M.E. Zion church's General Conference of 1844 in New York City formally moved to establish a connectional institution of learning. A committee was formed to draft a constitution, as a basis for the establishment of a connectional manual labor school, under the supervision of the General Conference (Walls 1974:302). According to Walls, "this action resulted in the calling of a Literary Connectional Convention at York, Pa., to be composed of delegates from the New York and Philadelphia Conferences to convene in 1847" (1974:302). Participants at the Pennsylvania Convention constructed a constitution and preamble, which they presented to the 1848 General Conference delineating plans for establishing and operating a connectional manual labor school known as Rush Academy in Essex County, New York. The preamble reflected the A.M.E. Zion church's confidence in education's ability to collectively transform African-Americans into religiously motivated missionaries of communal advancement:

> Whereas, We the ministry of the African Methodist Episcopal Zion Church in America, feeling as we do that many of the difficulties against which we have to labor, grow out of the fact that there is a great lack of education among us; and, Whereas, Man viewed as a being susceptible of happiness and capable of responsible action, sustains a thousand relations, involving as many duties; whatever, therefore, tends to increase this susceptibility and enlarge this capacity, must exalt his nature and promote the benevolent purpose for which he was created, as such is the tendency of a well directed education, of virtuous example, of sound philosophy and theology, indeed, of everything which gives the understanding a controlling influence over the grosser passions, of everything which purifies and regulates the feelings without diminishing their order or depriving them of their appropriate objects; and since among the many causes which conspire to produce this effect, none is so efficient as a well directed education; therefore, these persons whose names are here connected do agree to form an institution, having for its objects the establishment of prominent schools of education preparatory to the ministry, and for other useful information calculated to elevate our whole people. (Walls 1974:302–3)

When A.M.E. Zion churches in Arkansas organized their state Conference in 1870 they, like the General Conference, placed a high premium on educating African-Americans. This emphasis eventually led the Arkansas Conference to establish Arkansas High School in Parkdale and Ashley County High School in Wilmot in 1891 (Walls 1974:327). The establishment of these schools and several others in neighboring states moved the 1892 General Conference of the A.M.E. Zion Church to pass the following resolution:

> *Whereas*, We feel that education among the people whom we represent
> cannot be too strongly encouraged, and that too many schools for such
> education cannot be established, offering such advantages to the sub-
> jects of our common Church; and,
> *Whereas*, it seems to us that it is the disposition of the Church to enlarge
> upon the advantages given the youth in all the parts of this land and
> Whereas, The Tennessee Conference has established the Greenville
> High School; Arkansas Conferences, the Arkansas High School . . . be it
> *Resolved*, 1. To encourage, help, and stimulate such, and this General
> Conference accept and adopt these schools as connectional schools.
> (Walls 1974:324)[4]

The resolution expressed and reinforced beliefs about the necessity of education in creating a critical mass of people with the mental dispositions and skills
necessary for motivating political evangelism (Walls 1974). In other words,
church-sponsored schools provided students with opportunities for spiritual
nourishment, emotional support, friendships, and practical help in interpreting and acting on the Gospel's mandate for religious outreach and sociopolitical organizing and activism.

Politico-religious activism

Since religiously educated African-Americans possessed a commitment in
both belief and action to sociopolitical activism, some deemed it a part of their
Christian responsibility to participate in politics. James Poindexter, a Baptist
minister from Ohio, in an address to an audience entitled the *Pulpit and
Politics*, articulated the rationale for religious activism during Reconstruction:

> Nor can a preacher more than any other citizen plead his religious
> work as an exemption from duty. Going to the Bible to learn the rela-
> tion of the pulpit to politics, and accepting the prophets, Christ, and
> apostles, and the pulpit of their times, and their precepts and examples
> as the guide of the pulpit today, I think that their conclusion will be
> that wherever there is sin to be rebuked, no matter by whom commit-
> ted, and ill to be averted or good to be achieved by our country or
> mankind, there is a place for the pulpit to make itself felt and heard.

The truth is, all the help the preachers and all other worthy citizens can give by taking hold of politics is needed in order to keep the government out of bad hands and secure the ends for which governments are formed. (Woodson 1972:202)

Hence, when the commander of the Fourth Military District, in compliance with the provisions of the Reconstruction Acts of March 1867, ordered the registration of potential voters in Arkansas for the elections of representatives to frame a new state constitution to enfranchise African-Americans, some religiously educated African-Americans like Baptist minister James T. White of Helena, Arkansas, submitted their candidacy for state delegate for the 1868 Reconstruction constitutional convention. White believed, like Florida's A.M.E. minister-politician Charles Pearce: "A man . . . cannot do his whole duty as a minister except he looks out for the political interest of his people. They are like ships out to sea, and they must have somebody to guide them; and it is natural that they should get their best informed men to lead them" (Walker 1985:11–12). Moreover, White correctly surmised that the odds for his election were good given that the military order resulted in the enrollment of 66,805 voters, including 21,696 African-Americans into the state's new electorate (St. Hilaire 1974:38). In the November 1867 election these voters endorsed, in a vote of 25,576 to 13,558, convening a convention to form a new state constitution (St. Hilaire 1974:38). Due to the superior organizational skills of Republicans and the refusal of many European-American Arkansans to participate in the election, a majority of the seventy-five delegates elected were Republicans, including eight African-Americans of various abilities but all of whom were religiously affiliated in some way (St. Hilaire 1974:38).

There is considerable disagreement in the literature regarding the abilities and performance of newly freed African-Americans at southern state constitutional conventions. William Dunning (1962), for example, argued that Reconstruction allowed ignorant and propertyless African-Americans to secure control of the South. Thomas Staples (1923), a Dunning student from Arkansas who examined Reconstruction in the state, suggested that African-American convention delegates were mere puppets of European-American Republicans (St. Hilaire 1974). Before the constitutional convention convened, this view was conveyed in local newspapers around Arkansas such as the *Van Buren Press*, which in a December 13, 1867, article alleged that "the constitutional convention meetings in the state had been called for the purpose of 'giving silly Negroes and dishonest white men an opportunity of seeing a big town, free of expenses . . . and to sit in arm chairs in the state house, and look as knowingly owls' " (St. Hilaire 1974:40).

In contrast, W. E. B. Du Bois's (1935) and Kenneth Stampp's (1965) evaluations of African-American Reconstruction delegations found that they were by no means passive or irresponsible (Hume 1973). Considering the situation of newly freed blacks, Stampp concluded that their political performance on reconstruction issues was "relatively clear-cut. Given their condition and the limited political choices open to them, most Negroes responded to the appeals of rival politicians in a manner that had obvious logic to it" (1965:165). Du Bois (1935) documented and demonstrated the exceptional abilities of African-American members of the Arkansas convention through their articulate speeches and provided evidence that they were not simply voting as European-American Republican leaders suggested.

Contrary to Staples's (1923) findings, evidence suggests that African-American delegates were highly skilled, independent and effective politicians. The African-American delegation at the Arkansas constitutional convention comprised four educated ministers, two farmers, one planter, and one postmaster. All black members of the delegation were Christian, literate, and united in their determination and effort to secure citizenship rights for African-Americans. The names of four ministers attending the convention were William Grey and James White, Phillips County; Monroe Hawkins, Lafayette County; and Thomas Johnson, Pulaski County. The four nonclergy delegates were James Mason, Chicot County; William Murphy, Jefferson County; Henry Rector, (county represented unknown); and Richard Samuels, Hempstead County. Generally, African-American delegates represented counties in the central and southeastern sections of Arkansas that were majority African-American. Chicot County had the highest proportion of African-Americans in the state (87 percent) while Mississippi County had the smallest majority (51 percent) (Moneyhon 1985:223). Though Pulaski County, whose seat is Little Rock, did not have an African-American majority, its African-American population was sufficiently large to ensure that one of the four delegates from the county was an African-American.

Due to the rural character of the state, most African-Americans during Reconstruction worked as tenant farmers or sharecroppers who cultivated leased land from landowners in exchange for half the crops or profit from its sale (Raper and Reid 1971). However, sharecropping worked to the disadvantage of tenant farmers since it required that next year's crop be pledged to landowners in exchange for credit to purchase supplies that exacted exorbitant rates of interest. This credit arrangement created an environment of debt and poverty among sharecroppers that most found hard to escape. Understanding that their community could not advance far beyond illiteracy, farming, and poverty without the vote, African-American convention delegates, especially minister-delegates, argued skillfully and forcefully for an enfranchising constitution. For example, William Grey, chief spokesperson of the African-American delegation, replied to a European-American delegate's attempt to secure the adoption of the state's 1864 constitution, which failed to enfranchise African-Americans, by asserting: "I am here as the representative of a portion of the citizens of Arkansas, whose rights are not secured by the Ordinance offered by the gentleman. [The citizens I represent] . . . have stood by the Government and the old flag in times of trouble . . . From this and other considerations we are here not to ask charity . . . but to receive . . . the appointment of our rights, as assigned by the Reconstruction Acts of Congress" (St. Hilaire 1974:47–48).

In addition to discussing African-American enfranchisement, members of the convention also debated the merits of the Freedmen's Bureau and miscegenation. Southern white conservative delegates criticized the Freedmen's Bureau, which Congress established in 1865 as a postwar relief agency, as the corrupt arm of the Republican Party (St. Hilaire 1974). This assertion was made primarily because conservatives realized that the Freedmen's Bureau's effort to educate and advance African-Americans as full citizens threatened to inhibit their attempt to reestablish a quasi-feudal farm labor system. Several European-American conservatives in the convention developed arguments pushing for discontinuing the Bureau based on the illogical assertion that in their counties, where the Bureau was no longer operating, everyone "g[o]t along more peaceably and quietly then before" (St. Hilaire 1974:50).

To counter attempts to dismantle the Bureau prematurely, African-American delegates mounted an unrelenting defense that called for its extension. William Grey criticized European-American conservatives' prejudicial arguments with this remark:

> While gentlemen have expressed the kindest feelings, they have said they believed the organization of the Freedmen's Bureau to be the greatest curse that has been inflicted upon our race, *except our emancipation!* I believe there are many honorable exceptions to the prejudices that blind the minds of men . . . yet, while such antagonistic feelings still remain in the breasts of the leading men of our country, do you

think it would be wrong on our part to ask the Government to continue the only practical means by which we obtain a shadow of justice?
(St. Hilaire 1974:50)

Thomas Johnson, another member of the African-American delegation
also spoke in favor of continuing the Bureau. He asserted: "I do not think I
ever would vote for the Freedmen's Bureau to be done away with, until the
country is reconstructed. We need reconstruction—universal suffrage. Give us
that, and we don't ask for more—give us that, and we will not need the
Freedmen's Bureau" (St. Hilaire 1974:50).

African-Americans also used argumentative skills, honed in religious
schools and churches, to alter the direction of debates and votes regarding miscegenation laws. For example, William Grey's satirical yet convincing response
to a European-American conservative's miscegenation resolution helped to
reduce the measure to a motion with little impact (Palmer 1965:113). Grey
proposed that, if such a law be enacted, it include a severe punishment for
European American violators: "the provision is superfluous. I know that such
provisions have heretofore more or less obtained; but while the contract has
been kept on our part, it has not been kept upon the part of our friends; and
I propose, if such an enactment is inserted in the Constitution, to insist, also,
that if any white man shall be found cohabiting with a negro woman, the
penalty shall be death" (St. Hilaire 1974:52–53).

Grey presented two reasons for opposing the miscegenation clause.
First, he argued that a constitutional provision prohibiting unions between
Europeans and African-Americans was unnecessary because few people inter-
racially married in the state. Second, he asserted that the resolution, which
restricted only interracial marriage, failed to prohibit European-American
men from simply residing with African-American women (Hume 1973:188).
When another European-American delegate offered a substitute resolution
that maintained that the amalgamation of the "races" was "contrary to the
nature and law of God," Grey countered:

It seems some of our sages have made some extraordinary discoveries,
in their investigations of the last few years, in regard to the laws of God
on this subject; and having broken those laws, I should think they
ought first to repent, before proposing any amendments!

As far as the intercourse between the races is concerned, there is
no gentleman here, whatever may be his opinions, that objects to it

more than I. I am willing that you should make any enactment of this subject, outside of the organic law; but sir, let that be, *equality before the law*. Do not touch that sacred instrument, by inserting anything that puts in an entering wedge that may hereafter split the whole concern into a thousand pieces. (St. Hilaire 1974:54–56)

This unique way of deconstructing the legitimacy of the miscegenation motion suggests that African-American delegates looked to their experiences and religion rather than radical white Republicans for guidance in political debates and votes.

The constitution that the convention finally adopted by a vote of forty-six to twenty was one of the most progressive in the state's history. It guaranteed the equality of all persons before the law and the enfranchising of all male citizens with the exception of certain persons who had served the Confederacy (Hume 1973:203; St. Hilaire 1974:58). Despite congressional stipulation that voters in each of the ten ex-Confederate states ratify new constitutions granting full citizenship rights to African-American males as a criterion for readmittance into the union, throughout the convention European-American conservatives attempted to block any legal design to enhance African-American Arkansans' political and social position (St. Hilaire 1974). These obstructions frustrated and angered African-American delegates like William Murphy, who broke his silence at the convention to say: "I would never have spoken, here, but to say this to the men that have been our masters, men whom we have brought to the very condition they are in, and have not only fed them, but have clothed them, have tied their shoes, and finally have fought until they were obliged to surrender. Yet, now that they have surrendered, they say we have no rights!" (St. Hilaire 1974:58).

It was inconceivable to African-Americans that southern European-American conservatives, whom they had defeated during the Civil War, had the audacity to argue that blacks should not be granted political rights. Thomas Johnson suggested that conservatives' recalcitrance regarding African-American full rights as citizens implied they wished only "to let us stay in slavery" (St. Hilaire 1974:58–59). In this way, religiously politicized African-American delegates at the constitutional convention demonstrated their independent ability to represent their constituents' interests and played an important role in drafting Arkansas's 1868 constitution.

After the adjournment of the convention, all but one African-American delegate, Henry Rector, continued their involvement in politics. William Grey,

Monroe Hawkins, and James White all were elected to the state House of Representatives while other delegates like Thomas Johnson engaged in political activism outside of the state apparatus. Johnson attended a meeting at Wesley Chapel Church in Little Rock on June 20, 1869, with eight other African-American Christians to discuss how to use religious resources to mobilize community support for establishing an African-American newspaper. After a long discussion, a committee was formed—consisting of Rev. Hagan Green, Jerome Lewis, Rev. Thomas Johnson, Armstead Handy, Rev. John Peyton, Winfield Scott, David McWatters, Rev. Henry Gratton, and Emanuel Armstead—that announced plans for a benefit dinner at City Hall on June 24, for the formation of an African-American newspaper (Littlefield and McGraw 1979). In their public announcement, which was read in every black church, the committee appealed for communal support: "We are trying to sustain schools, and we believe that if we can support a paper, that it will encourage our people in the matter of knowledge, pride, and usefulness. . . . We are poor and weak; we ask for help. Give us help and in other days we will stand by the friends who help us now" (Littlefield and McGraw 1979:75).

The committee's appeal implicitly tapped deep religious sentiments that encouraged African-Americans to develop skills necessary for training and sustaining a cadre of individuals with reservoirs of ways of knowing, forms of struggle, and visions of the future important for undermining white supremacy's domination over their community. Four days after the benefit dinner, *The Arkansas Freeman* weekly newspapers begin publication under the editorship and proprietorship of Rev. Tabb Gross, an ex-bondsman from Kentucky who came to Arkansas "to assist in reconstructing the state" (Littlefield and McGraw 1979).

In early July, Gross published a prospectus for the newspaper in local papers that reflected its Christian founders' desire to use elements of religious culture as a crucible for guiding African-American political and economic advancement. The prospectus read, "The blacks of Arkansas needed a 'faithful and reliable newspaper, devoted particularly to their interests and conducted and controlled by men of their own race and color.' Being uneducated and 'by nature credulous and confiding,' they were 'easily deceived and imposed upon by false friends.' It was therefore highly important that they have as advisors and leaders honest and faithful men who were 'bound to them by the close ties of color, kindred, and a common destiny'" (Littlefield and McGraw 1979:77–78).

Furthermore, Littlefield and McGraw found that Gross made the following pledge as the *Arkansas Freeman's* editor: "I shall always use whatever political influence my position will give me, towards benefiting, in every possible way, my own race and color—by securing them the benefits of schools for their children, and churches to worship in—by procuring the passage of laws to protect them in their contracts, and secure to them the fruits of their labor; by lightening the burdens of taxation, and in every other possible way to promote their happiness and increase their prosperity" (Littlefield and McGraw 1979:78).

These excerpts suggest the *Arkansas Freeman* used religious principles as guideposts for broadening the space for creating political and organizational opportunities for advancing African-American Arkansans' socioeconomic and political independence.

Gross's pursuit of African-American independence encountered opposition from Radical Republicans who viewed his paper's commitment to universal suffrage as a threat to their political hegemony. He favored "Universal suffrage, and Universal Amnesty, and Equal and Exact Justice [for] all Men" because he believed that there would be no lasting peace in the South without the reenfranchisement of European-American conservatives (Littlefield and McGraw 1979:80). Gross's view reflected his religious belief in human equality and his naive belief that "it was just a matter of time . . . until the Democratic Party regained its political strength. The rights of blacks would be better secured by granting a boon to the Southern whites than by being compelled to yield to them thereafter. If blacks did not stand for universal suffrage, Gross predicted, they would later suffer retaliation" (Littlefield and McGraw 1979:82).

To avoid this political calamity Gross encouraged African-Americans to discard Radical Republican principles that advantage them while disadvantaging southern European-American conservatives. In addition Gross suggested in an editorial in the *Arkansas Freeman*: "Above all, we shall try to get our people to think for themselves; and not to be like a flock of sheep, to be driven all in a body, in one hole in a fence, and all out together at another, as a few party leaders may desire. We like party and party success, but we like intelligent and independent manhood more and more; but parties made up of men, who have no minds of their own, can never succeed long, or do any good to a people or a country" (Littlefield and McGraw 1979:81).

Gross's attack on Republican attempts to reduce party competition by disenfranchising European-American Democrats and making African-Americans politically subservient eventually forced Republicans to silence the *Arkansas Freeman* in 1870. However, before leaving the public scene, Gross delivered a speech to mainly African-Americans at a Republican rally in Little

Rock on August 8, 1870, in which he reiterated themes he expressed in editorials in the *Freeman*. Gross advised African-Americans "to elect honest men: 'When you send one to the legislature or to the congress to be certain and send a nigger along to watch him.' He warned them not to take sides in the current split of the Radical Republican Party into the factions of Governor Powell Clayton and the Reverend Joseph Brooks. Blacks held the balance of voting power and should let the factions come to them for help: 'They have been telling us these democrats would play h–l with us—now *they're* playing h–l—so our safe plan is to watch all'" (Littlefield and McGraw 1979:84).

These political altercations suggest that during Reconstruction the deeply felt religious commitments of a pool of individuals were instrumental in encouraging African-Americans to oppose white Republican attempts to garner political hegemony. Religiously motivated blacks took this position despite the fact they did not know what white southerners intended to do with their vote.

Post-Reconstruction Era

Religion as a mobilizing resource during post-reconstruction

Reconstruction ended in 1877 when the Democrats agreed to allow the electoral commission to declare Republican Rutherford B. Hayes the presidential victor, though he did not receive more popular votes than Democrat Samuel J. Tilden. In return Democrats were allowed to restore white supremacy in southern states. After this historic "agreement," legal restrictions were instituted that formalized African-American Arkansans' subordination and disenfranchisement. However, these laws did not immediately prohibit African-American participation in Arkansas politics. Moneyhon, a noted Arkansas historian, maintained that though "the return of the Democratic Party to power in the state limited the opportunities for black participation in politics, black voters continued to take part in elections, and their leaders developed methods and opportunities to represent the state's black population. Arkansas's black leaders effectively articulated and expressed the interests of their constituents up to the end of the century" (1985:222).

Since the church was the only institution owned and independently operated by African-American Arkansans, it provided the social context within which black Christians and non-Christians interacted with one another to express their grievance, forming relational bonds, identities, and meanings that encouraged participation not only in church work but also in political matters that concerned their community. Consequently, among the eight African-Americans elected to Arkansas's post-Reconstruction general assembly were four Baptists, two members of the A.M.E. Church, one Roman Catholic, and one Quaker (Moneyhon 1985:231).

Cultural exposure together with a political arrangement known as fusion politics helped to sustain and elevate African-Americans' participation in the political process during post-Reconstruction. John Graves's study, *Town and Country: Race Relations in an Urban and Rural Context, Arkansas, 1865–1905*, suggests that an attempt to reduce racial tensions and preserve order in heavily populated African-American counties led to the development of the "fusion principle." Under this system Republicans and Democrats agreed to meet prior to Election Day to allot each other places on the ballot; thus sharing political power. According to Graves the typical fusion system operated similar to this scheme implemented in Jefferson County in 1878: "Democratics usually named the county judge, county clerk, the assessor, and the state senator; while the Republicans chose the sheriff, the circuit clerk, and the three representatives in the lower house of the General Assembly; lesser county offices were similarly divided" (1990:54).

In view of the fact that African-Americans participating in the fusion system were educated in church schools that taught them to transform the world into God's beloved community, they frequently ran for office under this arrangement.

Fusion political arrangements increased African-Americans' participation in the political process for a period of time, since their votes enabled an unpopular Democratic leadership, whose laissez-faire economic program sparked party defection among European-American Democratic voters, with a means to maintain their ascendancy within the Democratic Party. When the agrarian European-American Democratic constituency, for example, abandoned their party to join the third party agrarian movement (for example, the Greenback Party, the Agricultural Wheel, and the Union Labor Party), the party leadership used African-American votes garnered from the fusion arrangement to fend off this serious challenge to their political hegemony (Graves 1967:201). Though conservative Democrats supported African-American officeholders through the agency of the fusion system, they attempted to arrest the development of nascent Republican leadership among native European-American Arkansans by branding the Republican Party a tool of African-American control (Graves

1967:201–2). As Democrats disparaged the fusion system they simultaneously made overtures for African-American support since the third party agrarian movement in 1888 and 1890 in the form of the Union Labor-Republican Party coalition posed a serious electoral threat to Democrats.[5] Democrats tried to reconcile this seeming contradiction in strategy by arguing that people should fear northern carpetbaggers more than African-American domination. Clarifying this view, the editor of the *Pine Bluff Press Eagle* wrote:

> Republics are proverbially ungrateful; so are republicans. It was the Negro vote that such men . . . were able to get possession of the southern states during the era of reconstruction and inaugurate systems of wholesale plunder that foisted debts upon the southern people which they are paying to this day. The white people of the south are intolerant of Negro domination, it is true; but [white] republicans . . . taught them to be so. They have learned from bitter experience in the past, that Negro domination is but another name for carpetbag radical domination and its attendant train of evils; and until the Negroes manifest wisdom and independence enough to cut loose from their old political bosses, the white people of the south will ever remain "solid" in their resistance of Negro domination in politics. (Graves 1990:148)

Although Democrats lobbied for African-American votes by welcoming them into their clubs, rallies, and parades, they did not endorse racial equality (Graves 1990:148). Consequently, African-Americans viewed the Democratic approach to include them in their party as a transparent attempt to "keep them in their place." As a result, the majority of blacks voted for the Union Labor-Republican ticket. This was a logical move considering that the Union Labor-Republican ticket advocated political and economic policies that directly benefited African-Americans such as the abolition of crop lien laws. Contrary to the *Pine Bluff Press Eagle* editor's assertion that African-Americans were being manipulated into supporting Republicans, blacks simply backed the party that they believed defended their interests. As we have seen, this independence of mind and politics was nurtured in struggle, churches, and sectarian educational institutions.

Democrats responded to the African-American refusal to join their party by sponsoring a series of legislative reforms designed to sharpen racial distinction and purge African-Americans from the active electorate. Consequently, when the *Arkansas Gazette*, the Democratic organ, announced that the 1891

General Assembly's passage of legislation designed to segregate public facilities and disenfranchise African-Americans was a certainty, some African-American members of the Assembly immediately solicited the help of black religious organizations like the Ladies Auxiliary of the Young Men's Christian Association (YMCA) to mobilize resistance against these measures.[6] The Ladies Auxiliary of the YMCA quickly formed a committee to draft resolutions protesting against segregationist legislation like the Separate Coach Bill (Gatewood 1974). African-American women's religious organizations (for example, female benevolent societies, reading groups, antislavery societies, and religious associations) had a tradition of engaging in collective action for the benefit of their community during the post-Reconstruction era.

The Ladies Auxiliary appointed a committee to draft a resolution and began circulating a petition in the community. Ministers J. P. Robinson and C. O. H. Thomas convened a mass meeting at First (Colored) Baptist Church in Little Rock on January 19, 1891, to discuss strategies for resisting the Separate Coach Bill. Representative John Lucas and other politicians attended.[7] This meeting was held at church for many reasons, but one of the most important was church culture's ability to invoke collective orientations that promoted political activism. In the church's organizational setting it was not enough for African-Americans to be hearers of the Gospel, they had to be implementers of it in society. After convening the meeting with a prayer and the hymn, *Fear Thou Not*, the Separate Coach Bill was read, followed by extensive discussion that culminated in the appointment of a committee consisting of Dr. J. H. Smith, dentist; Rev. C. O. H. Thomas, A.M.E. Church, and Y. B. Sims, First Congregational Church; John E. Bush, founder of the Mosaic Templars; W. H. Scott, landowner; Honorable J. Gray Lucas and attorney G. K. Perkins, Little Rock's Third Ward representative, to draft a resolution that reflected the sentiments of the meeting (Gatewood 1974:302; Kousser 1975:160; Graves 1990:153). While the committee was at work on its resolution, members of the Ladies Auxiliary of the YMCA and their secretary came forth to read their protest resolutions. This was accompanied by a massive petition, which "set up, in substance, that a quiet and respectable Negro was not more objectionable than a drunken and boisterous white man to the traveling public" (Kousser 1975:158). After reading their resolutions, a collection was taken to have the petition and declaration printed for distribution among more sympathetic European-American legislators for use in formulating arguments against enacting the Separate Coach Bill (Gatewood 1974:303).

The resolutions developed and eventually adopted by meeting attendees at First (Colored) Baptist Church read as follows:

We, the colored citizens of Little Rock in mass meeting assembled, adopt following resolutions:

Whereas, numerous bills have been introduced in the Arkansas Legislature, having for their avowed purpose and object the forcible separation and isolation of the "white and African races upon the passenger trains of the railway of the state," which bills in any form whatever, should any one them become a law, would operate with great discrimination against an injustice to the colored citizens of this State, and,

Whereas, Such a law, whatever its provisions may be, will invite the special insult, contumely and imposition of a certain well known class of white persons; and,

Whereas, The colored people generally, and the colored ladies especially, must if this law be passed, unavoidably encounter and unnecessarily be subjected to forcible usage, insult, injury and indignity, at the hands of the class of public servants usually entrusted with the enforcement of these laws upon common carriers; therefore, be it

Resolved, That we sincerely and strongly condemn all bills introduced in the Legislature, which have for their object for forcible separation of its citizens upon the railways of this State upon the basis of color or race, as caste and class legislation, which has no place in our country, and should find no expression upon the statutes of this, our State, and be it

Resolved, That any law in contemplation by our lawmakers which necessarily or incidentally require[s] an inquiry into race or color of its citizens, that its provisions may be enforced or which relegates to individual judgment on a question so nice and narrow as the question of the race of any citizen is contrary to good public policy, which must lead to serious blunders and which must prove odious in the extreme to all rightly and well constituted citizens; and be it

Resolved, That the object stated: "An act to promote the comfort of passengers on railway trains" can be better attained, with honor to the State and justice to all concerned, by compelling the railway companies to provide first and second class accommodations with charges accordingly, by which means, the respectable traveling public would be relieved of contact with objectionable persons of whatever race or class, and be it

Resolved, That the sentiment of these resolutions do apply to the question of separate waiting rooms, as well, and be it further

Resolved, That a copy of these resolutions be published in the newspapers of our city and a copy sent to the Arkansas Legislature with a request that they be read. (Kousser 1975:158–59)

Although the resolution was firmly against artificial barriers that maintained inequality, it condoned the inequities created by economic liberalism. When it became clear that the Separate Coach Bill would become law, a second meeting was held on January 27, chaired by George Perkins, in which leaders such as Rev. Asberry Whitman admitted that arguing against the Separate Coach Bill was a waste of time. Instead, he and others made economic appeals that asked "if it comes to pass that you [European-Americans] will have things your way, see to it that the better element of our race is protected" (Kousser 1975:163). This naive appeal for social class solidarity failed to consider the depth to which European-Americans' racial privilege and sensibilities trumped class identification. That is, "race was the basis of [European-American] personal and group identities; social and political values were translated into racial terms; thus race defined their 'duty,' their moral sensibility, and their legal and cultural place" (Fredrickson 1981; Griffin 1995:91).

In addition to this failed strategy, African-Americans inundated legislators with petitions, memorandums, and resolutions that African-American legislators in the house (for example, R. C. Weddington, J. N. Donohoo, and John G. Lucas) and in the senate (for example, George W. Bell) used to develop their arguments against passage of the Separate Coach Bill. The memorandum and resolution themes such as the right of the public to equal protection under the law provided Lucas with the rationale that segregation of public facilities (railways) violated the Constitution. Specifically, Lucas's exhortations against the Separate Coach Bill asserted that segregation undermined the fundamental principle of American personal liberty because "it prohibits and prevents free men [from the right] to choose their own company," thereby creating "an unlawful imprisonment" (Graves 1990:157). To further buttress his point, Lucas distinguished between civil and social equality. He maintained that social equality was a matter of private relations between two or more persons whereas no African-American expected social recognition or acceptance merely because she or he was a passenger on the train. However, civil equality stipulated that it was the right of every citizen to expect equal protection from government agencies charged with regulating public business such as railroads (Graves 1990:158). Armed with this rationale, Lucas illustrated the absurdity of the Separate Coach Bill's provisions by sarcastically arguing: "It would be just as reasonable and proper for the state to place a dividing line through its public roads for two races, or to require cities to divide their streets, or even to require all white people to live in one particular portion of our cities and colored in the other portion, or if you please, in different towns [as the Separate Coach Bill required]" (Graves 1990:158).

Lucas's satirical yet prophetic remark foreshadowed the irrational ends to which segregationists would later go to fix African-Americans in an inferior caste status permanently (Graves 1990).

John Lucas and George Bell used the YMCA Ladies Auxiliaries' petition wording to construct arguments that exposed the inconsistency of Separate Coach Bill advocates on their aversion to physical contact with African-Americans. This demonstrated that the real aim of the bill's sponsors was to sharpen the social distinction between African-Americans and European-Americans by inhibiting the former's social mobility. The bill also exposes its sponsors' irrational sexual taboos and phobias about miscegenation (Graves 1990:159). Bell constructed an argument that reflected a deep religious tradition of resistance to injustice and oppression. He

> claim[ed] that certain citizens of our state are not comfortable, because their eyes happen to espy a man or a women with African blood in his or her veins sitting at a distance from them within the same coach, seems to me, Mr. President, the height of inconsistency. The Negroes have been riding upon and within the same coaches, in common with all other races, in this State for more than eighteen years. And during that entire period they have had no race wars, but, in contrary, have behaved themselves quite as well, if not better, than some of the other races . . . To reason and conclude, that because a people have once lived in the lower state of degradation, or because their skins are different from ours, that they are not entitled to the same human and Christian rights that belong to other members of the human family is to destroy the very foundation stone upon which this mighty fabric rests so well planned by our ancestors, and so well built and protected by your and our fathers . . . We deny the assertion so often made by some of the friends of this bill, that the Negroes seek social equality with the white people, when he rides in a coach for which he holds a ticket, in common with other passengers. I am frank to say, that no

true Negro desires social equality with the white race, to the extent of losing his race pride, that which God seems to have fixed unalterable as a characteristic mark into the heart and soul of all nations. We have our churches separate and distinct from yours, our social entertainments and all our gatherings for pleasure. We have never sought to marry among you, though we have among us a peculiar people called mulattoes, the history of whom is a mystery to us, and an astonishment to the civilized and moral world. (Williams et al. 1984:154–56)

Lucas took Bell's rather mild comments about miscegenation a step further by scornfully assuring European-American legislators that they need not fear African-American fraternization with European-Americans but rather their own tendency to engage in immoral interactions with African-Americans. He observed: "Out of a bounty and plenty of culture and refinement we are satisfied and glad to wed amongst our own; for have we not samples of all complexions and features and texture of hair, if you please, that all the races afford, from the fair-haired daughter of the Caucasus to the raven-haired maid of voluptuous Spain? He or she among us must indeed be an epicure that from our goodly quantity and from among our differing qualities may not find satisfaction. It is the dissatisfaction of some of our neighborhoods with their own, it would seem, that their own restraint (which does not restrain) they must have laws to prevent this race antipathy of which love to prate" (Graves 1990:159).

Although the African-American church and its congregants orchestrated a courageous and well-organized protest, the Separate Coach Bill passed the General Assembly in February 1891. Representative R. C. Weddington correctly concluded that the Separate Coach legislation was introduced and passed "not for the benefit of the interest of the two races, but on account of politics. The Democrats were fretted because colored people voted the Republican ticket. What had the Democratic Party ever done for the Negro? Nothing. The more the colored man tried to get along with the whites the more the latter tried to humiliate him" (Kousser 1975:168).

Given this deduction, many African-American Arkansans relented in their protest against the bill.

Protest against the 1891 election bill

Having lost on the separate coach measure, African-Americans concluded they had no chance to defeat the 1891 election bill that sought to obliterate African-American political power through disenfranchisement. For example,

Moneyhon's election bill research found that the African-American Arkansan grassroots, especially the church, never mobilized against the bill (1985:243). However, members of African-American churches who were representatives in the General Assembly, though discouraged, once again tried to prevent the passage of segregation legislation. They realized its enactment would effectively disenfranchise their community. In the state House of Representatives Lucas defended African-Americans against old racist charges of political irresponsibility and ignorance while in the senate, Bell accused his colleagues of introducing a bill that placed control of elections in the hands of the Democratic party, which intended to disenfranchise members of other parties (Moneyhon 1985). Republicans tried to employ the same political tactic during Reconstruction over African-American objections.

In his opening challenge to the bill Bell warned against the inherent danger of giving a small group of European-American men vast powers and authority: "Mr. President—This bill comes to us so heavily sugar-coated until it appears at first sight harmless. But, however, upon closer scrutiny we find, sir, many things against which and upon which I shall stamp my solemn protest. The first section . . . provides that the Governor, Secretary and Auditor of the State shall constitute a 'State Board of Election Commissioners.' . . . When you thus place the election machinery into the hands of the governor, secretary and auditor of State that what will prevent them from appointing their satellites as County commissioners in every county in the State, who in turn, influenced by their political bosses . . . will do their bidding?" (Graves 1990:171).

Such questions went to the heart of the bill's objective to insure Democrats political power through the control of election mechanisms. However, such brilliant analyses and arguments were not enough to prevent the general assembly's passage of the election bill.

Despite these legislative setbacks, African-American participation in the struggle to defeat de jure segregation created collective identities and critiques about white supremacy that continuously motivated mass mobilization through the only institution they controlled, the church. For instance, in the structurally constraining politico-racial environment of 1897 Holly Grove, Arkansas, patriarchal activist ministers used their pulpit to mobilize their community against an affront to a *respectable* woman in their community. The Indianapolis, Indiana, African-American newspaper the *Freeman* reported March 20, 1897:

A few days ago a white man kicked a respectable colored lady out of his store here, because she gave him some impudence. The Negroes of this town made a great bluster and blow over the matter, but as usual like the catfish, his rantings amounted to all head and jaw. On the following Sunday all the ministers of this community, led by Rev. E. M. Argyle of the A.M.E. church, denounced the act as outrageous and [described it as] a test of Negro manhood. Rev. Argyle asked the Negroes to be men, and not be afraid of death. He said that the Negro who would spend his money in a store where a colored lady had been mistreated was an enemy of the race, and should be ostracized. Rev. B. Lee of the C.M.E. church took up the cudgel of denunciation at his night services and the result has been that this white man has gotten but little Negro patronage. (Gatewood 1974:322)

While there was group pressure for everyone to participate in the store boycott, the fear of social ostracism alone does not adequately explain why church members became protestors at the apex of the repressive powers of legalized segregation. For many church members, their participation in protest is best viewed as a product of religious cultural assets (for example, religiosity, social ties) that encouraged boycott participation. One element of these religious cultural assets called *hope* derived from deeply felt religious beliefs that temporal social change was possible with divine help. Hope inspired and motivated African-American boycotters to struggle in Arkansas's constraining socio-political environments. According to theologian James Cone, this strongly held religious culture of hope encouraged African-American Christians to believe that "God is a God of liberation, who calls to himself the oppressed and abused in the nation and assures them that his righteousness will vindicate their suffering. It is the Bible that tells [them] that God became man in Jesus Christ so that his kingdom would make freedom a reality for all. . . . [Hence African-Americans] no longer ha[ve] to be . . . slaves to anybody but must rebel against the principalities and powers which make [their] existence subhuman" (Cone 1974:118).

Thus, despite the fact that boycotters were in the midst of a hardening racial caste, their belief that God lives and presides over worldly affairs served as a resource in stimulating challenges to white supremacy. Moreover, the shared conviction and psychological satisfaction (that is, feelings of efficacy and righteousness) gained from the belief that it was their religious duty to participate in the long and continuous struggle to elevate African-Americans sustained a "collective memory" (Polletta 1999) of religious protest that strengthened boycotters' resolve and encouraged future activism.

Religion's influence on the streetcar boycott

The historical record suggests that around the turn of the twentieth century church culture content continued to serve as a resource in mobilizing resistance to de jure segregation throughout the South. In their research of Georgia streetcar boycotts in the early 1900s, Meier and Rudwick (1976) found a *Savannah Morning News* report on an African-American maid who refused to ride the segregated streetcar to deliver two heavy suitcases to the mayor's secretary in City Hall. When the maid arrived late soaked with perspiration, it was discovered that she had walked to town because her minister declared segregation was contrary to the Bible and the spirit of Christianity and had admonished parishioners to keep off the trolley cars (Meier and Rudwick 1976:272). African-Americans in Arkansas also heeded the words of their clergy after the state legislature in 1903 enacted a law extending the coach segregation requirement to streetcar transportation. African-American ministers, like their predecessors in the 1890s, used the church's cultural resources to frame the 1903 decree as an ungodly, "unjust, barbaric and . . . cowardly measure" to mobilize a communal boycott that worked very effectively in Little Rock with "less than five percent of the usual 60 percent of African-American riders using the streetcars" (Meier and Rudwick 1976:270, 272).

Most of the streetcar boycotters adhered to Booker T. Washington's bourgeois economic and social accommodation philosophy, which opposed "open agitation" against segregation and articulated that no "race" that makes itself economically indispensable can be politically and socially ostracized (Harlan 1972:219). Consequently, Little Rock's streetcar boycott organizers believed, as Washington's accommodation philosophy directed, that they were more likely to achieve the objective of their protest by avoiding open confrontation with segregation's legal and political foundations. For example, in the Little Rock streetcar boycott, facilitators told protestors, who were primarily Christians, to "be obedient to the law. Let no one get on the cars and attempt to undo what the legislature of the great state of Arkansas has done . . . Never mind framing resolutions or arguing the merits or demerits of the affair with anyone. Simply stay off the cars" (Meier and Rudwick 1976:280).

The boycott goal was to make the streetcar lines aware of how segregation hindered their economic prosperity. Streetcar protestors believed that economics, not lawsuits or legislation, would overturn streetcar segregation laws or create more palpable alternative approaches.

As the boycott dragged on and state officials revealed no desire to repeal the segregated streetcar law, it became clear to some African-Americans that

experiences with segregation breed associations within the community necessary for producing and sustaining social change agents. For instance, President
Boyd of the National Negro Business League, founded by Booker T.
Washington in 1900, asserted at the League's 1903 convention: "These dis-
criminations are only a blessing in disguise. They stimulate and encourage
rather than cower and humiliate the true ambitious, self-determined Negro"
(Meier and Rudwick 1976:281). Boyd argued that antagonism from without
could encourage the development of a sense of affective focus and solidarity
useful for creating innovative self-help solutions to combat effectively the realities of de jure racial segregation. When the streetcar boycott produced no
measurable result, the collective orientation aroused by the common struggle
against segregation motivated African-Americans to move beyond protest to
employing cooperative strategies for establishing their own transportation systems like those in Norfolk, Virginia, and Nashville, Tennessee (Meier and
Rudwick 1976).[8]

Though the streetcar boycotts in Arkansas did not lead to the development
of African-American streetcar companies, it precipitated the establishment of
local branches of the National Business League in 1902 that promoted the
development of African-American economic enterprises (Williams 1986:30).
A member of the local Business League, Mifflin Gibbs, opened the second
African-American-owned and -operated bank, Capital City Savings Bank, in
Little Rock in 1903 (Gordon 1995:77).[9] Capital City's assets grew from
$10,000 in the first year to $100,000 by 1905, and the institution later organized a subsidiary health insurance company called the People's Mutual Aid
Association (Williams 1986:30; Gordon 1995). However, mismanagement
combined with the Panic of 1907 forced the bank to close in 1908 (Gordon
1995:77). Though attempts to maintain banking institutions were usually
unsuccessful, they reflected the ascendancy of the African-American churches'
self-help economic strategy, which Booker T. Washington popularized. The
church, as we have seen, continuously encouraged self-reliance and challenged
African-Americans to save and invest their money to "pull themselves up" without the help of European-Americans (Cunningham 1985:274). Heeding this
call, African-American communities throughout Arkansas established various
types of businesses (for example, health, electrical, coal, ice, timber, beauty par-
lors, barber shops, and restaurants) that both white and African-Americans
patronized. However, as segregation expanded, African-American businesses
were limited to trading only with African-American customers, guaranteeing
these businesses a small but healthy share of the market (Williams 1986:30).

Consequently, an unintended outcome of segregation was that it provided short-term economic gains to some owners of African-American businesses.

Though some African-Americans gained economically from segregationist arrangements, for most African-Americans segregation caused economic and social problems. "Black workers were paid less than their white counterparts, and they needed to get the most for their money. But black businesses, with limited capital and few goods, could not always compete with larger white-owned stores. In the midst of growing segregation and hostility, many blacks had to patronize white merchants who sent them to the back door and called them 'boy,' 'auntie,' or 'uncle.' . . . [Moreover w]hen black businesses were forced to sell their merchandise at higher prices than those of white merchants—or when store owners took advantage of the situation to price gouge—some people came to see merchants as traitors to their race" (Williams 1986: 30–31).

Religion's effect on the exodus mobilization

Since the benefits of the philosophy of economic self-help were slow to materialize and the sociopolitical climate worsened, some African-Americans began calling for emigration to the African continent. These calls for repatriation originated with a small group of nonclerics within the African-American church during the post-Reconstruction era who maintained, like their group leader, Martin R. Delaney, that the "exodus movement is the uprising of poor but industrious and religious people, who desire to cultivate the land in Liberia, and do good to the natives, promoting peace and Christian civilization" (Patton 1992:166). The research of Adell Patton Jr. (1992) suggests that the calls for emigration to Africa were not new in Arkansas, especially in the predominant African-American eastern counties of the Mississippi Delta where the Liberian Exodus Arkansas Colony (LEAC) had been formed at Third Baptist Church in Helena, November 23, 1877 (Patton 1992:167). The movement's leadership consisted primarily of clergy like Rev. Anthony L. Stanford, who spent a lot time fighting back African-American ministers' opposition to emigration. Such ministers included Rev. J. T. Jenifer of Helena, who blasted LEAC ministers from his pulpit, saying "certain leaders of this movement, namely: [A.M.E. Bishop] Henry McNeil Turner, [ministers] R. H. Cain, B. F. Porter, and Anthony L. Stanford, should have a rope put on their necks, be led to the woods and be made to promise to leave the country, or the rope tightened until they did" (Patton 1992:167).

Supporters of the exodus movement responded to Jenifer's criticism by affirming their determination to undertake their mission and framing him as an enemy: "Long live the leaders of the Liberian Exodus. Long live the African Colonization Society . . . as Christ bade us pray for our enemies, Long live J. T. Jenifer to repent of his wickedness" (Patton 1992: 167). Emigrationists proceeded with their movement, but because they relied on the services of the nefarious American Colonization Society for resettling African-Americans in Liberia they obtained only marginal support in Arkansas. Only 105 people signed on to emigrate to Liberia in 1880 (Patton 1992). Like their antebellum predecessors, vast majorities of African-American Arkansans were convinced that it was best to pursue their rights in the United States rather than emigrating to Africa. Thus, calls for an African-American Arkansan African exodus were not isolated occurrences but part of an emigration impulse that emerged among some church members during calamitous political periods like that which existed throughout the post-Reconstruction era (Patton 1992).

Like its antecedents, the emigration movement in Arkansas appealed to Christians who believed that the "Redemption of Africa" would provide them with a homeland in which to implement the Gospel's imperative of human equality (Patton 1992). These Christians equated the common ancestry of humans with human equality and believed that God would not grant humanity peace until people ceased oppressing one another. Randall Burkett contends that these religious sentiments were one of the reasons that the Marcus Garvey emigration movement in 1917 emerged as the largest mass-based sociopolitical movement ever developed by blacks in the United States (1977:4, 7). Since it was impractical to call for wholesale emigration, Garvey pushed for the migration of a few skillful individuals who would build the nation that would serve as a refuge and defender of the rights of Africans and their descendants in the Diaspora (Bontemps and Conroy 1966:193). To encourage people to emigrate, Garvey tapped blacks' deep religious tradition of resisting racial oppression and injustice by suggesting that creating a nation in Africa to protect the rights of diasporic Africans was a means by which they could fulfill their Christian responsibility to uplift the oppressed. His main message was: "If the strong oppresses the weak confusion and discontent will ever mark the path of man, but with love, faith, and charity toward all that reign of peace and plenty will be heralded into the world and the generation of men shall be called Blessed" (Jacques-Garvey 1986:38).

That is, Garvey insisted, "Christ was the leader of a mass movement for the uplift of the oppressed . . . [and that his doctrine] was simple but revolutionary. He laid the foundations of a pure democracy and established the fact, not a theory, of the Universal Brotherhood of man" (Martin 1976:68). Mindful of the entrenched position of religion in the lives of blacks, Garvey sought to channel their religious passion into the path of racial salvation (Martin 1976: 70). He urged blacks to discard any religion that functioned as a spiritual and material tool for European-Americans and to replace it with a counterhegemonic Christianity of liberation. Specifically, he wrote in the *Negro World* in 1923: "The Negro is now accepting the religion of the real Christ, not the property-robbing, gold-stealing, diamond-exploiting Christ, but the Christ of Love, Justice and Mercy. The Negro wants no more of the white man's religion as it applies to his race, for it is a lie and a farce; it is propaganda pure and simple to make fools of a race and rob the precious world, the gift of God to man, and to make it the exclusive home of pleasure, prosperity and happiness for those who have enough intelligence to realize that God made them masters of their fate and architects of their own destinies" (Martin 1976:71).

According to Burkett (1977), Garvey's religious cultural appeals and interpretations stimulated the establishment of Universal Negro Improvement Association (UNIA) chapters in forty-two of the forty-eight states. Support for the movement was very strong throughout the South, especially in small towns. Burkett's limited examination of UNIA chapters in North Carolina found that whenever there were a sufficient number of blacks (ranging in population from 183 to 46,000), chapters were established (1977:5). This suggests that the Garvey movement played a very important role in facilitating the construction of efficacious religious identities, behaviors, and perceptions among blacks in the South.

What is abundantly clear is that African-Americans used religion's rich storehouse of rituals, symbols, and relational networks as a source for mobilizing resistance to white supremacy. These cultural assets fostered the development of collective politico-religious identities that renewed hope and motivated African-American Arkansans to work continuously for social, economic, and political change.

Appropriation of religious culture for union mobilization

Politicized religious identity construction also encouraged union participation among African-American sharecroppers in the early twentieth century. Labor mobilization was facilitated in part by union organizers openly informing tenant farmers of their rights as workers. O. A. Rogers, Jr. argues that the union's advocacy role was very important since

> The Negroes had been having trouble in getting settlements for cotton they raised on land owned by whites. Both the Negroes and the white owners were to share the profits when the crop was sold at the end of the year. Between the time of planting and selling the sharecroppers "took up" food, clothing, and necessities at excessive prices from the plantation store owned by the planter. It was not the practice of the landowner and share-croppers to go together to a market to dispose of the cotton when it was ready. Rather the landowner sold the crop whenever and however he saw fit. At the time of settlement neither an itemized statement of accounts owed nor an accounting of the money received for cotton and seed was, in most cases, given or shown the Negroes. The total amount owed was stated, and the Negroes then given settlement which inevitably kept many Negroes in debt with the landlord. The Negroes were afraid, because of intimidation and possible bodily harm, to protest openly the disadvantages of the system. (1960:143)

Although sharecroppers were afraid to challenge tenant system abuses and exploitation, some mustered the courage to organize the Progressive Farmers and Household Union of America in 1918, at Winchester, Arkansas. What explains this sudden interest in organizing and joining unions? According to Rogers (1960), part of the answer lies in the appeal of the Progressive Farmers and Household Union as a fraternal and social organization. For instance, Progressive Union circulars often used a mixture of religious and union rhetoric to promote African-American unionization: "The time is at hand that all men, all nations and tongues must receive a just reward. This union wants to know why it is that the laborers cannot control their just earnings . . . Remember the Holy World, when the Almighty took John up on the mountain . . . and John said, 'I see all nations and tongues coming up before God.' Now, we are a nation and a tongue. Why should we be cut off from fair play?" (Waskow 1966:122).

Moreover, union applicants submitted to an examination, and answered under oath such questions as: "Do you attend church?" "Do you believe in country?" and "Do you believe in God?" The Progressive Union was a secular-religious organization concerned with helping sharecroppers obtain relief from exploitation (Rogers 1960:145).

Rogers's (1960) research on Progressive Union organizing in Arkansas suggests that the aforementioned techniques were effective tools for organizing union branches (lodges) in 1919 at Ratio, Elaine, Hoop Spur, Old Town, Ferguson, Countiss, and Mellwood. Moreover, he credited the religious essence of the union with transforming members of the Hoop Spur in Phillips County into spirited protestors after their church agreed to let their organization use its facilities to promote and organize sharecroppers. In the church's organizational setting, African-American sharecroppers encountered religious language that linked Christianity to social action and relational networks that encouraged them to resist economic exploitation. That is, as Rogers (1960) contends, sharecroppers at Hoop Spur found strength through social interaction with other tenants and in numbers. "Each pledged to protect the other members as they sought to obtain their rights as citizens, knowing that to acquire these rights in Phillips County they would need to protect themselves and their families, for white man's law would not protect them against the abuses of white men. The Negroes were tired of being expected and 'forced to act as children.' In local meetings they denounced in inflammatory speeches the white planters, and armed themselves with rifles and pistols for defensive purposes, fully aware of the dangerous course they were taking" (Rogers 1960:146–47).

Evidence suggests that in the dialectical cultural setting of the church, union organizers and members interpreted religious culture content to facilitate the construction of efficacious identities, behaviors, and perceptions. This politicized disposition framed sharecroppers' experiences with the tenant system as a worldly injustice whose remediation was possible only through their mobilization. Consequently, despite sharecroppers' fear of plantation owners' economic and coercive threats against labor organizing, tenant farmers proceeded with their unionization effort to secure their rights as workers. To alleviate the individual fear of mobilizing against plantation owners, the church and union officials comforted and empowered sharecroppers by suggesting to them that though their struggle for justice occurred in hostile socio-political contexts, "God was on their side" and "would make a way out of no way." Believing in the rightness of their union cause, sharecroppers fought back fearlessly when deputy sheriffs, sent by plantation owners to break up an organizing meeting at a church in Hoop Spur, fired upon them. The resulting incident precipitated a bloody week of racial conflict at Elaine, Arkansas, in 1919 that left seventy-three African-Americans and two European-Americans dead (Waskow 1966:128).[10] While no European-Americans were tried for their role in the rioting, eighty-seven African-Americans were charged and convicted.

Seventy-five were ordered to serve one to twenty-one years in prison. The remaining twelve, who were identified as leaders, were sentenced to death for first-degree murder (*Arkansas Gazette*, Nov. 23, 1919:1). Arkansas's Supreme Court eventually overturned the death sentences in 1923 (Kirk 2002:20).

Though union support waned somewhat after the riot in Elaine, African-American tenant farmers' and church support for unionization remained constant because worker organization was crucial for their community's economic uplift. Moreover, African-American sharecroppers' support for unionizing remained steady because organizers appealed to tenant farmers not as individual laborers but rather as an African-American community and tapped their religious culture to invoke collective orientations to mobilize and sustain the union movement. Through the agency of church culture, union organizers engendered in African-American tenant farmers the collective confidence to organize continuously to rid themselves of tenant system abuses. This collective orientation was instrumental in encouraging African-American sharecroppers to renew their efforts in 1934 to unionize despite the odds against success. However, this time their organizing included a concerted effort to incorporate European-American sharecroppers into the union (Venkataramani 1960). Venkataramani contends that European-American farmers "had gradually been drawn into the [sharecropping] system until, in time, they [were] almost as numerous as Negroes. With little financial resources of their own," they found themselves heavily indebted to landlords and forced to pay high interest rates (1960:226). With the encouragement of Arkansas's Socialist Party secretary Henry Leland Mitchell, European-American sharecroppers became convinced that the only way they could escape peonage was by joining with African-American tenant farmers to organize a biracial union (Venkataramani 1960:232). The Southern Tenant Farmers Union (STFU) was formed in July 1934 in the eastern Arkansas county of Poinsett at a meeting composed of twenty-seven African-American and European-American men in a schoolhouse named Sunnyside (Kester 1936:55). Some European-Americans expressed reservations about joining an integrated union. Their apprehensions, however, were alleviated somewhat by an elderly African-American man's use of religious and class rhetoric to argue for a united organizing effort.

> We colored can't organize without you, and you white folks can't organize without us. Aren't we all brothers and ain't God the Father of us all? We live under the same sun, eat the same food, wear the same kind of clothing, work on the same land, raise the same crop for the

same landlord who oppresses and cheats us both. For a long time now the white folks and the colored folks have been fighting each other and both of us has been getting whipped all the time. We don't have nothing against one another but we got plenty against the landlord. The same chain that hold my people holds your people too. If we're chained together outside we ought to stay chained together in the union. It won't do no good for us to divide because there's where the trouble had been all the time. The landlord is always betwixt us, beatin' us starvin' us and makin' us fight each other. There ain't but one way for us to get him where he can't help himself that's for us to get together and stay together. (Kester 1936:56)

After this religiously constructed comment, the group formalized the STFU, electing a European-American as chairperson and an African-American minister as vice-chairperson (Kester 1936:56).

Among black Arkansans the main force behind the unionization effort, besides the STFU, was the black church. The church's support for the STFU enhanced its credibility among tenants and provided it with a communication network to inform sharecroppers about union activities and instruct them how to organize. Thus by way of the pulpit, the STFU membership expanded between 1934 and 1937 in northeast Arkansas from a mere 18 to 11,846 (Yard 1988:202). This astounding increase in union membership unnerved landlords, who initiated efforts to intimidate ministers with violence and threaten sharecroppers with eviction. Landlords promulgated ordinances making it unlawful for any person "to make or deliver a speech on any street, alley, park, or other place" without permission from local authorities and began padlocking and ransacking churches where union meetings were held (Kester 1936:61; Venkataramani 1960:234).[11] In many places, like Birdsong, Arkansas, armed intruders forcibly prevented union organizers from holding meetings with sharecroppers. Venkataramani (1960) maintained that it was not uncommon for planter vigilante squads to harass and beat members and supporters of the STFU. In eastern Arkansas, for instance, on March 25, 1935, a group of African-American men and women returning home from church in eastern Arkansas were mobbed by a collection of armed men, who "[beat] several of them with pistol butts, and flashlights" (Venkataramani 1960:234–35). On the same night of this incident a church was fired upon. These difficulties failed to inhibit the growth of the STFU primarily because it, like the Progressive Union, linked labor organizing to deeply felt and ingrained religious beliefs (Kester 1936:52). Though union appropriation of religious culture is not necessarily definitive evidence for explaining increased African-American involvement in unions, it certainly suggests that religion was a factor in transforming tenants' consciousness from fatalism to agency. Since union organizers' interests in integrating union and religious messages are consistent with this explanation, it is unlikely that they would have interpreted African-Americans' cultural experiences in ways that were not relevant for mobilizing participation. Considering this evidence and the expressions and actions of African-American union members, it appears that church culture was instrumental in producing an internal sense of political efficacy that encouraged African-Americans to join the STFU despite fears of retribution.

Conclusion

From Reconstruction through the first half of the twentieth century, black church culture continuously nourished enduring elements of an opposition. This suggests that sociopolitical movements contain cultural links and connections that can facilitate the mobilization of individuals for social action. Therefore many African-American sociopolitical movements in the South, particularly in Arkansas, cannot be explained only as a product of spontaneity or political opportunities but rather as a result of historical religious motivations and justification for political activism. In the next chapter we examine how church culture sustained a "collective memory" of protest that influenced the development of collective action preceding the civil rights struggle in Arkansas.

CHAPTER 4

Social Activism Preceding the Desegregation
Movement in Little Rock

————◦《◉》◦————

The school desegregation movement in Arkansas is typically presented
as if the 1954 *Brown v. Board of Education of Topeka* Supreme Court
ruling precipitated its emergence. This chapter describes how enduring religious culture and practices in ethnic institutions helped to facilitate the
desegregation movement in Arkansas. Religious culture was fundamentally
important in encouraging a cadre of African-Americans to mobilize for educational equality *before* the 1957 desegregation of Little Rock Central High
School.

Aldon Morris's (1984) research on the evolution of the Civil Rights
Movement found that various kinds of ethnic organizations and networks
were essential in mobilizing movement participation. Most important in this
regard was the African-American church. In the church many people encountered ministers and other church members who conveyed religious legitimation for political activism through tight-knit social networks (that is, friends,
acquaintances, church visits, or family) that gave them a deep sense of emotional security and a consciousness of self importance needed for social
activism. As we have seen, church social ties in Arkansas historically operated
in complex ways to encourage movement participation. However, there were
other indigenous organizations and groups whose membership was drawn primarily from churches that were central in mobilizing protest before the desegregation of Little Rock's Central High School.

Through hardships and the dehumanization of legalized white supremacy
during the first half of the twentieth century, churches remained the place

where African-Americans were tied together by common religious identities and ideas. That the church and its spirituals gave hope and inspiration to African-Americans is evident in early-twentieth-century eastern Arkansas where it was common to hear songs rising from small churches in the middle of farm fields such as: "My Lord, He calls me; He calls me by the thunder. The trumpet sounds within my soul; I ain't got long to stay here . . . I've had sorrows like this before, I've known heartaches by the score; I know that this cannot last; this, too, shall pass!" (Williams 1986:36). Such songs reflected the harshness of life in a white supremacist environment as well as African-Americans' hope for a better future. Pattillo-McCoy's (1998) research on political activism suggests that the collective orientation of indigenous organizational (for example, church) practices and rhetoric is an important cultural tool for constructing group consciousness and movement commitment. Individuals are exposed to others "having similar experiences . . . asking the same questions, [and] identifying with the same problems," making it possible for them to mobilize collectively to ameliorate their situation (Brecher et al. 2000:21).

During the late 1930s and 1940s church culture in Arkansas generated support for and participation in ethnic organizations like the National Association for the Advancement of Colored People (NAACP), which had been established by W. E. B. Du Bois and other prominent African-Americans in 1909 to pursue racial equality. The NAACP's local leadership consisted primarily of African-American ministers who used their churches' networks to portray the NAACP as an instrument for implementing God's beloved community on earth. In this way during the late thirties and early forties church culture cultivated participation in several local movement organizations and support for NAACP lawsuits seeking the abolition of segregated railways, political primaries, and education.

Movement to Integrate Railways and Political Primaries

The struggle against segregated railway accommodations in Arkansas had a long history, having begun during post-Reconstruction in Arkansas. Efforts to abolish railway segregation began anew in 1937 when Arthur W. Mitchell, an African-American Democratic member of the United States House of Representatives from Illinois, filed a lawsuit in Northern Illinois's Federal District Court against the railroad after he was forcibly ejected from the first-class section of a railcar in Arkansas while traveling from Chicago to Hot

Springs (Williams et al. 1984). When the Federal District Court denied Representative Mitchell relief under the Interstate Commerce Act of 1887, supposedly guaranteeing equal accommodation for passengers, he filed a complaint with the United States Supreme Court. In 1941, the United States Supreme Court concurred with the plaintiff and issued a directive for the Interstate Commerce Commission to provide African-Americans with railway accommodations "substantially equal" to those provided for European-American passengers (Williams et al. 1984:224). This decision required companies engaged in interstate commerce to implement both the "separate" and "equal" provisions of *Plessy v. Ferguson* law. Before the Supreme Court's ruling in *Mitchell v. United States*, no company seriously entertained complying with the "separate but equal" clause, since maintaining equal facilities for both African-American and European-Americans induced severe economic hardship. Consequently, the *Mitchell v. United States* ruling made it legally and financially burdensome to maintain de jure segregation. The legal foundation for the *Mitchell* case was formulated by Charles Houston, the first full-time paid special counsel to the NAACP, who crafted a strategy for ending segregation in graduate school based on the inequality of education. Houston's first legal victory, *University of Maryland v. Murray* in 1935, resulted in the United States Supreme Court ordering the University of Maryland to admit Donald Murray, an African-American, because there were no law schools for African-Americans in the state. Houston's victories provided a record of precedent based on inequality of facilities and were invaluable for facilitating the desegregation movement throughout the South.

Before this litigation was completed, African-American Arkansans formed the Arkansas Negro Democratic Association (ANDA) (later renamed the Arkansas Democratic Voters Association) in 1928 to push for the right of African-Americans who were affiliated with the Democratic Party to vote in the party's primary (Kirk 2002:23). One ANDA participant explained that African-Americans sought to vote in the Democratic Party's primary because "In Arkansas Negroes were Republicans for obvious reasons. [W]e didn't have a two-party system here as such [thus] if you were a Republican you could only vote four times a year. And by this being a Democratic [state], you couldn't vote in the Democratic primary. So you couldn't have any say. You didn't have any say in what went on politically. If they voted to cut . . . your salaries . . . you couldn't do anything about it because you were a Republican." Consequently, African-Americans organized as Democrats in an attempt to legally vote in Democratic primary elections where local, state, and national officeholders were actually chosen (Smith 1982:40). When members of the Arkansas Negro Democratic Association tried to vote in the Democratic primary election held July 28, 1942, election officials turned them away. After African-Americans were denied the primary ballot, ANDA, supported by the Little Rock branch of the NAACP, immediately filed suit against the Democratic Party of Arkansas (DPA) stipulating that since the DPA operated under the auspices of the state, African-American Democrats had the right to vote in its primaries for national officials under the Fifteenth Amendment, prohibiting racial discrimination by state (Smith 1982:43). On the basis of this constitutional violation, the Arkansas Negro Democratic Association requested that the United States Attorney intervene in Arkansas to force the Democratic Party of Arkansas to open its primaries to African-Americans; however, the appeals of the Arkansas Negro Democratic Association found no support in Washington, D.C.

Though the enfranchisement legal strategy of the Arkansas Negro Democratic Association made little headway, several people, like this earlier respondent, suggested that his faith motivated him to continue his struggle for the vote because "the Bible is the answer to all human problems . . . I don't drink, I don't smoke, I don't chew, I don't dip, and I'm a deacon in my church. I joined the church when I was a young man . . . and I've been a Christian ever since. And one thing we all ought to remember is that your life ought to be an example to somebody. It ought to be somebody who knows me . . . that know you that want to be like you. Your life is supposed to be an example to people and you're supposed to be a leader by precept and example."

This remark suggests that practicing Christianity provided Arkansas Negro Democratic Association participants with an identity, consciousness, efficacy, and commitment for justice and equality that promoted involvement in politics despite the tremendous odds against success. The respondent further suggested that though the movement to acquire the primary ballot was unsuccessful, it was not futile. The Arkansas Negro Democratic Association's effort to provide African-Americans nationally with the legal support for challenging segregated primaries moved the Supreme Court, on April 3, 1944, to rule favorably in a suit filed by dentist Lonnie E. Smith of Houston against the Democratic Party in Texas, maintaining S. E. Allwright, the election judge in Smith's precinct, wrongly denied him the opportunity to vote in the state Democratic primary (Smith 1982:45). In his research on *Smith v. Allwright*, Calvin Smith noted

the Court outlawed the all-white Democratic primary because the Democratic party was not a private organization, as it claimed to be, because it operated under state regulations. "If," said the Court, "the state requires a certain electoral procedure, prescribes a general election for state officers to those whose names appear on such a ballot, it endorses, adopts, and enforces discrimination against Negroes. This is state action within the meaning of the Fifteenth Amendment." Although the Court's decision focused on Texas Democratic Primaries, it . . . directly affected Arkansas because the DPA operated under state regulations . . ., claim[ed] . . . it was a private organization, and adopted a resolution asserting that the party "has as much right to restrict party voting to qualified white electors as a fraternal or religious order has to restrict its membership." (1982:45)

Before African-American Arkansans could celebrate their legal empowerment "to influence those political decisions that most affected their day-to-day lives, those made by state and local officials," the Democratic Party of Arkansas immediately moved to evade the Court's decision in *Smith v. Allwright* (Smith 1982:45). The Democratic State Committee held a special meeting on July 8, 1944, to amend Rule II of the Democratic Party of Arkansas that limited party membership and primary election voter participation to European-Americans only. The amended rule eliminated the "white only" and replaced it with a loyalty requirement designed to disqualify those African-Americans who might have voted for or supported any candidate for public office over the past two years who was not a Democrat (Smith 1982:46; Kirk 2002:37). Since the Republican Party was the only party open to African-Americans during this period, most blacks were excluded from Democratic membership and voting privileges. In addition, the Democratic Party of Arkansas amended Rule II to require that African-Americans who wanted to vote in the party's primaries as nonmembers accept the segregationist and discriminatory principles and laws outlined in the 1874 State Constitution in exchange for hollow participation in statewide elections where their numbers were not sufficiently large to influence the political arena (Smith 1982:47).

When the Arkansas legislature convened in January 1945, it also passed legislation such as Act 107 (Moore Bill) and the Trussell Bill to insure that the Democratic Party of Arkansas remained all white and in firm control of state politics. Act 107, sponsored by state Senator John Moore of Helena, stipulated that racially separate primaries and preferential runoffs be held for federal and state elections with African-Americans restricted to voting in primaries for federal officials (Smith 1982:48; Kirk 2002:37). The Trussell

Bill, sponsored by Senator L. Weems Trussell of Fordyce, gave every organized political party in Arkansas the right to prescribe qualifications for its members and establish qualifications for those who voted in primary elections. Governor Ben Laney signed both statutes into law on February 27, 1945.

African-American Arkansans utilized the organizational setting of the church to initiate formal protests against their community's de jure exclusion from the political process in Arkansas. "In November 1945, at the annual meeting of the black Arkansas Baptist Convention, a resolution was adopted which called upon the legislature to repeal [Act 107] because 'it is in direct opposition to those fundamental principles for which our great national government, in our recent World War, gave both her blood and wealth freely without respect to race, color, or creed for democracy and this law reflects discreditably upon the whole of our American citizenry'" (Smith 1982:49). The churches' appeal meant little to the Arkansas legislature.

In his study of *Smith v. Allwright*, Calvin Smith (1982) found that African-American voter registration increased in Arkansas despite the Democratic Party of Arkansas's efforts to evade implementation of the Supreme Court's decision. He found that African-American voter registration in Arkansas began to increase in 1940 when the Arkansas Negro Democratic Association appealed to the Democratic Party of Arkansas to modify its rules to allow African-Americans to vote in summer primaries for Democratic congresspersons and Democratic National Committee members. As Tarrow (1994) argues in *Power in Movements*, this suggests that a nucleus of early activists, like those in the Arkansas Negro Democratic Association was instrumental in broadening the sociopolitical terrain for future African-American participation and challenges. This cadre of early activists in the Arkansas Negro Democratic Association, as we have seen, were encouraged by their interpretation of church culture content to engage in social action when sociopolitical conditions were not conducive for such action. One Arkansas Negro Democratic Association participant maintained that during difficult sociopolitical times Arkansas Negro Democratic Association tapped the African-American community's familiarity with religious language, as religiously motivated activists did during the Reconstruction era, to promote voter mobilization. According to this participant's sister-in-law, the Arkansas Negro Democratic Association's religious calls for participation often reasoned: "You're [on earth], at least you ought to have an education that leads into another life. [In] school . . . [you] learn how to read, [you learn a] skill, [you] learn [a] new life, and [learn how] to live with your fellow man and how to make money. You got to have money to live . . . You need houses—beautiful houses. God did not mean for you to live in no shack . . . . He put pretty stuff on earth for [us] to have." Though the collective orientation (that is, practices and rhetoric) of religion was a factor in consistently mobilizing participation in Democratic Party primaries in Arkansas, it alone does not explain why the African-American voter registration increased from 1940 through 1957. Smith (1982) argues that the increase in African-American voter registration was also due to several changes in the structure of Democratic Party of Arkansas. "In 1947 the . . . [Act 107] primary system, due to the expense involved and other complaints from county officials, was abandoned. Although DPA rules were not changed to allow blacks to become party members and thus help select party nominees, over 20,000 blacks voted in the 1948 Democratic primaries for local, state, and federal officials. Two years later, the all-white primary was officially abolished. And in 1954, acting on the recommendations of the Democratic nominee for Governor, Orval E. Faubus, the State Democratic Convention admitted blacks as party officials for the first time" (Smith 1982:50).[1]

Smith's findings suggest that the Arkansas Negro Democratic Association's struggle for the primary ballot made the Democratic Party of Arkansas aware of the great financial and political cost of maintaining segregated primaries. More important, the above explanations show that religious culture partly accounted for people becoming and remaining involved in the Arkansas Negro Democratic Association during inhospitable periods. Furthermore, participation in the Arkansas Negro Democratic Association exposed people to others who interpreted religious culture content in ways that were conducive to sustaining the sense of community and solidarity essential for promoting social activism.

Teacher Salary Equalization Movement

In 1942, African-American Arkansans began their struggle for equal education when the Arkansas Teachers Association (ATA), an African-American teachers association founded in 1898, filed a suit against the Little Rock School District seeking the equalization of African-American and European-American teachers' salaries. Sue Cowan Morris (later known as Sue Cowan Williams), chairperson of the English department at Dunbar High School and a member of the Little Rock Classroom Teachers Association (an ATA affiliate), agreed to be the plaintiff for the lawsuit despite the fact that doing so caused her dismissal from her position. The court case *Sue Morris v. The Little Rock School District* was tried in U.S. District Court. The court ruled that the school district had not discriminated against African-American teachers in fixing salaries (Patterson 1981:90). When Morris appealed the court's decision to the U.S. Eighth District Court of Appeals in the fall of 1943, the superintendent of the Little Rock School Board refused to renew her teaching contract (Patterson 1981:90). His actions did not stop Morris from pressing forward with her appeal, which resulted in the District Court of Appeals reversal of the lower court's ruling in 1945, ordering equal pay scales for schoolteachers.

According to several respondents who were members of the Arkansas Teachers Association during the struggle for equal salaries, religious culture was vital in promoting and sustaining their commitment to organizational goals when opposition was fierce. Though the Arkansas Teachers Association was not a religious organization, respondents suggested that "it opened all its meetings with prayers [and] there were people in the [ATA]—a special group of ministers, and they participated but they were just regular participants, and did not sign out as religious leaders. . . . [E]verybody in [the organization] belonged to the church."

Pattillo-McCoy stresses the importance of religious practices such as prayer in creating collective goals expressed in the content of social action (1998:770). During periods of adversity, individuals like Sue Morris pressed forward with group goals because the bonds of friendship and family solidly grounded her in movement social support networks that urged her on (Kirk 2002:40). Hence, failure to carry through with group goals—in this case, ATA litigation—is tantamount to deserting one's friends and family (Bainbridge 1997:135). One respondent, who became an ATA litigant in the struggle for teacher salary equalization in 1952 when school districts throughout Arkansas either could not or refused to raise funds necessary to comply with the District Court of Appeals salary equalization order, maintained that his interactions with religious individuals in his family and church "gave me a strong sense of right and wrong. And I felt—for example, that a teacher that was my counterpart in the white school, back in the 1950s was making $100 a month more than I was . . . I just felt that was wrong. And the teacher organization and church . . . felt it was wrong too."

He continued: "In the earlier times—and I suppose now also—the church was one of the few institutions that was basically owned by blacks, controlled by blacks. It's an institution where you can gather and be free to express yourself. Find others that are supportive of your cause and even when they disagree you don't have to look over your shoulder for somebody going and undercutting you . . . Blacks have been freer and more comfortable in speaking their true beliefs in the sanctuary of the church."

This suggests that situating African-American protestors in indigenous institutions (that is, church, family, ATA) alleviates their sense of isolation because they belong to a group with whom they identify and share a common sense of obligation and responsibility for group principles. Several other respondents also explained that interacting with devout family members helped them construct and accept religious meanings and identities that encouraged their participation in the teacher salary equalization movement. "[M]y grandparents were both Methodist and Baptist, and they had strong feelings about civil rights. What was right and what was wrong. They passed that on to us, . . . my grandparents were strong believers in the Bible . . . [T]hey had the strong belief that God didn't create one to be a servant to the other. They always felt that coming in back doors was not a thing that God condoned. Treating one person less than human was not a thing that they believed in. They just believed that people, a man should be measured on his work or quality of his character rather than color of his skin."

Many respondents insisted that exposure to ministers and churchgoers who supported the ATA's goals and linked Gospel precepts with worldly action were also instrumental in promoting support for the organization. "[I]t's just thrown throughout the Bible where Christ did—I mean face the kinds of problems we [faced]. Trumped up charges in jail; [ministers] could always find something in the Bible. Civil disobedience, he could find that. . . . I can't think of a specific biblical scripture right now but there is just a world of material ministers . . . could talk about to get [people] aroused."

These accounts suggest social groups and individuals within indigenous organizations, interpreting religious culture in activist ways, persuaded some people to view their role as Christians not as mere carriers of faith but as implementers of it as well.

Another respondent and former president of the ATA maintained that since the church as a whole refused to get involved in the struggle for teacher salary equalization, the ATA, like the Civil Rights Movement, did not rely on churches for movement success. He asserted that the ATA depended on individual church members. "Those people were all right. They were people who—they didn't renounce their church affiliation to join the Civil Rights Movement but they did use the church as a base . . . That was the only place you could meet . . . So, therefore that was the forum. We couldn't have civil rights [meeting] over at our schools. You would have to go to church. So, the church actually served as a meeting place for civil rights groups. So, it served its purpose but as far as it taking a leadership role! They ain't done nothing. I mean they served as a base, a meeting place, moral support but that's it." The respondent's words suggest that, though overall churches were reluctant to get involved in the movement for the equalization of teacher's salaries, individuals in nonactive churches still developed a commitment to the movement. As we will see in the next chapter, Harris (1999) suggests it is possible for people intensely engaged in church activities within non-activist-oriented churches to cultivate sentiments and relationships engendering political efficacy. Individuals with this disposition viewed nonsupport for local movement organizations like the ATA as a violation of the Christian imperative to transform the world. As this respondent explained, "church is the savior of the world." It was left by "Jesus to straighten the world out," and it is necessary for "the church as a whole [to] take complete calling because its membership is made up of the community. And if the community goes down other members and their churches go down . . . So, the church members need to be in there strong, they're the ones who need to be there [struggling for communal uplift]."

The evidence suggests that though there was no coordinated church effort in Arkansas in support of teacher salary equalization, there were individuals within black churches whose interpretation of religious culture content led them to believe they were obligated to engage in social activism to rid society of division and oppression. Also, the above accounts indicate that family, church, and other indigenous social networks housed enduring meanings and ideas that consistently encouraged some people to struggle for equality during structurally constraining times. African-Americans bonded in relationships in indigenous organizational networks to cultivate emotional and other forms of support important for mobilizing and sustaining collective action.

Wartime Experience's Impact on Religious Interpretation During Desegregation

To avoid complying with the Supreme Court's directive in *Mitchell v. United States* to maintain "separate but equal" public facilities for African-Americans, the Arkansas state legislature passed Act 345 in 1943, which appropriated five thousand dollars for out-of-state "tuition costs for [each] Negro student desiring to work in fields not offered at [Arkansas] Agricultural, Mechanical and Normal College (AM&N), the only African-American higher education institution in the state" (Williams 1986:38). The amount allocated for the student was then withheld from funds allocated to Arkansas AM&N College. In effect, this arrangement required African-American Arkansans to finance the cost of maintaining racial segregation (Williams 1986).

This redirection of funds did little to abate African-American's drive for equal educational opportunity within their own state, especially after African-American veterans returned to Arkansas from World War II. As Payne's (1995) research on civil rights mobilization suggests, wartime experiences of returning veterans further emboldened African-American resistance to the racial inequities. Payne found that the wartime experiences of Amzie Moore, a member of the Student Nonviolent Coordinating Committee in Mississippi, helped him to develop a politicized religious perspective that negated his view of himself as well as his fellow African-Americans as appendages to European-American society.

> Before he went into the service, he had trouble reconciling Christianity with the reality of Mississippi: "You're standing there and you hear the word, the message, and you believe in it but you're wondering about whether God believes in it." At one point in his life, he had concluded that the degradation of his people must have been divinely ordained. White people were special, and God must have wanted them to have everything. It took his military experience to divest him of the idea that white people were special. God had put him on a ship and sent him around the world so that he could see that people were pretty much the same all over. He lost his fear of white folks and joined the NAACP while still in the service. (Payne 1995:30–31)

Essentially, Payne found that African-American soldiers experienced two conflicting phenomena during the war: equality with European-American soldiers and discrimination on the part of the military that transformed their consciousness. Several respondents like this one maintained that when he "came out of the Marines in 1946 . . . the . . . movement was in full flight . . . I would say the . . . movement, . . . if it had any spread of forwardness came when young GI's like myself came back determined to enjoy freedom for which we had just fought. You would look at the climate and you will find that was a great plus for the civil rights struggle, young . . . black soldiers who were determined."

Though veterans acknowledged the importance of their wartime experiences in promoting their activism after World War II, they also suggested that their protest was an extension of their earlier involvement in the *black struggle*. This is evident in this exchange:

> Q: As we were talking, you were saying that even before you went overseas, you were engaged in protest.
> A: Well, that's what I am talking about. As a youth—when I was fifteen [I attended] NAACP youth conferences . . . I was very active in the NAACP after I came [to Little Rock] from Gould, Arkansas and joined the NAACP . . . There were not many confrontations at that time because they had not been formulated. But our concern, our reason of issue, our demanding change came during that period. And, usually confrontation is a follow-up to a demand for change, if followed logically. First, demand change and when they won't do change then you come up with a method to insist that they do it. That was the process.
> Q: As far back as you can remember, even as a kid was there constant demand for change?
> A: Absolutely, and fortunately I was a part of it. Always conscious of— I remember when I was in the military, the Armed Forces were segregated at that time. [President] Truman desegregated the military in 1946 but all the time that I was in the Marines it was segregated. There was not a single black commissioned officer in the Marines when I was there. I bitterly resented that, I thought there was a bright—I thought of myself that way, a young black from Dunbar High School, the greatest high school in the world. That's the way I thought of it. I thought that I should have had the opportunity to go to OCS, Officer Candidate School. But I was not [granted this opportunity], and resented that, . . . that drove my concern in civil rights.

Veteran respondents also cited the enduring aspect of their families' religious devoutness as a factor in encouraging them to challenge racism while serving in the military. For instance, a respondent communicated in a lengthy response that after World War II ended in the Pacific, he refused to accept segregationist practices instituted aboard the ship, sent to return his unit to the United States.

> Well the aircraft carrier, Hornet showed up, it had been converted to a troop ship and they picked up units throughout the Pacific. The first

two or three days, we entered the general wash area, using the same facilities as all other Army, Marines, Navy and whatever. But about the third or fourth day out . . . the fourth morning out, I got up early and went to the wash area. There was a guard standing there with a gun. He said, "You can't enter." I said, "I beg your pardon?" He said, "You can't enter." He said, "Blacks are no longer permitted to use this, you will have to use that little makeshift facility in the area where your unit is occupied or stationed." I couldn't believe this. I said, "Oh, you say." He said, "Yes, you can't enter." So, I went back to my group . . . and I said, "look they're segregating this, we can't use that facility." I said, "Look, let's get a committee and look into this." Here was the response: "No, . . . I haven't seen my wife since we've been out here, I don't shake the boat . . ." Another said, "I've got a girlfriend and we are engaged for a long time . . . I don't want to shake the boat." So I struck out on my own, I went back to—I said, "Who directed you to keep the blacks out?" He said, "Well, the officer of the day." I said, "Where will I find him?" So, he pointed. So, when I got there the officer of the day says, "What can I do for you?" So, I told him what happened and he said, "Well, there's not a thing I can do, it came from above. The only thing I can tell you to do is see my superior." He said, "Have a seat. Do you want to see him?" I said, "Yes, I would like to see him." So, I think I sat there for about two or three hours. I thought, "Oh, my gosh, what are they trying to do, to see whether I am determined, whether or not this will cause me to drop what I am trying to accomplish?" So, at the end of two or three hours, he came in and he said, "Alright, you can go up to see the Ensign." . . . When I got there, they told me to have a seat, that he was tied up . . . it was during the noon hour or even beyond, so finally the door opened and it was a young, intelligent, radiant looking guy. He said, "Come in. What is the problem?" I related it to him. I could tell he was from the North and probably had come from one of the Ivy League schools. He said, "Look, you've got a point." I said, "Look, I given the better part of my years fighting for democracy and here I am being denied the opportunity to use a facility that the taxpayers have authorized and paid for." He said, "Yeah but there's nothing I can do." He said, "The only thing I can do is refer you to my supervisor." He said, "By the way, have you had anything to eat." I said, "No, matter-of-fact, I haven't even washed my face." He said, "I just returned from eating and I brought myself a sandwich and I'm going to give it to you." So, I thanked him. So, he pointed me to his superior. So, when I got up there, I was told that he was busy and it would take some time . . . if I was interested in seeing him, have a seat. So, I sat there for another couple of hours. Well, when he finally opened the door I got up. "What can I do for you?" I related to him what had happened. "What are you trying to do? You're the only one coming up here from your unit that is principally black. Where are you from? And you got segregation down there. What are you trying to do, rock the boat?" So, I related him that I had given the better part of my life fighting for democracy and was not admitted because of my race and this was most disturbing. Well, he went on to lecture me and what have you, trying to discourage me. So, well, "I'll tell you this, the only thing that— you'll have to see my superior, the Captain and I don't know if he will see you or not." So, I said, "I would like to see him." So, he directed me how to get to . . . where the Captain was located in the bridge. So, when I got there I had to sit a couple of more hours. Gosh, [I wondered], what are they trying to do, discourage me. . . . Then I thought, maybe what they are doing is looking at my records to see if I caused problems but I hadn't parenthetically . . . at that time, but years later . . . thought "my gosh, when I was walking along the ship's rails somebody could have pushed me over in the Pacific and told my parents that I died in service." I didn't think about that at that time but I have always felt that there is a supreme being and that He will look out for his followers . . . [F]inally the door opened and the Captain said, "What can I do for you." So, I related [my experience] to him. He looked me in the eye and said, "You are right." He said, "When you go back tomorrow morning there will not be a guard at that door." . . . When I got back to my area, here were northerners who were college graduates and what have you, asleep, stretched out, and this was most shocking. I said to myself, "My God, I see why Blacks do not achieve or acquire their desires." They do not take a firm logical, legal stand. I didn't threaten anybody, I wasn't loud. They told me to wait and I waited. I simply stated my position and that was it.

The respondent explained that he stood alone in his opposition against attempts to segregate African-American and European-American troops because "Well, my mother was a very strong Christian and my father who didn't have a formal education . . . was a Baptist minister. I was always told that whenever you are traveling the straight and truthful path, take a stand . . . If you have that self-confidence or that strength to take a stand, make sure you are right. We were taught that." In effect, the fundamental normative purpose and direction of familial religious values and beliefs provided respondents with the view that God supported those who put their faith into practice.

Taking this view, veterans like Wiley A. Branton, manager of a Pine Bluff taxi company, and Silas Hunt, a native of Ashdown and later a 1947 graduate of Arkansas AM&N College, returned home infused with hope for the future and faith in their own ability to create social change. With the help of Pine Bluff lawyer and NAACP state president W. Harold Flowers, both men submitted applications in 1948 for admission to the all European-American University of Arkansas Law School. Flowers used the United States Supreme Court's 1941 *Mitchell v. United States* decision mandating "separate but equal" educational facilities, equipment, and courses of study to force the University of Arkansas to integrate its graduate schools, and especially those academic fields that were not available at Arkansas AM&N College. Years after his retirement Lewis W. Jones, president of the University of Arkansas, recalled: "When I came to Arkansas in 1947, the anticipated applications of black students for admission to law school and possibly to other graduate schools, . . . occup[ied] the attention of the administration and the Board of Trustees. But, because of the emotional climate in the matter of race relations, both in the North and South, the political overtones especially in the South, this issue was a particularly sensitive one" (Williams 1986:38).

In 1947, Clifford Davis, the first African-American Arkansan admitted to the law school and a graduate of Philander Smith College in Little Rock, refused to enroll because of "the special classroom and study room" provision proposed for him at the law school (Williams 1986:38). Shortly before Silas Hunt submitted his formal application for admission in 1948, Robert A. Leflar, dean of the law school, reaffirmed the university's special contingency for enrollment. At a news conference he stated: "The Law School will, in accordance with plans approved by the Board of Trustees, admit a qualified Negro student if he applies for admission. This is required by the recent decision of the United States Supreme Court. A separate study and classroom will be provided in the law building. We believe that the facilities offered here will satisfy Supreme Court requirements" (*Arkansas Gazette*, Feb. 3, 1948). In order to expedite the integration of the law school, Hunt accepted this arrangement while Branton withdrew his application. Although Silas Hunt, after his first year in the law program, died of tuberculosis, he made it possible for African-Americans to attend and graduate from the law school. This indicates, as several respondents asserted, "The climate among young [returning] GIs was to fight for rights for which we had fought in the far islands of the South Pacific and Europe . . . We were determined that it was our time now; we had secured the rights of other folk, so we wanted to secure our own rights."

Since the Supreme Court's *Mitchell v. United States* directive to maintain "substantially equal" facilities proved to be an effective tool for integrating higher education in Arkansas, W. Harold Flowers filed suit in Federal District Court in Little Rock in January 1949 requesting that the DeWitt Special School District No. 1's Board of Directors provide equal educational facilities for African-American and European-American students (*Arkansas Gazette*, Mar. 17, 1949).[2] On July 8, 1949, Federal Judge Harry J. Lemley concurred with Flowers's "charge that facilities offered DeWitt Negro children were far below standards of those for white children . . . [and] an abridgment of national and state constitutional guarantees to Negro children," but believed that DeWitt Special School District No. 1's Board of Directors recognized the disparity and wanted to correct it (*Arkansas Gazette*, July 9, 1949). Consequently, the court allowed the directors a "reasonable time" to make specific adjustments but told them either to equalize educational terms and facilities for African-American students or reduce the school period and amenities of those maintained for European-American students until they are "substantially equal" (*Arkansas Gazette*, July 9, 1949). Moreover, the board of directors was also ordered not to allocate any more money for building or improving European-American schools unless a proportionate share of the funds were distributed for improvement of African-American schools (Cather, July 8, 1949; *Arkansas Gazette*, July 9, 1949).

Two days after the ruling, an editorial appeared in the *Arkansas Gazette* specifying that if European-Americans wanted to maintain segregated public educational facilities, it would cost them dearly financially. The editorial, titled *Sobering School Decision*, read:

A sobering decision to the school patrons and taxpayers of Arkansas was made by Federal Judge Harry J. Lemley, Friday.

It ordered DeWitt Special School District, No. 1 to provide school facilities for its Negro Children, "substantially equal" to those of its white children.

This means buildings, equipment, length of school terms and other such factors. A "reasonable time" is allowed for improving the Negro school buildings. But the length of terms must be equalized at the opening of the 1949–50 session.

The district has no Negro high school, and the Negro children have been going to one in another district, a C rated school. Judge Lemley says these children must have the same rating of high school as the district's white pupils.

In allowing a "reasonable time" for improving the Negro elementary school, the decree said it must be "substantially" as good as the white school, "taking into consideration the comparative average daily attendance of the students of each race, together with any other pertinent factors."

How much, if any, leeway that may allow, we don't know.

Apparently, the decision will apply to all districts having white and Negro schools. The cost would be high. To bring the school buildings and equipment up to standard may call for 10 million dollars, according to Ed McCuistion of the state Department of Education. And the per capita expenditure for Negro students, for upkeep, teachers' salaries and the like, will require about three and one-half million dollars more a year.

Some money can be raised by bringing property assessments in the districts up to where they belong. But many white schools also are below standard. The whole bill, for two school systems in many districts, will hit hard.

And where does this "equality" matter end? Will it result in a demand that all of the poorer white schools in the state be brought up to a level with the best ones? Will it apply to the colleges, as say, between the Negro AM&N College at Pine Bluff and the white colleges? How can Arkansas, 47th in per capita income, meet such a bill, and finance other urgent demands?

We are not finding fault with Judge Lemley's decision. It was a tempered pronouncement, in line with federal Supreme Court rulings, and essentially just.

But we do wonder about that "equality" standard. Some of our Negro schools are a disgrace, and cannot be too quickly improved. Yet the best schooling isn't always provided with the costliest facilities. A lot of mighty capable men and women have been turned out by plain, little schools; some mighty poor ones by imposing educational plants. (Editorial, July 10, 1949)

My interviews suggest that long before Judge Lemley's ruling in 1949, the religious relational links and culture in indigenous institutions (that is, churches, families, ATA, and ANDA) served as resources in mobilizing committed groups of African-Americans for participation in the desegregation movement. As discussed in chapter 1, Tarrow (1994) calls these small insurgent groups "early risers" who, despite restraining political conditions, worked continuously to construct political opportunities for change that larger movement groups later exploit. During the first half of the twentieth century in Arkansas these "early risers" did not allow the harsh segregative environment to impede their efforts to bring about desegregation. Rather, in their churches and other indigenous organizations, these individuals bonded in relationships that fostered the creation of social support and enduring self-understandings that gave them confidence in their own efforts to desegregate public facilities. Their long struggle and legal victories eventually made it economically impractical for European-American Arkansans to continue practicing segregation, especially in the educational arena. Estimates were that it would cost $13.5 to $20 million to equalize educational facilities, per pupil expenditures, and teacher salaries (*Arkansas Gazette*, Jul 9, 1949; Bosson, May 31, 1953). For a state with a small population of approximately 1.8 million and a per capita income around $3,000 to $4,000, raising another $13 to $20 million to equalize education was virtually impossible. However European-Americans refused to give up on segregation. They adopted a divide and conquer strategy by raising sufficient funds to equalize facilities and teacher salaries in the most problematic school districts in the hopes that protesters would stop the desegregation movement after these schools complied with court orders. Their strategy did not succeed, given that religious cultural practices (that is, singing, praying) and meanings invoked a collective orientation (that is, group identity and consciousness) among African-Americans that continuously encouraged the social application of religious teachings. Moreover, the DeWitt Public School District, No. 1 court ruling and President Harry S. Truman's lackluster support for antilynching legislation, action against employment discrimination and segregation in interstate transportation, and push for voting rights legislation cued African-Americans to continue their struggle for societal integration. African-Americans used Truman's weak political gestures of support to further legitimate and garner more support for political change.

Sustaining Movement Momentum

Continuous agitation for school desegregation eventually forced the University of Arkansas to open its undergraduate school to African-Americans in 1951 and to maintain its annual admission of one to two African-Americans to its law school (*Arkansas Democrat*, Aug. 26, 1951).[3] As a result of these admissions, Jackie L. Shrosphire became the first African-American to receive a degree from the university's law school in 1951 (Williams 1986:38). Some months after Shrosphire's graduation, a Little Rock interracial school study found that though African-American and European-American children started school with the same abilities, the low quality of education at African-American schools inhibited their learning over time (*Arkansas Democrat*, Feb. 3, 1952). This finding in combination with integration of the University of Arkansas further emboldened African-Americans and stimulated further use of church culture and organization as an agent for securing socioeconomic equality. During this period, the respondent below, like several others I interviewed, maintained that it was perfectly clear to him "that anybody who accepts Christ as [his or her] leader has the obligation to make sure that the rule of law is applied equally across the broad, irrespective of ethnicity or gender. The church has that obligation because Christ gave his life for humanity to make sure that there was an opportunity to enjoy eternity . . . Yes, I think there is an obligation. Now, I don't say that they've got to get out there and demonstrate, I think it is left up to each unit as to what approach to take."

The respondent's observation that "it is left up to each unit as to what approach to take" in fulfilling the church's social mission suggests that there were multiple discourses on the church's social obligation. Individuals drew a variety of meanings about the extent to which their church should be involved in the desegregation movement. Respondents, like the one below, argued that it was common to find churches like the one he attended, simultaneously limiting church involvement in the movement while encouraging churchgoers' participation. "Well, the pastor did not believe in involving the religion or the church in politics or what have you, but [the church] would have these funds and make contributions to the chapter as well as national organization. So, he was active and he would encourage the members to take out a membership with the local [NAACP] branch. [Let's not go out and demonstrate,] let's take the legal course. That was his view . . . he was a Christian."

Though wholesale church and congregant involvement in the desegregation effort was not evident, their obtuse support for the movement played a crucial role in providing protest participants with emotional and social support, which, according to Mamphela Ramphele, encouraged activists to believe "in a future which might be better than the present, a desire to be engaged in the establishment of a better order, and compassion for the underdog. Secondly, [it gives political activists] a share[d] sense of fellowship with others who are similarly committed" to cement bonds that are instrumental in reaffirming their commitment to the movement (1999:106). Moreover, the tacit support of inactive churches allowed their members to take comfort in the belief that the church's minimal institutional, emotional, and social support for the movement fulfilled their religious mission to transform the world.

Given the multiplicity of church discourses on fulfilling religion's social mission, some churches, like the above, espoused a more restrained sponsorship of the desegregation movement, while others took a more activist stance in carrying out the Gospel's call for secular transformation. The former perspective was found in a Methodist church in south central Arkansas that one respondent identified as "St. John A.M.E. Church in Pine Bluff, where the NAACP held its monthly meetings. There was a St. Paul Baptist Church in Pine Bluff, where Wiley [Branton] used to conduct programs to enlighten our people on how to execute a vote. In other words, back then in order to qualify to vote, you had to pay a $1.00 poll tax . . . So those educational meetings that I participated in with Wiley Branton at those churches were designed to enlighten our people on what to do when you get to the poll . . . Those meetings were designed to encourage them to pay that poll tax [to] vote."

Though the culture of these churches promoted movement involvement, this respondent reported that some church members believed that their church had no role to play in temporal affairs: "If there were members who didn't appreciate it, I got the impression that they just didn't attend [the meetings] . . . [Usually] the pastor and the deacon board . . . in . . . [the] church are in charge. [They] usually control the situation. If you got that pastor [or board] on your side, you've got it." Respondents also credited church members' involvement in local movement organizations for the willingness of some churches to allow civil rights groups like the NAACP and Arkansas Christian Movement to hold meetings in their buildings. According to one respondent, members who disagreed with the church's open door policy toward local movement organizations were ineffective in blocking other members from using the church as a transformative agent "because the officers [in organizations like] the NAACP [were] members of . . . churches. If I am the president of the NAACP and I wanted to go to Mt. Pleasant, I [am a member] in good standing. I am a paying member, and have some political clout in the community. The pastor, nine times out of ten, is not going to deny me the right to bring the group into the church." The presence of these religious activists reminded church people of their religion's moral imperative to uplift the oppressed and culturally cajoled some to participate in and open their churches for movement organizing. One respondent maintained that this pressure was applied gently from the pulpit of his inactive church when the pastor routinely acknowledged social activist congregants to let them know he valued their participation in the desegregation movement. "Now, Reverend [Fred T.] Guy [pastor of Mount Zion Baptist church] was not going to get personally involved in any type of confrontation, but he always would lend his support, and most especially did he lend his support to me. He called me, 'Young Prince.' [He would say,] 'Young Prince we are proud of you.' He would say that from the pulpit . . . and he would walk up to me after church and put his arm around my shoulder and say 'we are proud of you.'" Such public shows of support from prominent members of the African-American community proved important in mobilizing and sustaining the desegregation movement in Arkansas. Respondents, like this one, repeatedly asserted that movement organizers "knew who to go to in a particular community . . . knew who to touch in the community," and whose opinions the community valued, so they tried to persuade these individuals to support the desegregation effort under the assumption that they would use their influence to encourage protest mobilization.

While using prominent communal figures to mobilize political action, movement organizers also tapped the deep tradition of religious resistance to injustice and oppression to incite and sustain the desegregation struggle. This process is demonstrated in a respondent's religious activist frame, which identified the church as "[a]n instrument of God . . . We are all God's children; we are God's prize possessions [and] inasmuch as he has given us the ability to think . . . he's given us a part of him. That's the part he wants back, [and] . . . that's the part that the church per se is based on . . . [Thus the role of the church is] to take care of the whole man, total man . . . The church is supposed to reach out to mankind." Since many respondents saw themselves as the divine's living spirit, they tended to view their faith as a blueprint for living, requiring them to participate actively in the process of ensuring the well-being and holistic development of humanity. As this respondent explained: "religion is just a vehicle, just like any other car, to get you from point A to point B . . . So, a religion only gets you through this life to God. That's all religion is for." Consequently, respondents had few problems using churches as resources in political organizing and activism. The respondent maintained: "I feel that blacks are a church-oriented people. That's the only area where the white man wouldn't bother you. That's why everything went on in church. . . . [E]ach minister would say 'well you know election time is coming up and they're going to have this such and such thing on the ballot.' . . . He (the minister) wouldn't tell you which way to [vote]; you would use your own mind." Through the aforementioned cultural processes, the desegregation movement in the 1940s and early 1950s was sustained in Arkansas. These same cultural processes inspired further movement activity after the U.S. Supreme Court's 1954 *Brown v. Board of Education of Topeka* ruling declared segregation in education unconstitutional.

Conclusion

In this chapter I used secondary historical and personal interview data to argue that culture is a key link between organization and political activism. Specifically, I maintained that crucial cultural elements of religion were influential in helping African-American Arkansans construct relationships and meanings that predisposed some to mobilize collectively to struggle for equality during the oppressive heyday of segregation. This suggests that the prevailing social movement theory's focus on indigenous organizations' functions in mobilizing protest must be expanded to include a general emphasis on the role of culture and also a specific focus on the process by which various groups and individuals interpret religious meanings and practices. In the next chapter I continue my investigation of culture's effect on movements by exploring how religious culture content mattered in mobilizing the school desegregation movement during the 1950s in Arkansas.

CHAPTER 5

Religion's Effect on Mobilizing Civil Rights Protest

————⊷((◦))⊶————

On May 17, 1954, the United State Supreme Court unanimously ruled in *Brown v. Board of Education of Topeka* "that segregation 'solely on the basis of race' violates the Constitution, regardless of whether schools for Negroes appear to be as good as those for whites" (*Arkansas Democrat*, May 18, 1954:1A). Arkansas's public school superintendents reacted to the decision with concern but not alarm. Their responses followed the general theme articulated by C. S. Blackburn, superintendent of North Little Rock schools: "Most of us have felt it (the antisegregation decision) was only a matter of time" (*Arkansas Democrat*, May 18, 1954:2A). A good number of school district superintendents realized, like their colleagues in Texarkana and Conway, that despite the fact that they "were doing everything . . . to equalize [their] program . . . the problem [could not] be worked out satisfactorily . . . without some readjustments" (*Arkansas Democrat*, May 18, 1954:2A). They reached this conclusion after African-American Arkansans' litigation successfully established, in the late 1940s and early 1950s, that segregated education was unequal, and in violation of the Supreme Court's 1941 "separate but equal" facility order issued in *Mitchell v. United States*. Moreover, superintendents correctly judged that African-Americans' persistent legal challenges would eventually erode de jure segregation's viability.

Although the assessments of these superintendents were correct, the state's refusal to enforce laws that undermined segregation proved to be a formidable desegregation obstacle. Given this state of affairs, what motivated African-Americans to continue their struggle for desegregation? In what follows I explore how and why religion mattered in the desegregation struggle in Arkansas. In short: can persistent activism in oppressive sociopolitical environments be viewed as a manifestation of meanings and actions expressed by religious discourse and institutions? The purpose of this endeavor is to look for connections rather than assume them, and thereby specify the mechanisms by which religion influenced individual action within the Civil Rights Movement in Arkansas. Before proceeding with this examination, it is worthwhile to discuss briefly the sociopolitical context in Arkansas just before the desegregation of Little Rock Central High School.

State Response to Court Decision

Shortly after the Supreme Court declared segregation unconstitutional in 1954, Arkansas's political leadership expressed its willingness to obey the law. Francis Cherry, Arkansas's governor at the time of the decision, pledged that the state "would approach problems relating to the U.S. Supreme Court's anti-segregation ruling not as 'outlaws,' but would seek to work out solutions that would meet legal requirements" (*Arkansas Democrat*, May 18, 1954:1A). This promise came during the gubernatorial campaign; Governor Cherry, who was seeking a second term, expressed his desire not to make integration an issue in the campaign (Bates 1986:48). However, Cherry's opponent, Orval Faubus, saw political advantage in making integration an issue. In a formal statement, he declared:

> It is evident to me that Arkansas is not ready for a complete and sudden mixing of the races in the public schools and that any attempt to solve this problem by pressure or mandatory methods will jeopardize, in many communities, the good relations which exist between whites and Negroes.
>
> In my opinion, desegregation is the No. 1 issue in this gubernatorial campaign and I am therefore making my position clear at the outset with the expressed hope that this issue does not become a temptation to acts and declarations of *demagoguery* [italics mine] on the part of those who might seek to play upon racial prejudice for selfish ends or, as in the case of communism, to create ill will between whites and Negroes and disrupt this country. (Bates 1986:48–49)

When Faubus uttered these words it was he, not Cherry, who used racial prejudice and made false claims to secure political power. Though he knew the Supreme Court had ordered rearguments concerning implementation of its

integration decision, Faubus deliberately implied that *Brown* called for immediate integration. Not until the May 1955 reargument ruling (known as *Brown
II*) did the Court grant localities maximum flexibility to make a "prompt and
reasonable start" toward integration (Freyer 1981). In practical terms, this
meant that state officials, local school boards, and federal district judges were
given an ambiguous mandate that they construed to justify delay and gradualism (Freyer 1981:197). Faubus's deceptive representation of the *Brown* decision was enough to convince the majority of the European-American electorate
to vote him into office four months before the *Brown II* decision.

Before the gubernatorial campaign, many school districts sought to obey
Governor Cherry's directive to comply with the court's ruling. Five days after
the May 17, 1954, ruling, the Little Rock School Board issued this statement:
"It is our responsibility to comply with the federal constitutional requirements
and we intend to do so when the Supreme Court of the United States outlines
the method to be followed" (*Arkansas Gazette*, July 29, 1955). The fall after
the *Brown* ruling, two northwest Arkansas communities, Fayetteville and
Charleston, opened their European-American schools to African-Americans.
Since their African-American population was small, European-Americans' fears
about integrating public schools in Fayetteville and Charleston were not apparent. Seven African-American students were admitted to Fayetteville's high
school while twelve African-Americans were integrated into Charleston's district
(*Arkansas Gazette*, June 26, 1955). All but one or two of the twelve students
admitted in Charleston were at the elementary school level (*Arkansas Gazette*,
June 26, 1955). One of the most noteworthy attempts to conform to the
Supreme Court's decision outlawing public school segregation occurred in the
southernmost edge of eastern Arkansas in the delta town of Hoxie in July 1955.
Hoxie's school superintendent, K. E. Vance, announced prior to integration,
"we are making no special preparation and are expecting no trouble of any
kind . . . We will try to begin the new program without fanfare" (*Arkansas
State Press*, Jul 14, 1955, v. 15, no. 11). Desegregation was full—extending to
classrooms, lunchrooms, playgrounds, and school buses—and immediate—
beginning with the 1955 summer session designed for the convenience of
cotton growing counties (*Arkansas State Press*, July 14, 1955, v. 15, no. 11). The
Arkansas State Press informed readers: "Superintendent Vance [explained] that
the board reached the decision to proceed with full integration because: 1)
integration is right in the sight of God; 2) it is in accord with the Supreme
Court's ruling that segregation in public schools is unconstitutional, and; 3) it is
cheaper [than segregation]" (*Arkansas State Press*, July 14, 1955, v. 15, no. 11).

Like Fayetteville and Charleston, Hoxie's African-American population was small; therefore, it was more economical to integrate. But unlike these northwest Arkansas communities, it was located in the heart of the delta with its unwavering southern segregation practices and planters' interest in keeping laborers ignorant and in the cotton fields. Thus integration in Hoxie encountered organized white racists that opposed admitting twenty African-Americans into the town's public school (*Arkansas Gazette*, July 12, 1955; *Arkansas Gazette*, Nov. 13, 1955). On August 3, 1955, approximately two hundred segregationists met at Hoxie City Hall where they adopted a resolution demanding a return to segregated public schools. European-American parents were encouraged to withdraw their children from the school until the withdrawal of African-American students (Bates 1986:50–51). In her book *The Long Shadow of Little Rock: A Memoir*, Daisy Bates, president of Arkansas's NAACP and the organizer of the desegregation movement in Little Rock, indicated that African-American parents in Hoxie "were subjected to threats of intimidation, and were even called upon to put their names to a petition demanding the return to the segregated school system. The Negro parents stood firm in their determination to abide by the school board decision to integrate the school" (1986:51).

Given the opposition's strength, the Hoxie School Board filed for a temporary injunction in the Jonesboro Division of the United States District Court to stop interference with racial integration in their schools. The *Arkansas Gazette* identified "defendants in the case as Herbert Brewer, leader of the Hoxie group opposing integration; Amis Guthridge of Little Rock, attorney for White America, Inc.; former state Senator James D. Johnson of Crossett and Curt Copeland of Hot Springs, both leaders in the White Citizens Council and the Committee Representing Segregation in the Hoxie Schools" (Nov. 13, 1955; Oct. 23, 1955).

On November 1, 1955, the court ruled that defendants had "planned and conspired" to prevent integration at Hoxie and issued a temporary injunction ordering them to cease interfering with the desegregation of Hoxie's schools (*Arkansas Gazette*, Nov. 13, 1955).

Prosegregationists took their cue to resist integration from individuals like Richard McCulloch, attorney for the Hughes Special School District, who collaborated in writing the state's amicus curiae brief in *Brown v. Board of Education of Topeka*, which stipulated that segregation was solely a school problem rather than a legal or political concern. Though McCulloch advised school districts to "act promptly to conform to the spirit of the Supreme Court's decision," he specified they do so with reference to local conditions (Harris, Aug. 4,

1955:1A). In addition, he suggested that communities that did not want to desegregate their schools had to find other means to fulfill "the spirit of the Supreme Court's decision," like Hughes School District's construction of new facilities for its African-American school in lieu of full integration (Harris, Aug. 4, 1955:1A). Though the *Brown* decision declared "separate but equal" illegal, McCulloch and Hughes's school board assumed the Supreme Court would interpret incremental moves to upgrade African-American public schools as a crucial first step towards full integration since enlarged districts would eventually need additional facilities. However, in practice, the Hughes strategy legitimated the implementation of gradualism, which obstructed integration and perpetuated pre-*Brown* school arrangements.

Orval Faubus also advocated state policies that motivated resistance to integration. Faubus, like McCulloch, maintained, "segregation in some form could be maintained if teachers' salaries and [school] facilities were equalized to the point that . . . Negroes would be reluctant to seek integration through court action" (*Arkansas Gazette*, Feb. 17, 1955). Faubus's equalization strategy underestimated African-Americans' collective determination and desire to challenge segregation's structures and value system that sustained and legitimated inequality. Fatmagül Berktay (1998), in her discussion on gender and oppression in *Women and Religion*, contends that challenging oppressive structures and value systems requires that oppressed groups construct their own forms of expression and processes for creating meanings and images that order society. Since dominant groups usually use these cultural elements to encourage subordinate groups' acceptance and internalization of hierarchical definitions, these groups often struggle against external pressures and obstructions as well as prevailing cultural meanings they carry within themselves (Berktay 1998:3, 5). Noted philosopher Maurice Godelier (1982) contends that subordinate group members can surmount cultural hegemony through interactions with others having similar experiences, making it possible to construct and sustain a sense of community, solidarity, and culture needed to stimulate opposition against domination. Thus rather than Faubus's equalization strategy creating division between among African-Americans, it heightened their sense of community and commitment to secure full integration. The following discusses at length how struggle against segregation gave rise to social bonds and ideas among blacks that delegitimized the existing racial order and inspired collective resistance.

The decision of several Arkansas colleges (that is, Arkansas Tech, Henderson State Teachers College, and University of Arkansas's College of Engineering) to admit African-Americans, on the assumption that the Supreme Court's ruling applied to tax-supported colleges, further emboldened movement participants to continue on with their struggle (*Arkansas Gazette*, Sept. 16, 1955:1A). These admissions in higher education occurred despite Arkansas attorney general, T. J. Gentry's ruling that the Supreme Court's decision outlawing public school segregation "directly applied to the parties in those cases, and . . . not . . . directly to any Arkansas . . . district college or university" (*Arkansas Gazette*, Sept. 16, 1955:1A). Although Gentry's comments implied segregation in higher education was legal, it also offered African-Americans hope, when he suggested the possibility "that the Supreme Court would follow the precedent set by the other decisions if an Arkansas case came up, even with 'separate but equal' facilities, and . . . that such a decision then would apply to any institution supported by public funds" (*Arkansas Gazette*, Sept. 16, 1955:1A). After these remarks Gentry spent a month carefully examining the Supreme Court's decision before reversing his initial legal assessment in a letter to the presidents of the University of Arkansas and six state-supported "all-white" colleges: Arkansas Tech, Henderson State Teachers College, Arkansas State College, Arkansas AM&N at Monticello, and Arkansas State Teachers College at Conway. The attorney general stated, "the Supreme Court would make the decisions of May 17, 1954, and May 31, 1955, applicable if an Arkansas segregation case came before it, although separate but equal facilities were provided . . . Therefore, the decision would be the same if the question were presented to the Court concerning a state-supported university, college, high school, grammar school or kindergarten" (*Arkansas Gazette*, Aug. 4, 1955:1A).

These developments led the State NAACP executive board and branch presidents to convene on June 11, 1955, in Little Rock at Phyllis Wheatley YMCA in order to adopt a four-point program designed to hasten the pace of integration (Sutton, June 12, 1955:1A). The new NAACP policy ordered the president and chairperson of the legal redress committee to:

1. Draft letters to every school district in the state where Negroes are enrolled asking that integration begin immediately.
2. File petitions with the various school boards similar to those filed in several districts some months ago by the organization seeking a hearing on the plans for integration.
3. Seek conferences with Governor Faubus, Attorney General Gentry and Education Commissioner Arch Ford on the integration of the Arkansas schools.

4. To actually file suit against school districts which refuse to act "in good faith" in initiating the integration process. (Sutton, Jun 12, 1955:1A)

In regard to point 2, the NAACP requested that school districts announce their plans for integration before September 1955 or face lawsuits. As one organizational official stated: "We want to know what the boards have in mind before September [because] if they don't announce their plan by that time we will know that they are stalling and not working in good faith" (Sutton, June 12, 1955:1A).

Since the school board of the northwest Arkansas city of Van Buren declined to submit an integration plan to the NAACP and refused to admit nineteen African-American students in fall 1955, the NAACP petitioned the Federal District Court in Fort Smith to force immediate racial integration of Van Buren's public schools. The *Arkansas Gazette*, in an article titled "Van Buren Integration Suit Filed," reported:

> The suit, charg[ed] the Van Buren School Board and Supt. Everett Kelley with denying admittance to all-white schools, asks for a temporary injunction, to be made permanent later, to keep the school officials "from denying the plaintiffs and the class they represent their rights, privileges and immunities" under the U.S. constitution and laws.
>
> It also asks that the Court rule unconstitutional a 1947 Arkansas statute giving public school trustees the power and authority to "establish separate schools for white and colored persons." (Oct. 29, 1955:7B)

Before going to trial, a settlement was reached requiring Van Buren to integrate its schools fully by fall 1957 (*Arkansas State Press*, Sept. 12, 1958).

The Van Buren suit was followed on January 28, 1956, by the NAACP's announcement that it would attempt to enroll African-American students at all grade levels in local schools, commencing in Little Rock. When students attempting to enroll were denied entry, the NAACP filed suit in federal court asking for integration without delay, like what occurred in Fayetteville and Charleston (*Arkansas Democrat*, Jan. 29, 1956). Wiley A. Branton, state NAACP attorney from Pine Bluff, was appointed by the organization as lead attorney for the plaintiffs. Others on the legal team included NAACP regional counsel U. Simpson Tate of Dallas, Texas, and national counsels Robert L. Carter and future Supreme Court justice Thurgood Marshall of New York.

After the NAACP's unsuccessful sixteen-day attempt to enroll thirty-three African-American students at four "all-white" Little Rock public schools, it filed suit in federal district court in Little Rock on February 8, 1956, "contending that the children were denied admittance solely on the basis of race" (Childress, Jan. 23, 1956; Frick, Feb. 8, 1956; Craig, Feb. 9, 1956:1A). More precisely, the *Arkansas Gazette* reported: "The four NAACP attorneys who brought the suit asked specifically that Arkansas laws and School Board rules requiring segregation be declared unconstitutional and void, and that school officials be restrained from enforcing such regulations" (Craig, Feb. 9, 1956:1A).

The NAACP deemed the Little Rock public school suit necessary after the school board denied their request for immediate integration on August 5, 1955, and after their unsuccessful January 23, 1956, attempt to enroll African-American students (*Arkansas Gazette*, Aug. 5, 1955; Childress, Jan. 23, 1956:1A). Superintendent Virgil Blossom denied African-American students admission to "all-white" schools adjacent to their neighborhoods on the basis of the Little Rock School Board's gradual integration policy that was drafted ten days after the Supreme Court's *Brown* decision. The plan called for the implementation of integration in three phases:

> *First phase*: Integration should begin at the senior high school level (Grades 10–12).
> *Second phase*: Following successful integration at the senior high school level, it should then be started in the junior high school (Grades 7–9).
> *Third phase*: After successful integration in junior and senior high schools, it should be started in elementary schools (Grades 1–6). (Bates 1986:49)

School officials suggested that integration *might* start in September 1957 *if* a proposed new high school were completed by that time (Allbright, May 5, 1956:1A). No dates for the start of integration at other school levels were set.

Reverend J. C. Crenchaw, president of the Little Rock NAACP branch, and Daisy Bates, state NAACP president, maintained they "were not interested or impressed by the school board's plan for integration given it was 'vague and indecisive and could be implemented in 1956 or 1960'" (Allbright, May 5, 1956:1A). Moreover, Bates observed:

> Many Negro parents became convinced that Superintendent Blossom was more interested in appeasing the segregationists by advocating that only a limited number of Negroes be admitted than in complying with the Supreme Court's decision. The only assurance Negroes had that the school board would put the highly publicized plan into effect in the foreseeable future was the word of the school board. But years of

bitter and tragic experience had taught the Negro that the word of the Southern white man meant very little when it came to granting the Negro . . . constitutional rights . . . Negro parents felt the phrase "may start in 1957" was especially vague and left them no alternative except to go into court. (Bates 1986: 51–52)

As the NAACP pursued court orders for immediate integration, a group of black ministers led by Rev. Roland S. Smith, pastor of First Baptist Church of Little Rock, publicly announced their support for desegregation during a meeting with Governor Faubus on February 23, 1956. The declaration's primary goal was to convince Faubus to comply with the Supreme Court's antisegregation decision. In a prepared statement, the ministerial group urged the governor "as the elected leader of our state through the suffrage of all the people, without regard to race, to use your influence and power as our governor to uphold the constitution of the United States and to abide by the laws of the land as interpreted by the Supreme Court of the United States" (*Arkansas Democrat*, Feb. 24, 1956).

Faubus replied to the appeal by referring ministers to his January 28 statement in the *New York Times*, where he said, "85 percent of all Arkansans opposed racial integration" (*Arkansas Democrat*, Feb. 24, 1956). Unbeknownst to the ministerial group, Faubus was in the process of forming a five-person committee that included R. B. McCulloch to propose "laws—by legislative or initiated act—to prevent 'complete and sudden integration' " (*Arkansas Democrat*, Feb. 26, 1956). Specifically, the governor charged the committee to "recommend laws by which the people of Arkansas would be given an opportunity either by direct vote . . . or by the vote of their representatives in the General Assembly to affirm or reject" the Supreme Court's *Brown* decision (*Arkansas Democrat*, Feb. 26, 1956). On March 22, 1956, Faubus disclosed that his committee suggested that two legislative acts be developed calling for interposition—protecting the state against encroachment by the Supreme Court's decision and for school assignment provisions that ordered African-American and European-American students to attend separate schools (*Arkansas Democrat*, Mar. 23, 1956). In a prepared statement the governor said:

The measures will be in accord with the policy previously stated by myself and first made public early in 1954, and which state in substance:
   "Integration is a local problem and can best be solved on the local level according to the peculiar circumstances and conditions of each local school district.

The people of the state are overwhelmingly opposed to any effort to bring about sudden and complete integration.

Time is needed, in fact is absolutely necessary, to allow the citizens to cope with the most difficult problem that has faced the people of the state in many years. How much time is needed can be determined only by the events and developments of the future. . . .

The measures will be subject to the will of the people at a legally and orderly election. To me, there is no finer way to determine the will of the people on any measure than by the exercise of their franchise at the ballot box." (*Arkansas Democrat*, Mar. 23, 1956)

Since most African-Americans were disenfranchised and segregationists controlled election mechanisms, these measures were certain to pass if they were placed on the ballot. Awareness of this possibility induced African-Americans, like the president of the Arkansas Democratic Voters Association (ADVA), to become, as he claimed, "a wasp in the governor's pants." The *Arkansas Democrat* informed its readers that the ADVA president accused the governor of "encouraging open defiance of the law and the constitution when [he] endorsed petitions [and measures] for interposition and similar matters. [In addition . . . he] accused public officials . . . of violating their oath of office. Every elected official—including school board members—took an oath of office to uphold the law. Now they are trying to get around the law [using] delay tactics . . . The [S]upreme [C]ourt meant what it said and we might as well conform to the decision. I think it is a little unethical for one branch of the government to cast aspersions on another" (Mar. 23, 1956).

While Governor Faubus was deciding whether or not to impede integration through elections or legislation, pretrial depositions were taken for the integration suit filed against the Little Rock School Board. African-American desegregation activists retained their resolve for integration despite efforts by more powerful prosegregationist attorneys to undermine their credibility through invasive questioning and characterizations meant to destroy their unity and determination. When Leon B. Catlett, one of four school board attorneys present at the hearing, asked Daisy Bates whether or not she favored immediate integration, she replied she favored immediate and total integration because sufficient time had lapsed since the Supreme Court's decision and nothing had been done in Little Rock (Allbright, May 5, 1956:2A). Catlett's question sought to depict Bates as unreasonable and bent on using integration to disrupt the public school system, but her responses to his queries indicated she was quite sensible. Bates maintained that she and others had met several times with superintendent Blossom and that the meetings had always been courteous, but nothing had come of them (Allbright, May 5, 1956:2A). Catlett later asked Bates about her position on total and immediate integration, she replied, "I am for it." He then asked her: "When?" At that point *Gazette* reporter Charles Allbright, wrote she "leaned forward . . . and answered, almost incredulously, 'Now' " (Allbright, May 5, 1956:2A). An even more spirited exchange occurred between Catlett and Rev. J. C. Crenchaw. Catlett asked Crenchaw which he considered more important—immediate integration of schools or the educational welfare of both races?

Crenchaw: Integration for the betterment of the public over-all.
Catlett: Would integration be better?
Crenchaw: Integration should come immediately.
Catlett: Why?
Crenchaw: A law is a law {referring to the Supreme Court's anti-segregation ruling}
Catlett: There is no law that says integration will be immediate.
Crenchaw: There is none that says it will be gradual either.
          (Allbright, May 5, 1956:1A)

Though Bates and Crenchaw's testimonies were practical and logically sound, on August 28, 1956, the Federal District Court upheld the Little Rock School Board's plan for gradual integration. The decision maintained: "It would be an abuse of discretion for this court to fail to approve the plan or to interfere with its consummation so long as the defendants (the school board) move in good faith, as they have done since immediately after the decision of May 17, 1954, to inaugurate and make effective a racially nondiscriminatory school system" (Frick, Aug. 28, 1956:1A).

NAACP attorneys appealed the decision to the Eighth Circuit Court of Appeals, which in April 1957 upheld the lower court's ruling but in doing so decreed that the Federal District Court retain jurisdiction of the case for the purpose of entering such further orders as might be necessary (Bates 1986:52–53). Though the court did not order immediate integration, plaintiffs correctly understood that the judicial decree left the school board little choice but to integrate Little Rock's public schools.

Though desegregationist activists found solace in the court's ruling, it was short-lived given that, in the general election in November 1956, voters by a substantial margin adopted:

> a) Amendment No. 44 to the Arkansas Constitution of 1874, which amendment direct[ed] the Arkansas Legislature to take appropriate action and pass laws opposing "in every Constitutional manner" the decisions of the Supreme Court in the Brown cases;
> b) A resolution of interposition [that] . . . called upon the people of the United States and the governments of all separate states to join the people of Arkansas in securing adoption of an amendment to the Constitution of the United States which . . . provided that the powers of the federal government should not be construed to extend to the regulation of the public schools of any state, or to include a prohibition to any state to provide for the maintenance of racially separate but substantially equal public schools within such state; and,
> c) A pupil assignment law dealing with the assignment of individual pupils to individual public schools. (Williams et al. 1984:296)

Moreover, two months after Arkansans voted to amend the state constitution, four prosegregationist bills were introduced to the General Assembly of the Legislature: House Bill 322, which established the State Sovereignty Commission with the duty to "perform any and all acts and things deemed necessary" to protect the sovereignty of Arkansas and other states from encroachments by the federal government; House Bill 323, which relieved school children of compulsory attendance in integrated public schools; House Bill 324, which required persons and organizations engaged in certain activities to register with and make periodic reports to the State Sovereignty Commission; and House Bill 325, which authorized school boards to expend district funds in employing legal counsel to assist them in integration suits (Williams et al. 1984:296; Bates 1986:53). Since these bills, without much debate, easily passed the house eighty-eight to one, African-American activists concentrated on defeating the legislation in the senate. The senate's Constitutional Amendment Committee held hearings on February 18, 1957, which nine hundred people attended, the majority of whom were against passage of the bills (Bates 1986:54). They listened intently as speakers representing church and labor groups passionately argued against passage of the legislation. The only African-American to speak was Rev. Roland S. Smith, who like his post-Reconstruction predecessors, delivered an impassioned speech against the bills that echoed deep religious sensibilities for justice and equality. In Bates's summary of Smith's remarks, she specified, "he noted that Negroes had been 'separate but equal' for more than sixty years, during which time they had demonstrated love and loyalty for the United States. He said he thanked God that he was an American citizen, and that faith in God would bring justice and righteousness between the races. [He concluded,] 'We have nothing to fear but fear itself' " (1986:54–55).

A month after delivering this speech, Roland Smith and about three hundred black ministers from around Arkansas met at Little Rock's Union A.M.E. church on March 2, 1957, to organize the Arkansas Christian Movement to challenge the legality of the recently enacted prosegregationist laws.

Immediately after the *Brown* decision, African-American Arkansans reasonably believed the state would comply with the ruling; however, the subsequent *Brown II* ruling deflated their hopes with a vague implementation order that provided government officials with a means to impede integration. Despite this devastating setback, African-American activists, especially Christians like Roland Smith, persisted in their efforts to topple segregation. I turn now to examining religion's effect on desegregation movement participation.

Religious Culture's Substantive Role in Facilitating the Desegregation Movement

Berktay contends that, from its inception, Christianity contained contradictions that allowed it to promote and teach sometimes radical, sometimes reformist and conciliatory attitudes towards oppression (1998:80). Christianity's multivalent character, according to Lincoln and Mamiya (1990), makes it possible for African-Americans within the context of the church, to engage in an active process of socio-cultural appropriation and interpretation to construct their actions either to encourage or discourage religiously motivated protest. Deeply felt commitments, aspirations, and hope that religion engenders, directly and independently encouraged desegregation movement participation and strengthened protestors' resolve during difficult times. Interviewees consistently attributed their decisions to participate in the desegregation movement to religious mediated interpretive processes: "One of my favorite scriptures *Michael* verse 6 and 8, says 'I have told you old man what is good but do justly and to love mercy and to walk with man.' That means that's the sum total of my religious responsibility, to do justly, love mercy . . . There is another scripture that comes to mind with me all the time: 'Choose you this day whom you will serve but as for me and my house, I will serve the Lord.' So, I [said], 'Choose you, who you will serve but as for me, I will serve' the Civil Rights Movement. Now I am hoping I can inspire [others] with my actions, my convictions . . . [b]ut as for me and my house, we will serve the Lord."

Respondents, like this individual, asserted that religious sentiments regarding the implementation of faith in the world were an important factor in encouraging her Civil Rights Movement participation: "There is a scripture in the Bible, 'faith without work is dead.' You can't sit around here and talk about you're going to pray and the Lord is going to provide. No, he's not. You've got to get up and work. All my life I have been taught that . . . faith without work is dead . . . [W]e always studied the Bible, even when I was a kid . . . our family was a family of stalwarts." James Cone maintained that religious worldviews along these lines frequently led some adherents to believe, " 'If you're right, God will fight your battle.' God did not promise that we would not have troubles or that freedom would be easy to achieve. Rather God promised that we would not be left alone in the struggle" (1986:30). That is the faith and hope that sustained African-Americans' struggle for equality and enabled protestors to enunciate as Martin Luther King Jr. declared: "I tell you, I've seen the lightning flash. I've heard the thunder roar. I've felt sinbreakers dashing, trying to conquer my soul, but I heard the voice of Jesus saying, 'Still to fight on.' He promised never to leave me, never to leave me alone. He promised never to leave. Never to leave me alone" (Cone 1986:30).

Jean Cohen (1985) argued convincingly that to be culturally and politically effective, movements must construct and maintain collective identities that signify to themselves and the world who they are, what they stand for, and what kind of society they hope to create (Smith 1996:17). According to several respondents, religion engendered in them collective identities and meanings that imbued a sense of purpose that inspired the construction of perspectives proclaiming, "people who were products of segregation must be viewed theologically as the poor, the handicapped, the downtrodden. And theologically we have a responsibility to use our faith—to not be afraid to confront the oppressor."

The respondent continued; since church culture content "had always related the importance of civic responsibility in relationship to civil rights [I] appealed, confronted, advocated, encouraged, [and] nurtured others to stand up for their theological convictions." These remarks suggest that religion as a social phenomenon played a central role in generating values and social relations important for mobilizing Civil Rights Movement participation. Stark and Bainbridge (1980), in their analysis of new religious movements, found that processes of social bonding alone can be central in securing individuals' commitment to movements and helping them to feel they have the power to create ideas, organizations, and ways of living that are important for mobilizing social movements. Pattillo-McCoy's (1998) research on religion and activism in Chicago also established that religious discourse and practices (that is, sermons, prayer, singing, call-and-response interactions, and so forth) generated social relations, identities, and consciousness among African-Americans that are central in initiating and sustaining political action. These findings suggest that social movements, at their fundamental level, are expressions of cultural symbols and practices that can provide individuals with social support and meaning for collective action (Harris 1999).

To ascertain more fully which forms of religious culture were important for motivating participation in civil rights actions, I propose three configurations to examine religion's effect on protest activity. The sequence of each model is summarized in figures 5.1 through 5.3. Expressed verbally, all three models connect both reluctance and willingness to participate in collective action to how churches construe religious culture content. The first model suggests that if church cultural settings promote involvement in transforming the world, individuals are more likely to express their religious beliefs through participation in social action. The second model suggests that if church cultural settings communicate noninvolvement in the world, individuals are more likely

Figure 5.1 Collective Action

religious cultural setting → promote involvement in world → collective action

Figure 5.2 Non-Involvement in Collective Action

religious cultural setting → promote non-involvement in world → lack of action

Figure 5.3 Participation in Church Acivities Promote Collective Action

inactive and active religious cultural settings → individuals intensely involved in church activities → interpret religious culture to promote involvement → collective action to abstain from protest participation. The third model posits that in both inactive and active church cultural settings, people intensively involved in church activities are more likely to interpret religious culture content to promote social action. In short, rather than these configurations insinuating the centrality of resources and narrow self-interest in motivating involvement in collective action, they stress the importance of religious culture's effect on movement participation. Now let's explore how these models help us to explicate the effect of religious culture on civil rights participation in Arkansas.

Interview data suggests there is some support for the first model's expectations and conclusion. Broadly speaking, it does appear that aspects of religious culture motivated participation in civil rights struggle. Generally, people interviewed maintained that religious culture's symbolic meanings and practices were useful in organizing and creating particular "strategies of action." As the preceding chapter delineated, interview data indicates that social interactions within churches and religious-oriented families significantly influenced how respondents interpreted religion's culture content. In the case of the desegregation activities in Little Rock, for example, several respondents, like the following, stressed the importance of church social relations and familial religious values in promoting movement involvement: "From the time that I could talk, my parents always tried to . . . instill in us a belief in God and that since we were blessed we had an obligation to do something; translate our blessings into helping other people. One of the best ways you could ever find to do that was through the fight for our people in this country."

Likewise, this individual maintained that in some Little Rock churches during the desegregation movement "black folks began to say our theology is not to look for justice in the by and by but to look for justice right now. Then in fact that meant that the individual had to become actively a part of trying to make that come to reality. And what happened during that time was that it kind of changed the whole theology. In terms of 'God's going to fix it,' everything is going to be alright and all you have to do is wait on the salvation of the Lord . . . That theology began to change."

Interview data suggests that though only a small number of churches linked religion to activism in Arkansas, their religious cultural narratives resonated enough among some people to motivate desegregation movement participation. As one Little Rock movement participant explained: "there was just a few [churches]—Bethel A.M.E., Wesley Chapel United Methodist, First Baptist—[that were] basically the hub in terms of the whole movement in Little Rock. The other churches—I don't think you find much history where a lot of [them participated]." He continued: "Mount Pleasant Baptist Church has some members who were involved . . . I know of three or four members who were involved in the movement . . . I am not aware of much action that came out of that church. I think they had some people who served in the NAACP [and] Urban League."

Similarly, this respondent maintained that only a few churches were actively involved in the desegregation movement: "First Baptist, on seventh and Gaines Street had Roland Smith, who at the time was a strong activist, . . . and he took that position, and I am sure there are others who did the same thing. But in terms of who laid their whole piece on the line. A.M.E. and A.M.E. Zion [as] a body . . . came out strongly [in support of the movement]."

Although a vast majority of churches did not actively promote movement participation, respondents, like this individual, asserted there was no organized attempt to inhibit use of church facilities to promote the movement because "there were those that feared . . . the unknown, and we were about to start treading in uncharted waters . . . there were those unwilling to take the risk for what it was that was about to happen." Another respondent simply stated, "You knew there were some ministers that would not be there and others who would not participate but lend you their church. [However, a] vast majority of blacks never [did] anything [in the movement] . . . The vast majority of people were very, very docile . . . [Y]ou . . . know that in all kinds of revolutions it is not the majority [who participate], they stay out of the fray."

Meanings, identities, and social relations arising from religious culture encouraged the activism of a small cadre of early activists who reminded church people of religion's moral imperative to uplift the oppressed. This cadre succeeded in culturally cajoling others to engage in socio-political struggle against segregation in constraining racial environments (Tarrow 1994). Christian Smith contends:

> When a movement recruits members through religious networks and organizations, along come the well-established structures of solidarity incentives embedded in those networks of relationships. The movement can then rely less on selective incentives and the promise of public goods to induce participation, since the new activists now participate, in part, because other members of their religious networks are participating and expect or encourage them to participate. The camaraderie, shared experience, and collective affirmation of moral

commitments and personal and group identity (i.e., through a process of lived experience groups and individuals draw on available cultural codes, ideologies, worldviews, values, symbols, and traditions to develop and sustain a meaningful sense of their own character and purpose vis-à-vis their social environment) all become rewarding in and of themselves, beyond what the movement may or may not achieve. (1996:15–16)

Later in the chapter I will examine the social processes through which African-American Arkansans translated religious culture to motivate desegregation movement participation.

Inaction versus Action

In regards to the second model's (see fig. 5.2) presupposition that members of churches expressing noninvolvement in the world are less likely to participate in movement protest, interview data generally affirm this premise but, more important, corroborate the third model's (see fig. 5.3) theory that it is possible for some individuals to develop politicized religious consciousness within church cultural settings promoting inaction. My interview data suggests that though most churches in Arkansas constructed conservative readings of religious texts that encouraged nonparticipation in the desegregation movement, church culture's multivalent character enabled various groups and individuals within inactive churches to hold different interpretations about religious ideas. As Gamson and Modigliani (1989) and Lincoln and Mamiya (1990) argue, beliefs are always found in "dynamic tension" that is characterized by multiple conversations contesting, reformulating, defending, and refuting ideas within as well as between groups. In the church's cultural context of dialectical tensions, people engage in an active process of social/cultural appropriation and interpretation that constructs their actions. As Klandermans argues, "individual beliefs may be properly viewed as the internalized by-product of socialization and shared public discourse. Since no two people experience socialization and public discourse in exactly the same way," one typically finds that shared beliefs within groups vary from individual to individual (1997:4). Like all ideas, religious beliefs are constructed and reconstructed through interpersonal interaction to produce variant interpretations of the Gospel's directive to exert moral influence in the world. My in-depth interviews suggest that three factors are crucial in transforming religious faith into protest participation: religious conviction, involvement in church work, and the presence of individuals in church networks who are involved in movement organizations.

Despite the fact that relatively few churches and congregants became involved in the school desegregation movement, the central importance of faith for some individuals motivated them to view racism as an affront to God's vision of human equality in the beloved community. One interviewee stated: "I am the kind of person who is not very condemning of other folk . . . [They must choose whom they] will serve but for me, I will serve the Lord." Social activism for this respondent was an expression of his commitment to God: "One of the reasons I went to law school was to try to come back and practice civil rights law. That is what I did for a while. That's in part based on how you view the structure of this country and how you can affect it. That comes from your own view of what man's importance is and what rights one has and how those are being dealt with in this country. If it comes from a religious view of—it leaves a spiritual view of what mankind is and what mankind has to do. So, all of that sorta melts into how one becomes what he is and what he does."

Because respondents interpreted life as Christians as engaging society, several interviewees, like this one, asserted: "You can't look at religion and not see other things. You can't be a Christian, you can't put God first, and you can't be an advocate or see the advocacy of religion unless you look at the whole person. My educational well being, my economic well being, my social well being, all those things enter into the picture. You got to be concerned about housing even though you're living fair; you're making a living fine. But really you can't be a Christian and enjoy being comfortable without being concerned about what I'm doing over here and how I'm making it or the fact that I'm living in substandard housing."

Many others, however, believed the church had no active role to play in society. This position is evident in this exchange between some church members and a respondent, who, while addressing the church on civil rights activities, encountered congregants who "thought [the church] wasn't the place—they [would] say 'what's your problem? Saying all that in here.' We had a minister who used to tell us all the time, . . . 'Praise his name, tell God about it! AAAAmen! You want that done, you can march all you want to! Unless you tell God . . . ! Amen, Amen!!'" The respondent continued: "My interpretation was that God put me here . . . to help develop this earth. And I have read the Bible some. The Bible tells me 'out of one blood one nation came to dwell on all the face of the earth.' All nations of men are to dwell on the face of the earth. That was in me, I couldn't get it out of me. Sometimes I'll get up—I'll have members of my church—I'll say, 'Brother pastor' somebody would say, 'There he go.' We just kept on at it."

Though desegregation movement participants attended a church that encouraged inaction, one person explained: "At that time I belonged to the Church of God in Christ [but] I didn't have [church support]. Nobody said anything about [my civil rights activities]. In that sense I [got involved because] I thought it was right . . . Jesus Christ . . . is for right and I know that, he is for right! . . . [Therefore] I thought it was right [to participate]."

According to another respondent, the tremendous sense of personal responsibility religiously motivated movement participants felt for changing society was derived in part from

> the Gospel of Luke, where Jesus c[a]me to his hometown and went to the synagogue on Sabbath day. He was given the book from Jeremiah and Isaiah to read. Jesus stood and read "the spirit of the Lord is upon me, he has anointed me to preach the Gospel to the poor. He has sent me to heal the broken hearted, to preach deliverance to the captives and to recover the sight of the blind, to set at liberty them that are bruised and to preach the word of the Lord" . . . That diminution of Jesus that God is on the side of the oppressed.

In the Book of Exodus God told Moses, "I hear the cries of my people by reason of their affliction, the cast down, and I come down to deliver" (3:7–8). Wherever God is revealed in the Bible, he is revealed as being on the side of the oppressed, the poor, the downtrodden, the outcast. "I come to preach, to liberate them". . .. The thrust of the Civil Rights Movement . . . was that God was on the side of the oppressed, side of the downtrodden, the outcast, the persecuted, the exploited. God is on the side of justice. It [is] commanded: "Do unto others, as you will have them do unto you."

The personal efficacy inspired by commitment to religious faith frequently emerged through involvement in church and religious association work. Involvement "in church life," as Harris notes, "beyond the regular weekly service, may cultivate and nurture organizational skills that can be used for . . . political activism" (1994:64). Involvement in church life in inactive places of worship, then, is a crucial social setting for generating movement participation. One respondent describes this link between involvement in church activities and activism: "Most of the people who were doing the [movement] work were people who were active in their church. That's what brought the politicians and social work into each person's immediate church . . . The reason [there was a] close connection [was because the] church was the leading organization [and] because most of the people who were active in church went out and were the ones who . . . were active in politics and social issues."

Another individual elaborated upon this point, stating that while fulfilling his duties as a deacon: "the Christian religion [got me involved]. I may be false on it, but that involved me . . . You see I couldn't join church like they do now. I had to feel what we call the Holy Spirit, then we had to make a confession, and then we had to try to live by it. And in trying to live by it, seeing how certain folks: the privilege was treating the under-privilege . . . Finally I decided, let's organize. Back there in 1948 we organized what was known [in Little Rock] as the Eastend Civic League. It's in operation now. [It's] no big thing but a lot of little things we tried to do to help out (several of us together). However, there might have been a few things I kind of took on myself."

While engaged in church work, a respondent insisted that she developed a politicized religious consciousness that "guided me in everything I did. [It] had a lot of bearing on my [participation]. Knowing that God made everybody equal and that I had the [same rights as] anybody else no matter my skin color. [To me] the church is responsible for humanity. That's really the bottom line."

Similarly, a Methodist man insisted that his work in affiliated church groups exposed him to a religious cultural setting that espoused, "God is on the side of the oppressed." Exposure to others articulating and acting on "this faith piece," he noted, gave him the self-confidence, courage, and commitment to work for social change. "[I]f the faith piece was there and you kept persevering, then something good would come out of it in the end. Not that if you just lay back, just leave it alone. But you have to keep nibbling at the rock in order for that whole piece to come down. That's where I stand . . . I don't give up. I think that sometimes we [are] go[ing] to get shot down. But in fact you have to continue to put somebody out there to be the target in order to draw the enemy for you to get a good shot at him."

Church activism, Harris (1994) maintains, creates and promotes discursive or culture content that directly encourages individual and collective action. While involved in church activities, people can generate internal religiosities that cultivate efficacy and interests in political matters. As Harris contends: "It might be that internal religiosity fosters political efficaciousness through a belief in divine inspiration, while the relationship of internal religiosity to interest in politics might be associated with interest in morally defined political issues or with racial identity and consciousness" (1994:62). This finding may help us understand, as respondents noted, why "religious people['s] . . . sympathy [for] the movement did not guarantee . . . they would consider taking part in protest activity." Interview data suggests that intensive and extensive involvement in church life frequently distinguished participants from non-movement participants. Involvement in church activities apparently nurtured social ties, beliefs, moral ideas, and skills that gave individuals the confidence, social support, and commitment essential for stimulating collective organizing and activism. As Harris argues, "religious ideals are potentially powerful sources of commitment and motivation" that can lead "human beings [to] make enormous sacrifices if they believe themselves to be driven by a divine force" (1994:48).

Class Influence on Religion

When I asked respondents why churches varied in their commitment to social activism, they almost invariably pointed to the congregation's class composition. A woman, stated: "Our church had a high concentration of black men . . . who worked on the railroad as porters and as coachman, postal employees of the railroad who recognized the importance of being members and participating in civil rights organizations like the NAACP and Urban League."

Yet others maintained that financial considerations tended to deter middle-class rather than working-class spouses' participation in the movement. A Baptist woman noted: "[w]hen you have nothing you have more to gain. When you think you have something you're cautious. The lawyer's wife thinks in terms of pleasing the [establishment]. The waiter's wife [is] always thinking in the other way."

Bluntly another respondent stated that "people felt they had too much to lose. They depended very largely upon white folks for their livelihood. And then if my church is identified and involved, then in fact, Miss Ann or Mr. Bubba might fire me next week. So, therefore, they just didn't want to be identified."

These comments indicate, first, economic status shapes people's interpretation of religious culture content; and second, drawing individuals into desegregation movement depended to some degree on the presence of individuals within churches who were involved in activist organizations. In regard to the first observation, my data offers contrasting views. Some respondents, like the aforementioned, suggested that church people's middle-class status predisposed them to translate religious culture content conservatively while others suggested that segregation's debilitating effect on class mobility facilitated the creation of politico-religious frames among African-Americans that promoted activism. Still others, like this woman whose father was postman, offered a more complex explanation of the interaction between religion and economic status that suggests that though class influences religious behavior and interpretations, religion also can mediate class experiences:

> [After I] married my husband, [h]e couldn't get a job or anything because we were black . . . My husband couldn't make ends meet, so he sent me down to the farm where his mother was. I stayed down there [with our two children for] two or three weeks. I came back . . . I went and found a job for $4 a week. First place I did a stupid thing, my people were sending me to school . . . all I had to do [was graduate but] I . . . quit. I couldn't get a job because I didn't have a high school education. Okay, I went to this white woman and got a job [as a domestic] for $4 a week. That was good [since] . . . everybody else was making $1.50 or $2 or $3 . . . I would come late in the morning to get dinner and clean the house, and stayed there until her little girl came home from school. Then see after her, and fix dinner, serve it, and wash dishes and then go take the garbage out with me when [I left for home] . . . [L]ooking out the window, watching that child on her bicycle, I would come home to my kids looking up at me crying [with their] hair uncombed. My husband came in after me saying "I didn't make anything today."

She insisted that she came to understand why her family experienced such class deprivation and how to transcend and change the situation through religious culture that emphasized reforming socio-economic condition through political participation. "When I was coming along . . . our church would have concerts, educational programs [or] in those days what you call debates . . . We would raise money—and it was the fellowship that we would have . . . All those things in the community brought people together . . . [W]hen [I attended my uncle's] rural church, during the political [campaign season]. . . . We would be sittin' up there eating dinner. 'Ya'll hurry up and get through eating so we all can go to the meeting at the church.' So . . . I went too. 'Alright you know the governor race is coming up [so] let's decide right now who we are going to vote for. Everybody decided because we're going out solid.' And they went out solid."

At this point, she suggested that because religion encompassed practically every aspect of African-American life, it was often used as a political organizing and discursive resource that directed people to express class experiences in religious terms that specified Christian responsibility: "To take care of the whole man, total man. . . . The church is supposed to reach to mankind; it ought to educate the whole community. Educate them! You're here; at least you ought to have an education that leads into another life. In school [you're supposed to] learn how to read, [acquire] new skills, . . . [learn how] to live with your fellow man and how to make money. You got to have money to live on earth. You need houses—beautiful houses—God didn't mean for you to live in no shack . . . He put pretty stuff on earth for you to have. School is supposed to let you learn all you can."

Given religion's centrality in African-Americans' lives, it was within and through religious discourse that African-Americans expressed themselves, negotiated their status, and acted out their interests. Some African-Americans, using this discourse, developed a sense of purpose, efficacy, and feelings of social equality that promoted involvement in movements for egalitarianism outside the church. The notion of religious discourse motivating practical activism is captured well in this respondent's explanation for why Christians were involved in the civil rights struggle: "We are first a Christian nation; Christianity means we are followers of Jesus Christ. Everybody at [that] time, affiliated with [the desegregation movement] were believers in Jesus Christ." They acted on their religious belief that they were obligated to engage in social actions designed to rid society of inequality and oppression. Furthermore, the respondent maintained:

I got involved because black students were seen as inferior. The black teachers weren't paid as much as the white teachers and [black teachers] had white supervisors that didn't have as much education as they had. It was a travesty. . . . Then when I got to teaching and got around [I realized that black children in the community] had no place to play. No playground, no swimming pool. Alright, here we go to the church for the meeting, where all the denominations came. Reverend Harry Bass was right there. He got up and gave a speech. Harry Bass said, 'Mrs. ____ will you go with me to the Mayor's office tomorrow?" Trying to get a swimming pool for these black kids.

Likewise, when other respondents explained their activism, they invariably provided religious rather than class explanations. One respondent stated:

I think my reason for being politically active is due to the fact [that] my upbringing was one of mere survival. Though I was reared in a two-parent family, my parents were poor. My father was uneducated. My mother had the education. . . . So with that being the case . . . the two of them . . . worked together very well and each leaned on the other person's strengths . . . As a result the two us . . . children were able to benefit from that. And [since] the church was always first in my home . . . [and] my [religious] upbringing caused me to want to participate in the different arenas in life (whether social, educational, economic or what have you) to call for improving opportunity, particularly for us. And in this case "us" means blacks. No man is an island. You can't stand-alone; you have to do something . . . about being a part of the church. God is always there with me. I've always put him first in what I did. Whatever I involved myself in, I did it with all the will and effort . . . but I always put God first.

Pausing to note that Christianity was not merely a belief system but also a blueprint that adherents were expected to employ in everyday life, the respondent continued: "I had to look at myself and say to myself; here I'm a Christian and how can I best serve God? Can I serve God just by going to church everyday or every Sunday or to various other board meetings I'm a part of? Is that it? And the answer came back to me naw, that's not it. You know, it's like praying and getting up and doing something about the prayer. So you go to church. You got to do something about being a part of the church or carrying out the function or role . . . So you've got to implement your hopes, your desires, your dreams, your commitment to Jesus Christ."

In light of these religious frames many respondents, as evident in the exchange below, developed politico-religious rationales for their involvement in the desegregation movement:

Q: Let me get this straight . . . For you serving the Lord, then, entails that there be justice in the world? That you have to work for justice in the world?
R: Well, that's what "thus saith the Lord" is. Now, even that is not the only reference to that point. That's what Patrick Henry said. "I know not what course others may take, but for me, 'give me liberty or give

me death.'" So, you see what Patrick Henry was saying was the same thing the scripture says . . . The scripture had said that almost 1700 years before Patrick Henry came along. He said that "I know not what course others may take." I use to recite that when I was a boy: "but for me give me liberty or give me death." And, ain't that the same thing the old prophet said, "choose you this day, who you will serve, as for me, I will serve the Lord?" In other words, the same kind of resolution.

Linking scripture to social action helped to generate a sense of how the world should be ordered. The respondent continued:

We were sharecroppers, my mother and her eight children. And the kind of treatment we received—I walked three miles to school . . . and as my sister, brother and I walked to school . . . the school bus came right by but it didn't pickup black children, only white children. We walked in the rain and cold [while] they rode the bus. . . . [S]chool for blacks in Gould [Arkansas] didn't go but seven months of the year. We went to school from late November—this time of the year we would be picking cotton; white kids would be going to school. High school didn't start until late November, when cotton crops were gathered and then we went to school. Then our school closed early so that we could stop to chop cotton. In May, high school closed; white schools didn't close until June. It was just a combination of things instead of one dramatic thing that got me involved in the movement.

I . . . complained to [my mother] about the school bus passing us by . . . [in] the cold and she said, "Yes, I know." I said, "When I grow up, the school bus is not going to pass by children." [She said], "What are you going to do boy?" I said, "I'm going to do something, even if I have to throw a brick at [the bus]." So, I think my commitment to civil rights is rooted in those kinds of experiences . . . [which] deepen my commitment to the black struggle.

These kinds of experiences, together with a religious worldview, suggest that religion is not merely an epiphenomenal cloak for essentially material and political interests; the substance of religion helps to constitute social movement identities, grievances, and organization (Smith 1996). When respondents, for example, struggled to secure equal rights for African-Americans, their actions were often prompted and guided by their hopes, dreams, and commitment to Christianity that found resources and space to organize within religious organization. Several respondents, like this individual, explained that she became involved in the desegregation movement in Gould because "I've always believed Jesus had no respect of person. That in His sight we were all created equally and it was pleasing to Him what I was doing because He didn't intend for any of us to go through with what we were [experiencing], the way we were living and things we had to do at that time."

Thus far evidence suggests that African-American activism in constricted socio-political contexts in Arkansas was driven in part by religious cultural meanings and experiences that played pivotal roles in helping African-American Arkansans define their social situation as unjust, and that persuaded some to act during inhospitable periods. In other words, the saliency of participating in the desegregation movement for some African-Americans became germane through internalized religious feelings of responsibility and moral obligations. According to this man, and several other respondents, these sentiments played a significant role in mobilizing a small cadre of "early risers," with few resources, whose confrontations with racial elites and authorities were important for initiating enduring forms of political struggle:

> I can assure you . . . there was no real beginning to our activism. I keep telling folks that the Civil Rights Movement did not start with Rosa Parks; that was not even the start of Rosa Parks' activism; it was just the timing in what she did . . . [W]e had been active long before, and Rosa Parks was nowhere near the first person who refused to give up [her] seat.
>
> I remember three of us going to an NAACP Youth Conference in Dayton, Ohio. Before [Rosa Parks' action, we] refused to ride on the back of the bus at L. C. Bates's directions. So, you see, the incidents that we cite are usually those that caught the public's eye. It was nowhere near the first time that a black person did that. We did it all the time.

As Klandermans argues, long-term socialization/social interaction processes generate ideology, beliefs, and values important for creating movement commitment that is necessary for collective action continuity (1997:33).

Link Between Church and Activism

Several respondents maintained that a key factor in the link between organization and activism is the presence of a select group of individuals in the church's social network who are involved in movement organizations and inter-pret church "culture content" to promote mobilization. These individuals, as Robnett (1997) found in her research on African-American women in the Civil Rights Movement, used their social links in the church and community to facilitate movement mobilization. This woman, like several other key individ-uals within her church, was an important intermediary between the church and activism:

> my church had a history of activism. Its activism is related to the com-position of its membership . . . The pastors were there for over fifty years: Dr. J. P. Gaines and the assistant pastor Reverend Crenchaw was the president of the NAACP's [Little Rock chapter] . . . So, I don't know anything but a church that has dealt with its responsibilities . . . What I saw was that from a religious standpoint it was strictly God's, as I understand, purpose for religion to prove that God creates everybody equal. The Civil Rights Movement was one of the vehicles we used to do that. One of the ways we did that was [to] always give recognition to those who were in the trenches . . . [C]ivil rights people . . . were always exposed to our congregation.

Yet, another respondent explained that through her membership in Little Rock's Mount Zion Baptist church, she interacted with Rev. Fred T. Guy, "a warrior in the community. I mean, everybody respect him [both] black and white. [Though] he was not [directly] involved [in the movement]." An addi-tional respondent maintained that Guy used his pulpit to "say that some critical things are happening [in the community] that the church needed to be mindful of." This respondent noted that Guy frequently drew attention to church mem-bers involved in desegregation effort to show his support for the movement. Although Reverend Guy did not actively participate in the desegregation move-ment in Little Rock, one respondent explained, he "was the sort of preacher who related the actions of Amos to justice today: Amos said 'Let justice roll down like the waters and righteousness flow like a stream.' He didn't relate that to some-where yonder, never. He used to say all the time that we won't need anybody to do anything unjustly in heaven; so he was just talking about here."

Respondents also highlighted the politico-religious urgings of ministers like J. C. Crenchaw and Negail Riley of Wesley Chapel United Methodist Church as factors in inspiring their desegregation movement participation. The previous respondent, a member of Crenchaw's church, maintained that

"When I arrived in Little Rock in 1945 I joined Mount Pleasant Baptist Church, one of our historic churches that's been involved in the Civil Rights Movement from its [inception] . . . Our church was organized by seventeen slaves. And, so as a result of our church history, all our leadership has been leadership that took an active role . . . [Consequently,] [o]ur church had the major actors in the movement for integration. J. C. Crenchaw was one of the ones that w[as] involved in the key leadership in the 1950s and 1960s. And so that activism—action of the religious community was important."

Crenchaw, she explained, always equated Moses leading the Israelites out of the wilderness of the Sinai to Christian responsibility in relation to the Civil Rights Movement. When people were exposed to these ministers, particularly Riley, one respondent observed that they would began "[t]o say if things are going to change, we're going to have to be God's instrument, and that God has no hands but our hands, and no feet but our feet. We're going to have to do things ourselves. And that was the kind of theology Negail Riley had."

Moreover, the respondent asserted: "He was the first person who really challenged our church, in terms of linking its mission [to civil rights issues. In fact] those churches that had strong pastors with strong theological beliefs were able to persuade their people [to support and participate in the movement]."

These preceding responses suggest, as previously established, that the desire to remake the world in accordance with God's will, when coupled with religion's rich storehouse of interpersonal interactions and moral standards, nurtured collective identities, solidarity, and understandings of reality that often played an important role in desegregation movement mobilization; particularly in constraining socio-political environments. For example, religion provided groups of desegregation movement participants with cognitive understandings about their relationship to the sociopolitical environment. These understandings sustained their commitment to the movement after Orval Faubus's administration decreased the odds of achieving "full and immediate" school integration. Respondents, like this individual, frequently quoted Paul's interesting biblical utterance in I Corinthians 15:10—"But by the Grace of God I am what I am; and his grace which was bestowed upon me was not in vain; but I labored more abundantly than they all; yet not I, but grace of God which was with me"—to convey religion's effect on his commitment to the movement: "Grace woke me up this morning, grace started me on my way, grace will help you love your enemy and above all grace will brighten your day. In other words, Jesus Christ allowed us to do things through his grace. All the things you may do in life . . . you're depending on God's grace to give you strength . . . Grace, grace, grace! You got to do that despite those persons who say you can't do it, the doubters."

In addition, the presence of key individuals within the church who were involved in secular activist organizations, and interpreted religious culture content in ways that encouraged activism, helped to predispose some people to participate in, and open their churches to, civil rights organizing. This Little Rock woman, for example, insisted that the movement organizational meetings in her church were owing in large part to the presence of activist minister J. C. Crenchaw: "The Urban League was real strong in my church [and] NAACP meetings [were convened] in [the] church . . . But Mount Pleasant Baptist church ha[d] members in the NAACP because of Reverend Crenchaw. He was called the father of the NAACP."

She also asserted that membership in church affiliated organizations such as the Young Men's and Women's Christian Association (YMCA and YWCA), Urban League, NAACP, and the Southern Christian Leadership Conference (SCLC) also influenced her desire to participate in civil rights actions given that most of these organizations' leaders came from "the leadership of the black church. And most of their fundraising [was] through the church." More precisely, membership in church-affiliated groups enabled churchgoers to interact with religiously motivated activists and to create enduring interpersonal relationships and meanings that persuaded some to mobilize for desegregation. The respondent specifically identified Phyllis Wheatley YWCA in Little Rock, an important church-affiliated organization that promoted movement participation. She explained: "YMCAs were legally segregated institutions, [but their] very name denotes civil rights activism and strong religious beliefs that gave these institutions connections to and a forum in the church" where individuals interacted with activists who approached social reform questions from their perspective as Christians committed to the possibility of divinely aided social progress (Weisenfeld 1997; Kirk 2002). One respondent said, "[faith] kept me from being afraid to march on the school board with placards . . . I went to sleep at night knowing God was there. I was doing what was good in his sight that is what we had to do . . . I felt what we were doing was morally right . . . in the quest of those who give their lives for that in which they believe is right . . . that's been my strength."

When asked whether or not her church group membership influenced her willingness to engage in protest in Little Rock's difficult socio-political environment, the respondent replied: "[Although] many people lost their job; there were people who couldn't get loans . . . they continued to [struggle] until others were ready to move the vanguard of hope. I think I am a part of the vanguard of hope. [One keeps working at achieving and having faith that something will happen. Eventually your faith and perseverance will win out] . . . Based on that continuous building, credibility of . . . faith is rewarded. It's to the point where people rejoice that they took the risk."

Another respondent explained that church-affiliated movement organizations like the NAACP, and later the Leadership Roundtable of Little Rock, provided "a small core of . . . concerned, committed people willing to act beyond the ordinary." They fostered a movement culture environment that motivated, comforted, and supported social action when socio-political environments were not conducive to protest. Moreover, he asserted that the Leadership Roundtable

> name came from the old story of Camelot [and] its righteous, just leader King Arthur [who] gathered around him devoted young men . . . he called . . . Knights of the Roundtable. Well, that's how the Leadership Roundtable was established . . . Devoted young men and women, who were willing to fight the fight for justice and freedom, in that sense. . . .
>
> [T]here was a committee of the Leadership Roundtable that met every Monday morning over a cup of coffee and discussed what problems existed in the community. What we needed to turn our attention to.

Church affiliated groups like these contained social relationships, meanings, and cultural practices that helped buttress respondents' commitment to the desegregation movement and the courage to join Daisy Bates's effort to secure students willing to integrate Central High School. This respondent, like many others I interviewed, credited social processes within church-affiliated groups for giving him the courage to join Bates's endeavor:

> we had to comb the whole Central High School area, and visit with— I bet we visited 200 families trying to [convince] them to enroll their children in Central High School. So, we didn't just start with nine going to Central High School. We started a year before with us [scouring the neighborhood for students willing to integrate Central]. Th[e] order of visitation was organized by a young white man, who coached the soccer team for Philander Smith College, Georg Iggers . . . Iggers got into the records of the school system under the pretense of working

on his doctorate (when he already had a doctorate) and he got into the records. He came up with names [and] locations of students . . . already in the Central High School jurisdiction who lived west of Central, who had to pass right by Central to get to [all black] Dunbar . . . Well, a whole bunch of black students then lived past Central . . . Anyway, we went into homes of hundreds of students, trying to get parents to enroll their kids in Central High School. When they found out what we were doing, the school moved from a jurisdictional system to a system of assignment . . . [called] pupil placement. And, many of the people we signed up . . . had to have an interview when they signed up to go to Central. That meant you had to come before the Little Rock School Board. At first we had from seventy to eighty students . . . ready to go, but when they came up with these interviews, that busted it down to about half that many, and then students started to get cold feet. All these processes you had to go through. We were falling so low that we were scared we weren't going to have anybody to try to go to Central High School. But out of the process, we came up with nine.

Conclusion

One of the key mechanisms for promoting African-American Civil Rights Movement participation was a religious culture maintained by churches, affiliated church groups, and families. Culture's role in movement mobilization is more complex and dynamic than is typically portrayed by resource mobilization theory. Rather than treating culture as external to movement mobilization, my study reveals that cultural processes are sources of interactions and meanings that people use to encourage social action. Some African-American movement participants in Arkansas actively appropriated/interpreted church culture content in activist ways. Respondents consistently suggested that the main thrust of Christianity is, as one respondent said, to "teach people how to live for God in whatever respect in life that you have to deal with. It's to teach people how to live from day to day in whatever circumstances that come about . . . [I]t is also the instigator of things that are good and things that are right."

Individuals with activist religious orientations frequently developed social ties, from which groups emerged, whose moral and political views promoted resistance to the organization of social relations in the racially ordered South. I have also substantiated the significance of religious culture as an independent factor in motivating desegregation movement participation. Specifically, interviews demonstrated that churches with key congregants involved in activist organizations were more likely than congregations that lacked these individuals to persuade the church or some of its members to engage in collective action out of moral obligation and personal responsibility. Moreover, evidence indicates that the centrality of religion in African-American lives often led some African-Americans to express class experiences, especially those promulgated by segregation, through politico-religious discourse that promoted involvement in organizations and movements seeking to remedy class inequality. Thus, what is abundantly clear is that religious culture was central to the mobilization and sustenance of Arkansas's desegregation movement.

CHAPTER 6

Culture's Centrality in African-American Women's Civil Rights Activism

———)(◎)(———

The aim of this chapter is to explain African-American women's civil rights activism in Arkansas within the framework of this study. Though scholars have repeatedly documented the importance of community organizations like churches in the initiation of social protest (McAdam 1982; Morris 1984; Lincoln and Mamiya 1990), researchers have only recently begun to evaluate how institutions mobilize women's collective action. While sociological research (Barnett 1993; Higginbotham 1994, 1997; Robnett 1997) increasingly considers culture's centrality in facilitating African-American women's activism, its importance remains underexamined. This chapter explores how cultural processes endemic to indigenous institutions (that is, churches, families, and other local groups) serve as sources of distinct meanings and patterns of interaction that encourage African-American women's mobilization. In addition, this study considers how women's experience within indigenous institutions contributed to the construction of gendered social relations and networks that promoted Civil Rights Movement participation in Arkansas. African-American women's considerable socio-historical experiences with sexual, racial, and economic exploitation, however, must be discussed first. Women's individual acts of resistance to sexism, racism, and classism were fueled in part by deeply held religious sentiments and understandings that increased their protest activities. These religiously motivated acts of resistance engendered in women efficacious beliefs suggesting that God would help them implement social change through collective action. This perspective gave African-American women the resolve to participate in numerous protest actions throughout history, including the Civil Rights Movement.

During the antebellum era slaveholders viewed enslaved African women as property from which to extract profit. Specifically, enslaved women, like men, were used as expendable commodities for accumulating capital (profit) derived from their labor. As Marx argues, profits are derived from unpaid laborers' involuntary contributions to exploiters (Tucker 1978). Marx's assumption is that the value of any commodity is equivalent to the amount of average labor time necessary to produce that product; in other words, the value of one day's labor as a commodity is the monetary equivalent of the amount of resources required to keep the worker alive, at work and able to reproduce his/her kind (Tucker 1978). Thus, according to Marx labor is capable of producing a certain amount of value over and above its own value. He termed this *surplus value* or profit that labor exploiters extract from workers by paying them nothing or less than the value of the labor for production. Labor exploiters (slaveholders) did little to deserve the surplus value that rightfully belonged to workers, but the economic system of social relations under slavery created an exploitive social arrangement enabling many to secure wealth. Moreover, Reid argues, enslaved African-American women were exploited as "the sexual property of the owner, his friends, visitors and relatives" and as commodities of slave breeding, a practice that burgeoned after the United States outlawed importation of Africans in 1808 (1976:7). As a result of these exploitive arrangements, Angela Davis argues, "the black woman had to be released from the chains of the myth of femininity . . . In order to function as slave, the black woman had to be annulled as woman, that is, as woman in her historical stance of wardship under the entire male hierarchy. The sheer force of things rendered her equal to her man . . . Stripped of the palliative feminine veneer which might have encouraged a passive performance of domestic tasks, she was now uniquely capable of weaving into the warp and woof of domestic life, a profound consciousness of resistance . . . The slave system would have to deal with the black woman as the custodian of a house of resistance" (1971:7–8).

As harborers of a resistance consciousness, some enslaved African-American women in major social institutions like the church and the family, passed down through the generations religious cultural meanings about everyday life that specified, as their ancestors taught, divine involvement in temporal affairs. According to Krass, for example, enslaved women like abolitionist and feminist Sojourner Truth frequently encouraged their children to believe that "'there is a God who hears and sees you.' The children asked her where God lived. 'He lives in the sky, . . . and when you are beaten, or cruelly treated, or fall into any trouble, you must ask help of him, and he will always hear and help you'" (1990:28–29). Such worldviews motivated some women to believe and act on the belief that, in the context of the oppressive socio-political environment in which they lived, Christianity's "chief task is to be to the world that visible possibility of God's intention for [humans]. It is not possible to be for Christ and not be for his people, the oppressed and unwanted in society" (Cone 1970:53).

Religious cultural meanings were pivotal in transforming Harriet Tubman, a prominent former bondsperson and Christian, into a religiously motivated social activist. Tubman's experiences as a bondsperson informed her desire to undertake a divinely inspired political mission to free enslaved African-Americans. Tubman claimed that her experiences in slavery and her frequent religious visions admonishing her to fulfill the Gospel of Luke's promise to deliver captives to freedom, encouraged her to initiate the mass runaway movement known as the Underground Railroad, which freed thousands of enslaved Africans before the Civil War. As already discussed, such religious outlooks were created by people whose daily existence entailed confronting an oppressive reality. In other words, African-Americans constructed oppositional ideas "about the reconstruction of a new humanity wherein people are no longer defined by oppression but by freedom" in indigenous religious settings (Cone 1978:150). These cultural frames facilitated women's construction and articulation of an activist gender consciousness that expressed their desire to participate in the struggle for equality with men and shaped their view that liberating religious dogma is not exclusively defined by a struggle against racism. As Grant notes, these women believed that for Christianity's mission of liberating the oppressed to be authentic, it must also include women's struggle against oppression (1989:195).

Such religious conviction had a profound effect on the political behavior of former enslaved African-American women like Sojourner Truth, who used speaking engagements at religious and women's rights conventions to explain to primarily European-American audiences that Gospel tenets demanded that Christians be crusaders against racial and gender oppression. For instance, at one women's rights convention in Akron, Ohio, Sojourner Truth delivered a speech that challenged religion's legitimation of patriarchy and white supremacy and urged women to mobilize to transform these exploitive social arrangements. In the talk entitled "Ain't I A Woman," delivered after an attempt by ministers at the convention to use the Bible to discredit women's quest for equal rights, Sojourner Truth used her gendered and racial experiences to construct this poignant and inspirational speech:

> Wall, chilern, whar dar is so much racket dar must be somethin' out o' kilter. I tink dat 'twixt de niggers of de Souf and de womin at de Norf, all talkin' 'bout rights, de white men will be in a fix pretty soon. But what's all dis here talkin' 'bout?
>
> Dat man ober dar say dat womin needs to be helped into carriages, and lifted ober ditches, and to hab de best place everywhar. Nobody eber helps me into carriages, or ober mud-puddles, or gibs me any best place! And ain't I a woman?
>
> Look at me! Look at my arm! (and she bared her right arm to the shoulder, showing her tremendous muscular power). I have ploughed, and planted, and gathered into barns, and no man could head me! And ain't I a woman?
>
> I could work as much and eat as much as a man—when I could get it—and bear de lash as well! And ain't I a woman? I have borne thirteen chilern, and seen 'em mos' all sold off to slavery, and when I cried out with my mother's grief, none but Jesus heard me! And ain't I a woman?
>
> Den dey talks 'bout dis ting in de head; what dis dey call it? ("Intellect," whispered a woman). Dat's it, honey. What's dat got to do wid womin's rights or nigger's rights? If my cup won't hold but a pint, and yourn holds a quart, wouldn't ye be mean not to let me have my little half-measure full?
>
> Den dat little man in black dar, he say women can't have as much rights as men, 'cause Christ wan't a woman! Whar did your Christ come from? Whar did your Christ come from? From God and a woman! Man had nothin' to do wid Him.
>
> If de fust woman God ever made was strong enough to turn de world upside down all alone, dese women togedder (and she glanced her eye over the platform) ought to be able to turn it back, and get it right side up again! And now dey is asking to do it, de men better let 'em. Bleeged to ye for hearin' on me, and now ole Sojourner han't got nothin' more to say. (Bernard 1967:165–66)[1]

In her speech Sojourner Truth expressed a religious, racial, and gender identity that was instrumental in helping her and other enslaved and freed African-American women develop and articulate a political analysis of how race, gender, and class simultaneously operate to oppress their community. In 1832 Maria Stewart, the first American-born woman to deliver public lectures to mix gendered audiences, offered biblical precedents in denunciation of sexism, slavery, and other forms of oppression (Higginbotham 1994:123). In her speeches she specifically argued that economic and gender oppression are immoral and that slave labor "deadens the energies of the soul and benumbs the faculties of the mind" (Giddings 1984:50). Moreover, Stewart asserted in her farewell address to the people in Boston, Massachusetts, in 1833, that women were divinely sanctioned to participate in political and religious affairs. She called forth names of biblical women who, with divine sanction, acted religiously and politically to lead the Israelites, and then asked: "What if such women as are here described should rise among our sable race?" Stewart insisted that employing women's talent was important in the effort to achieve political and economic liberation for African-Americans. As a result she declared: "God at this eventful period should raise up your females to strive . . . both in public and private, to assist those who are endeavoring to stop the strong current of prejudice that flows so profusely against *us* at present" (Giddings 1984:53).[2] In this way, Higginbotham (1994) argues, religion shaped Stewart's sociopolitical gendered consciousness and was central in her public pronouncements.

Women possessing a gendered politicized religious consciousness established church-affiliated clubs after it became clear that the racial movement for equality within the church harbored gender divisions and proscriptions that inhibited employing their talents in the struggle. These church clubs served to unite women with men in the movement for racial equality and fostered the development of separate gender-based communities reflective and supportive of women's and African-American equality (Higginbotham 1994: 153). In essence church clubs provided women with organizational meeting spaces to cultivate relationships, values, commitment, and organizational and leadership skills crucial in facilitating a collective quest to dismantle the triple oppression of race, gender, and class (Higginbotham 1994:183). In club societies, Higginbotham argues, gendered social relations imbued in women a sense of purpose and feelings of social equality that engendered political efficacy. She continues: "Missionary societies had early on brought together women with little knowledge of each other and created bonds of sisterly cooperation at the city and local levels. Not only Baptists but black Methodists, Presbyterians, and women in other denominations came together in associations that transformed unknown and unconfident women into leaders and agents of social service and racial self-help in their communities" (Higginbotham 1994:17).

As Hazel Carby (1987) notes, it was not until the 1892 antilynching campaign, initiated by religious activists and journalist Ida B. Wells-Barnett, that a rudimentary nationwide interactional network arose among local clubs to coordinate a national clubwomen's movement to pursue multiple social reforms such as an end to racial discrimination and violence; women's suffrage; equality of education and employment opportunities; better working conditions and wages; and numerous other reforms. Three years after creating these networks, church clubs in twelve states merged to form the National Federation of Afro-American Women (NFAAW). One year after merger in 1896, the NFAAW merged with the smaller National League of Colored Women headquartered in Washington, D.C., to create the National Association of Colored Women (NACW) with the goal of securing the moral, spiritual, industrial, and intellectual uplift of women and the African-American community in general. The NACW's objectives were influenced by the church's self-help strategy and historical/cultural tradition of articulating an African-American collective identity, dignity, self-respect and will for human equality.

In clubwomen's organizations, African-American women sustained inherited religious attitudes, social relations, and commitments that comforted and motivated them to struggle continuously and collectively in constraining sociopolitical environments to secure political, social, and economic equality. In Arkansas, we will see, women's clubs cultivated sentiments and identities that were indispensable in organizing civil rights activism.

Theorizing on Culture's Link to Women's Movement Participation

Numerous studies have recently established the importance of culture for women's movement mobilization (Sacks 1988; Payne 1990, 1995; Higginbotham 1994; Robnett 1996, 1997).[3] These studies suggest that social links and connections among individuals are critical resources in persuading women to join a movement. For example, Robnett's (1997) examination of the Civil Rights Movement reveals that its movement organizations housed an informal substructure of female "bridge leaders" who used their social links in the African-American community to build trust between civil rights leaders and community members to facilitate community mobilization. Although Robnett's

(1996, 1997) research suggests that culture is an important factor in movement mobilization, it neglects to explore fully the actual processes by which organizational culture content encourages women's social action. Robnett's research does not adequately examine how cultural meanings become transformed through interaction in organizations to foster movement mobilization.

Taylor and Whittier's (1995) research on the feminist movement also suggests that indigenous organizational culture is an important resource for mobilizing movement participation. Their study found that women's organizations and alternative institutions (for example, bookstores, publishing houses, rape crisis centers) fostered cultures that helped women construct movement communities to inspire them to continuously mobilize movements for change. However, like Robnett (1997), Taylor and Whittier also fail to specify how cultural content encourages activism.

As already discussed, scholars like Melucci (1985, 1995), Klandermans (1997), Polletta (1997, 1999) and Pattillo-McCoy (1998) have begun to explore how culturally mediated meanings within organizations encourage (or discourage) collective action. Polletta (1999), for instance, contends that organizations are cultural, although not merely cultural, because they are invested with a symbolic dimension that is given meaning and significance through social interaction. Through their interactions with others in institutions, individuals construct identities and meanings about everyday life that can incline them to identify with or be more willing to adopt the beliefs and norms that define a particular movement organization (Melucci 1989; Klandermans 1997:5). This literature brings us closer to understanding culture in an interactive and interpretive way.

This emphasis on understanding how culture content within organizations works to mobilize collective action has moved researchers to examine more specifically how these processes facilitate African-American women's activism (Sacks 1988; Barnett 1993; Mills 1993; Payne 1995; Gilkes 1997; Higginbotham 1994, 1997). In her study of the women's movement in the African-American Baptist church, Higginbotham (1994) found that when women came together in institutional associations, they constructed meanings that helped transform them into activists. In essence, women's church work fostered the creation of interpersonal bonds of cooperation, meaning, confidence, and obligation that engendered in them political efficacy. Payne's (1995) preliminary account of this process in women's Civil Rights Movement mobilization in rural Mississippi seems to corroborate Higginbotham's earlier research findings. Payne found that women became involved in the movement primarily through their deep investment in indigenous institutional social networks (that is, church and family) where they encountered others who were likely to draw them into the Civil Rights Movement (1995:271, 274). Payne's and Higginbotham's findings suggest that a broader definition of culture as a relational and interpretive resource may illuminate how indigenous institutional culture like religion provided African-American women with meanings that shaped their moral and political views about the kind of society that should exist. I turn now to exploring how cultural meanings in indigenous organizations encouraged and sustained African-American women's civil rights protest in Arkansas.

Women Civil Rights Activism as an Inherited Tradition of Protest

In this study of the Civil Rights Movement in Arkansas, both male and female respondents consistently maintained that women comprised a substantial portion of the participants within the movement. These accounts support the findings of numerous studies (Giddings 1984; Crawford, et al. 1990; Payne 1990; Barnett 1993; Robnett 1997) on women's involvement in the Civil Rights Movement. Though the research literature acknowledges African-American women's participation in the movement, researchers are only now beginning to analyze the social processes that inspired their participation. Respondents in my study attributed women's high level of participation in the Civil Rights Movement to their investment in indigenous institutional work. One respondent, like many others I interviewed, asserted, "Women have always been active in what black men did. You look at most of [the] church[es], the leadership are women. Women will put their money where their mouth is . . . [F]or every man you found in leadership roles in the civil rights movement, . . . you [could] find several women. When you go out in the community. It were [sic] the women that got out." This suggests that indigenous organizations were important cultural places where women engaged in interactions that provided them with meanings that promoted movement participation.

In view of the fact that the church was the only institution truly accessible to African-Americans during the segregation era in Arkansas, and women constituted the majority of its membership, the work roles they fulfilled were crucial in cultivating meanings to develop a political consciousness (Higginbotham 1997:216).[4] Through active membership in religious auxiliaries, administration of church affairs, teaching Sunday school, and founding national, state, and local church auxiliaries and clubs, women generated relational networks that encouraged people to link religious values and symbols to social activism (Grant 1986:199). To make this connection women constructed and communicated a collective will and culture maintaining "that [women's] efforts were essential for reform and progress, and that their moral standing was a steady rock upon which race could lean . . . black women saw their role in almost ecclesiastical terms. They were 'the fundamental agency under God in the regeneration . . . of the race, as well as the groundwork and starting point of its progress upward' " (Giddings 1984:81).

Motivated in part by the efficacy of church work, early-twentieth-century church women in Arkansas organized state and local church auxiliary organizations and women's clubs to raise funds to build and support colleges, night schools, and day care facilities and to provide aid to churches and other social welfare services (Gordon 1987).[5] In her study of Baptist church women, Higginbotham found that club leaders like Fannie Barrier Williams, a founding member of the National Association of Colored Women, readily admitted that women brought their church-related values, "social order, mutual trustfulness . . . [and] meaning of unity of effort for the common good" to their other organizations and relied on them to drive their social activism (1997:216). Likewise, in her research on Arkansas, Higginbotham found that women such as Sophia Shanks, the president of the Arkansas women's auxiliary of the State Baptist Association, acknowledged that several clubs and associations established by church women in Little Rock during the height of segregation owed their existence to the skills and social networks women developed during church work (1994:74).

My study, similar to Higginbotham's findings, suggests that indigenous institutions consistently provided women with the opportunity to interact on a regular basis and share common values, moral commitments, and interpersonal ties that cultivated their movement mobilization. The most influential members in church auxiliary and club organizations were teachers like Mary Harris Speight, who served as the first female president of the Arkansas Teachers Association (ATA) in 1919–20, and Mame Stewart Josenberger, president of Fort Smith's Phyllis Wheatley Club and vice-president of the state NACW during the early twentieth century.[6] These women supported and encouraged educators in their organizations to use their teaching to instill in students literacy and social advancement skills to counter racial caste intentions (Gordon 1987:30; Higginbotham 1994:42). Through their teaching, Speight, Josenberger, and others like them, created classroom cultures that inspired some students to become educational and community activists. For example, Speight encouraged one of her former students at Dunbar High School in Little Rock, Gwendolyn McConico Floyd, to pursue a career in education. After completing her undergraduate studies at Fisk University in Nashville, Tennessee, Floyd returned to Arkansas in 1927 to teach American history at Dunbar High School for sixteen years (Gordon 1987:31). Like Speight, Floyd used her classes as an interactive forum for critically examining students' social experiences. When teaching what may well have been the first African-American history course offered in a public school curriculum in the south in 1936, Floyd remembered, "in allowing [students] to speak and write, [students became] aware that we [Blacks] were being manipulated; that there were certain jobs we could not get; that we lived in an isolated society. Many of the boys in the classes worked downtown in hotels, at stores where Blacks could not come in unless they worked there. And then they had to come in a side door or back door. In nearly every class [I] had one or two males that would show anger. And usually they were the ones working downtown and had to go through it, [meaning that they had first-hand experiences with racial prejudice and insults]" (Gordon 1987:32–33).[7]

Through classroom discourse, students became aware that systems of ideas and practices shaped their lives and resigned them to the status quo. As in Melucci's (1989) and Klandermans's (1997) studies of interpersonal inter- action and mobilization, Floyd found that meanings and social awareness emerging from interaction could encourage collective action. Ernest Green's decision to participate in the integration of Little Rock Central High School in 1957 reflects the influence these culturally mediated meanings and identi- ties had on some students.[8] In her memoir of the Central High School inte- gration crisis, Civil Rights leader Daisy Bates (1986) suggests that Green's aunt and mother, both teachers, instilled in him educational and familial val- ues encouraging him to construct and accept classroom meanings and identi- ties that later led to his sense of obligation to the Civil Rights Movement. Green's aunt, who taught at Horace Mann High School in Little Rock, offered these words of support when he announced his intention to participate in school desegregation, "If you really want to go to Central High, we stand with you. If you have faith in what you are doing and the courage of your con- victions, we'll help you see it through" (Bates 1986:145). Contrary to Klandermans's (1997) contention that cost-benefit considerations inform individuals' decisions to participate in collective action, these data highlight the important role of culturally mediated interpretive processes.

The dialogue between teachers and students also served to heighten teachers' awareness of segregation's retarding effect upon their professional development as educators. Since teachers viewed segregation as a threat to communal advancement, individual grievances about inadequate professional preparation and development were transformed into collective concerns that encouraged teachers to seek redress through lawsuits. As already discussed, Sue Cowan Morris (later Sue Cowan Williams), chairperson of the English department at Dunbar High School, for example, agreed to be the plaintiff for a 1942 Little Rock Classroom Teachers Association (an ATA affiliate) lawsuit seeking equalization of teacher salaries despite the fact that she knew participating was grounds for dismissal from her position.[9] A year after filing the suit, the Little Rock School Board superintendent fired Morris (Patterson 1981). Rather than the school board's firing lessening her will to continue, it strengthened Morris's desire to move forward with court appeals. Interpersonal networks in the ATA, other community institutions, and the broader African-American community provided Morris with the social support she needed to affirm and intensify her commitment for social change throughout her ordeal (Kirk 2002:40). Morris's firing moved the ATA and other community institutions like the church to hold fundraisers to offset her financial strain. Moreover, people like L. M. Christophe, principal of Dunbar Junior High School, ensured that Morris knew he and others supported her and constantly pressured the superintendent to reinstate her (Patterson 1981:90–91).[10] These accounts suggest that prevailing movement theory's (McCarthy 1973; McCarthy and Zald 1976, 1976; McAdam 1982; Morris, 1984) focus on community organizations as embodiments of material resources must be expanded to include an emphasis not only on cultural resources but also on the interactive and interpretive nature of those resources.

In community organizations African-American women in Arkansas encountered extant relationships, meanings, and beliefs that altered their sociopolitical awareness to encourage them to initiate, organize, and participate in various socio-economic and political struggles throughout Arkansas's history. For example, after the Southern Tenant Farmers Union (STFU) linked union participation to religious values and beliefs, women, who composed a majority of the church's membership and skilled leadership, became strong members and central figures in organizing the STFU in 1934. The STFU's religious interpretations, as discussed earlier, engendered in African-Americans, and particularly in women, the efficacy needed to mobilize for union participation despite fears of reprisals from local authorities. According to Henry L. Mitchell, one of the socialist founders of the STFU, "women always had more courage than men and were usually able to get more done than men" (1973:364–65).[11] The point is not that men were reluctant to participate but that women found themselves in unique social positions promoting participation in movements against oppression. According to several respondents like this one, women's leadership and organizational skills ensured that their Civil Rights Movement contribution involved "go[ing] different places to talk about organizing . . . Most [of the] time you got women . . . just a lot of them were very good . . . at [organizing]. But you know, the men w[ere] very good, some of them, but sometimes they [weren't]." Specifically, the respondent asserted that women did the "telephoning, speaking, secretarial work or typing . . . [or] whatever it took to get the job done" to usher in the Gospel promise of human equality.

This idea of doing "whatever it takes" to help the movement meant African-American women performed an assortment of tasks and occupied various positions throughout the Civil Rights Movement's organizational strata. Women conducted fundraisers usually through the church in the form of fish fries and bake sales to support movement actions, and they headed state and local branches of numerous movement organizations such as the ATA and NAACP, where they were the predominant members. The state president of the NAACP during the desegregation era in Arkansas was Daisy Bates, newspaperwoman and organizer of the 1957 integration of Little Rock Central High School. She used the *Arkansas State Press*, a newspaper she and her husband, L. C. Bates, owned and operated to mobilize support for the Civil Rights Movement in Arkansas.

African-American women have a long history of linking religious values to social activism in community organization networks. Although delineation of this history is beyond the scope of this book, this chapter provides some insight into how social processes within indigenous organizations like churches and women's clubs led women to construct themselves as moral agents of social change decades preceding civil rights movement activity in the 1950s and 1960s. Specifically, we have seen that women transformed cultural meanings in indigenous organizations to promote Civil Rights Movement mobilization, a process that was instrumental in sustaining protest during inhospitable times.

Centrality of Cultural Processes in Movement Mobilization

Contrary to some movement scholars' contentions that organizational resources and cost-benefit calculations are more important in mobilizing protest, my analysis of the Civil Rights Movement in Arkansas suggests that culture and relational processes were central in women's decisions to participate in civil rights activism. Interviews indicate that though institutional culture, especially that of the church and family, can be a conservative force, the strong emotional and social bonds formed within cultural networks can serve as important mobilizing resources (Lincoln and Mamiya 1990). For example, several respondents, like this one, maintained that indigenous institutions, in this case, the family, were central in generating movement participation among women: "Because the home has always been built around the female . . . she's been the decision maker for the most part . . . All I'm saying is that because of the role that women played in the family, they were more decisive [about their commitment to the movement]."

In Arkansas familial network ties contributed significantly to women's mobilization through appeals to women's sensibilities as parents and their relationships with relatives active in the movement. These two factors played a significant role in mobilizing women for movement activities in Gould, Arkansas. When the Student Non-Violent Coordinating Committee (SNCC) arrived to initiate a voter registration drive in the small delta town of Gould in 1964, only a few people, primarily women, supported their effort. Payne (1995) and Robnett (1997) suggest that women's early support for SNCC was a product of SNCC's policy of developing nontraditional sources of leadership and exploiting their interpersonal networks. However, the respondents I interviewed maintained that SNCC's attempt to mobilize community support using women's interpersonal ties and networks in Gould initially floundered but later had some success when SNCC linked voter registration to familial concerns such as obtaining better educational opportunities for African-American children. Several respondents, like this mother, explained that this connection was an important mobilizing factor: "Basically because . . . we were being oppressed, depressed, held back, kept down, all those things. . . . I was looking at the future generation. The children that was coming on after me and I wanted them to have better opportunity than I had because at that time there were no opportunities at all for black people. Very limited opportunity for people to succeed. When you g[o]t out of school, you had to migrate to the North or just be stuck in a rut here . . . and I didn't see that as very good future for our people."

Since some women strongly believed that their parental positions obligated them to secure better life chances for their children, they joined the Gould Citizens for Progress Committee to challenge the legality of de facto school segregation. At the age of sixty-five, longtime community activist Carrie Dilworth and SNCC field workers organized the Citizens for Progress Committee after the school board adopted a freedom of choice plan in 1965 allowing parents to choose schools for their children.[12] European-American parents opted to keep their children in all European-American schools; consequently, there was no classroom space for African-American students in these schools.

In Evans's (1980) terms, Carrie Dilworth was a movement "mama" who served as a model of courage and leadership for community women. She was the first person to invite young SNCC organizers into her home in an effort to encourage community support for SNCC. Moreover, Dilworth volunteered to be the lead plaintiff for the Citizens for Progress Committee lawsuit on behalf of her two grandchildren, who were refused admittance to the all European-American Gould schools (*Arkansas Gazette*, Sept. 14, 1965). According to Dilworth's granddaughter, her grandmother agreed to be lead plaintiff for the suit because she wanted to ensure children had "an opportunity to be whatever [they] wanted to be. She knew that without a sound education" they would not have the self-confidence and skills required to advance themselves and their community. Moreover, her granddaughter explained that she herself became involved in the Civil Rights Movement through her grandmother, who helped her "lay out what I wanted for myself, so I felt [my participation in the movement] was the right thing to do." She continued: "[My grandmother] laid out that white children were no better than myself . . . we were the same, we were equal. So we should [be] treated equal[ly]. So, . . . what [my grandmother] was moving towards was fine, . . . equality between everyone. So, I felt . . . if they could go to school where they had good books and air conditioning, we should too." In this way the respondent's close connection to her grandmother engendered in her a sense of right and wrong, and the efficacy necessary to resist injustice. After joining the movement, Dilworth's granddaughter became a committed young activist who went door-to-door registering people to vote.

Another respondent I interviewed became involved in the movement out of a sense of parental responsibility to her children and loyalty to her aunt, who served as president of the Gould Citizens for Progress Committee. Her strong social links helped to generate a belief that segregation was wrong and motivated this respondent to become one of three women leaders of the movement in Gould. The respondent's brother was drawn into the movement by her activities, and her daughter got involved in the movement because her "mother was one of the civil rights leaders. So, I don't think I never gave it any thought [to] whether [participating] was something I wanted to do or not." Moreover, the daughter asserted that a friend's involvement in organizing activities also piqued her interest in the movement. Similar to the research findings of Rupp and Taylor (1987) and Payne (1995), these respondents suggest that they were initially drawn into the movement by relatives and friends with whom they maintained strong social ties.

Because African-Americans could not gain access to the material resources of European-American schools, and churches in Gould refused to get involved in the movement, SNCC organizers helped Dilworth and a few other committed women in the community establish a Freedom School in a building Dilworth owned. The school's primary goal was to serve as an after-school program for African-American children, but it also served as a place to organize and promote civil rights activities such as demonstrations, boycotts, and voter registration drives (*Arkansas Gazette*, Jan. 3, 1967:1B2). Moreover, because a vast majority of those in the larger African-American community, including those in churches, labeled movement participants as troublemakers, the activist culture maintained within the Freedom School played a crucial role in helping women construct and sustain movement community and solidarity.

The shared experiences and collective moral commitment cultivated through interactions with other women in the Freedom School gave one respondent courage to ignore her church's accommodationist racial advice and stand up for her religious conviction that segregation was morally wrong. A few congregants, like this one, possessed the moral courage to assert: "I know God for myself . . . [and] the few people [in] town that knew right from wrong . . . pulled together [in the Freedom School to work for civil rights]." In the Freedom School SNCC organizers helped these women develop skills as leaders, organizers and strategists, and according to the previous respondent, "helped us and motivated us, sold us dreams, that really weren't dreams they were just the way things should have been." This suggests that the cultural and relational processes found within indigenous organizations were crucial in promoting African-American women's civil rights protest.

Conclusion

This chapter presents evidence demonstrating how culture content and interactive processes in indigenous institutions (that is, churches, clubs, families, and other associations) informed African-American women's participation in the Civil Rights Movement. Data suggests cultural meanings emerging from gendered interactions with others within secular-religious organizations and institutions independently facilitated women's movement participation. Rather than explaining their decision to join movements in terms of personal gain, respondents in my study suggested that social ties within indigenous organizations facilitated their involvement. Specifically, I found that extant relationships, meanings, and beliefs in the church, religious affiliated women's clubs, and local movement centers (for example, ATA and Gould Citizens for Progress) reinforced protest commitment and provided women with self-confidence and identities that gave them the courage to engage in activism. This finding suggests that it may be useful to pursue further analysis of the role of culturally mediated interpretive processes in engendering movement efficacy.

CHAPTER 7

Theoretical Conclusions

━━━━◉━━━━

Once you change your philosophy you change your thought pattern,
once you change your thought pattern you change your attitude.
Once you change your attitude it changes your behavior pattern.
Then you go on into some action.

—Malcolm X (1964)

I would like to remind the black ministry,
and indeed all black people that God is not in the habit
of coming down from heaven to solve people's problems on earth.

—Steve Biko (1972)

In the above quotations, Malcolm X and Steve Biko indirectly suggest that culture, especially ideas and social relations, is important in mobilizing political action. Through culture, individuals form various social relations through which they construct meanings, feelings, and interpretations that help them traverse their social environment. What is apparent is that it can no longer be suggested, as previous scholars have done, that culture plays a peripheral role in social movement mobilization. Aldon Morris's (1984) research on the Civil Rights Movement identifies clergy social networks as important elements in movement mobilization, his work's organizational bias leads him to assign culture a mediating role between political opportunity and civil rights protest. Belinda Robnett (1997) disagrees with Morris's assessment, arguing for the centrality of social links, especially women's networks, in mobilizing African-American support for, and participation in, civil rights activities.

149

The present study illustrates that mobilizing collective action requires much more than gaining access to organizational resources; it also necessitates constructing cultural meanings through social relations to promote political action. Contrary to some movement scholars' views of culture as a perceptual cue mediating between political opportunity and social action, my study of the Civil Rights Movement in Arkansas sees organizational culture as a resource in engendering deeply felt meaning, commitment, and hope that directly mobilized civil rights protest. In Arkansas shared experiences and collective moral commitment (cultivated in preexisting indigenous organizations through extant interactions) motivated many African-Americans to participate in civil rights protest. By engaging others in dialectical relationships, African-Americans reconstructed their identities and interpretations of their situation into meanings that translated into collective action. Some African-American church members in Arkansas, for example, tapped the church's deep tradition of resisting injustice and oppression to construct religious meanings that helped them define their social situation as unjust and persuaded some to act.

It is clear that culture's reservoir of extant meanings, relationships, and practices are central in micromobilization. During the civil rights era, cultural reservoirs were found in indigenous organizations like churches, clubs, and movement centers where African-Americans interacted to create and sustain social ties and identities that predisposed them to join the movement. Respondents in my study repeatedly asserted that involvement in indigenous organizational work promoted feelings of self-esteem and interests in politics and social change. More precisely, this study presents evidence demonstrating that individuals who were actively involved in church-based organizations were more likely to be involved in social movement activities.

This study also provides insight into the ways in which culture can simultaneously politicize and depoliticize people for collective action. Culture is the product of multiple and conflicting meanings from which pluralities of meanings are created that can either discourage or encourage movement participation. In the multivalent cultural context of indigenous organizations, individual beliefs and meanings regarding collective action varied from individual to individual. Some people construct discourses that support social action whiles others do not. My analysis of the Civil Rights Movement in Arkansas illustrates that a crucial determinant in how individuals employ discourse was their involvement in organizational work that exposed them to others involved in activist networks. This suggests that relational processes are important factors in the link between organization and activism that shape and reinforce people's moral and political views about how society should be ordered and that inspire collective action and make conceptions concrete in reality.

Beyond Culture's Mediating Role in Social Movement Theory

Since this study focuses on culture's effect in the Civil Rights Movement, theoretical insights are drawn from two principal social movement theories: collective behavior and resource mobilization. Generally, collective behavior theorists argue that social movements are irrational, spontaneous events that emerge when societal institutions that guide social behavior disintegrate, leading atomized people to engage in noninstitutionalized collective efforts to reconstitute a sense of social order and shared meaning. My study finds conceptual utility in the relative deprivation/collective behavior theoretical variant because it posits that beliefs and meanings arising from socioeconomic institutional processes motivate people to make rational demands of power holders through collective action. Though relative deprivation theory identifies culture as an important determinant in movement mobilization, it offers no explanation for how individual beliefs and meanings are transformed into organized collective action.

Rather than conceptualizing African-American civil rights protest as emerging from isolated individuals banding together to form a movement group, I argue that the Civil Rights Movement in Arkansas evolved from rational organizational repositories of a historical/cultural tradition of protest. After arriving in the United States, Africans and their descendants' experiences with oppression moved them to establish numerous indigenous organizations/institutions such as churches, secular and church-affiliated clubs, and other groups that translated their religious beliefs about injustice into sociopolitical cultures of resistance. My study identifies churches in Arkansas, for example, during and after the antebellum period as sites of cultural practices, relationships, and meanings about everyday life that invoked collective orientations among African-Americans. These served to promote collective resistance against political disenfranchisement, de jure segregation in streetcar boycotts, and economic exploitation. These cultural elements contributed to the construction of enduring religious beliefs, values, and meanings that, in turn, helped to produce a cadre of early activists who constantly tested and probed the sociopolitical system, even during periods when protest was believed to be quiescent.

Decades preceding major civil rights activity in Arkansas, for instance, these individuals employed their inherited religious sensibilities as cultural assets to persuade people to resist the social, economic, and political ravages of the sharecropping tenant system through participation in the STFU.

Until recently, the principal theoretical approach that has dominated thought about social movements was resource mobilization theory and its variants. While resource mobilization theories generally acknowledge that ideas are significant in collective action, their assumption is that social movements arise first in populations that are sufficiently organized and in possession of resources needed to sustain social action. Since money, persons with free time, and other such pragmatic elements are essential for movements to develop, the resource mobilization approach minimizes the strategic significance of ideas and historical/cultural "memory" (Robnett 1997:12). A variant of the resource mobilization model, political process theory suggests that culture plays an important mediating role between political opportunity and collective action. Political process theorist Doug McAdam maintains, "movement emergence implies a transformation of consciousness within a significant segment of the aggrieved population. Before protest can get under way, people must collectively define their situations as unjust and subject to change through group action. The likelihood of this necessary transformation occurring is conditioned . . . by . . . [s]hifting political conditions [that] supply the necessary 'cognitive cues' capable of triggering the process of cognitive liberation while existent organizations afford insurgents the stable group-settings within which that process is most likely to occur" (1982:51).

Political process proponents, like McAdam (1982) and Morris (1984), contend that cultural processes in preexisting indigenous organizations like churches and other institutions played small but important roles in persuading people to take advantage of political opportunity for group protest. McAdam argues that the generation of collective action reflects the favorable confluence of three sets of factors: "expanding political opportunities combine with indigenous organizations . . . to provide actors the 'structural potential' for successful collective action"; this potential is then transformed into collective action by means of crucial intervening cultural processes that generate political efficacy (1982:51). All three factors are regarded as necessary but insufficient alone to generate collective action. Although political process theorists recognized the importance of cultural dynamics in mobilizing collective action, their dependence on improved political opportunities to trigger sociopolitical efficacy directs them to concentrate very little on understanding how preexisting organizations' culture directly engender in people who ordinarily consider themselves helpless a belief in their capacity to alter their lot.

In the preceding analysis, I suggest, like the political process model, that resources and opportunity alone are not enough to ensure movement genesis. Collective action development is contingent in part upon the deployment of organizational cultures as interpretive resources for organizing socio-political action. As this study demonstrates, social relations, cultural practices, and meanings in African-American indigenous organizations produce religiously constructed political identities and consciousness among African-Americans that motivated some to become committed civil rights participants in oppressive segregated contexts that dramatically reduced the odds for action success. My study found that African-American churches and other institutions housed religious meanings, practices, and relationships that empowered some African-Americans to cultivate a politicized religious consciousness that was passed down through the generations. In the multivalent cultural context of indigenous organizations, some African-Americans constructed politico-religious cultural meanings that insisted, as Martin Luther King Jr. asserted, "a religion true to its nature must also be concerned about man's social conditions . . . Any religion that professes to be concerned with the souls of men and is not concerned with the slums that damn them, and the economic conditions that strangle them, and the social conditions that cripple them is a dry as dust religion" (1958:36).

My findings indicate that acquisition of activist religious dispositions among African-Americans was facilitated through organizational social networks. This process is driven by the strength of affective and integrative ties in indigenous organizations. In other words, research findings suggest that sociopolitical efficacy can be generated through social ties that serve to eliminate people's tendency to explain their oppressive situation as a function of individual rather than systemic factors. These relational networks produced cultural resources that motivated African-Americans to engage in civil rights protest when resources were scarce and the sociopolitical environment was not conducive to action. Consider the example of the African-American women in the secular and religious club movement in Arkansas during the late nineteenth and early twentieth century: women in this religious-inspired movement did not allow a structurally constraining environment to impede their efforts to work for African-American equality. Rather, as discussed earlier, in their club organizations women bonded to create relationships and religious meanings and identities that sustained their commitment in the face of strong opposition.

Since resource mobilization theory and its political process variants assert that culture is a mere by-product of political opportunity and resource availability, they undervalue the importance of social dynamics in generating social movement. On the other hand, new social movement theory emphasizes culture's centrality in transforming potential participants into movement supporters. Their attention to how collective identity and solidarity are created produces space for discussing and investigating the socio-cultural processes through which individuals and groups develop politicized identities.

This study reinserts culture as a critical component of social movement mobilization. While previous accounts of movements present culture as a crucial intervening variable that has no direct role in facilitating collective action, this analysis suggests that culture's role in movement mobilization is more complex and dynamic than commonly portrayed in the literature. Rather than viewing culture as a mere framer of people's definition of their social situation, this study presents a broader view that defines culture as both content (that is, shared meanings, beliefs, values, norms, and symbols) and the interpretive processes that transform content into collective action. Consequently, my study encourages movement researchers to approach analyses of organizations as carriers not simply of material resources but also of immaterial cultural resources that directly stimulate efficacy and movement mobilization.

With this in mind, it is useful to examine how cultural content serves to link organization and activism. That is, a key factor to analyze is the relationships between individuals in organizations and the institutions in which they interact, communicate, influence each other, negotiate sociopolitical environments, and make decisions. Within this relational system of dialectical tensions and interactions, people construct multiple and conflicting meanings within organizations, producing a multitude of beliefs that both incite and pacify movement involvement. Evidence indicates that rather than explaining their decision to join movements in terms of personal gain, African-Americans suggested that social ties within indigenous organizations were more important factors in facilitating their movement participation. I found that relationships in churches, the ATA, clubs, and other local movement organizations reinforced protest commitment and provided African-American civil rights participants with meanings, values, self-confidence, and social support that gave them courage to take action. This finding suggests that indigenous organizations (that is, churches, ATA, women's clubs, local movement organizations), as rich storehouses of symbolic expressions and interpersonal networks, can engender feelings of moral obligation and commitment to a movement community.

As Klandermans notes, "feelings of responsibility or moral obligation play a crucial role in determining movement participation, especially when it comes to enduring forms of participation (1997:33).

Although class and gender influenced African-Americans' movement participation decisions, my interview data suggest that individual and subjective experiences of oppression were understood and transcended through a religious culture that emphasized reforming socio-economic condition through political participation. Since religion provided African-Americans with a blueprint for living, it was within and through religious, rather than class, discourse that African-Americans expressed themselves, negotiated their status, and acted out their interests. Throughout this study, respondents suggested that their interpretation of religious faith directed them to get involved with activities that challenged class oppression. One respondent noted: "You have to get involved in those [processes] that cause people [to live in substandard] hous[ing], and other persons similarly disadvantaged . . . to the point where we can afford efficient housing . . . You have to be concerned about where we live to a point where you would try to engage yourself in those activities that will call for improved housing . . . What I'm saying is that . . . a person should have an opportunity to progress . . . So, that's why I always put God in front." In this effort to advance African-Americans economically, he continued: "I believed that I could succeed at whatever I tried. And [yes] I [encountered] . . . stumbling blocks along the way or difficulties along the way [but] I just leaned on God."

As has been discussed, women established separate indigenous organizations that fostered the development of gendered relationships, values, commitment, and organizational and leadership skills providing support for their pursuit of equality. In church-affiliated clubs in Arkansas, for example, African-American women encountered extant relationships that supplied them with meanings and beliefs that encouraged them to initiate, organize, and participate in various socio-economic and political struggles throughout Arkansas history. Though the level of movement involvement varied, women from these separate organizations, who worked primarily as teachers, used their understanding of racial, class, and gender oppression to create classroom cultures that produced a new generation of educational and community activists who proved indispensable in advancing the Civil Rights Movement.

Alberto Melucci (1989) and Nancy Whittier (1995) argue that the understanding of social movements cannot be reduced to analyses of formal organizations and resources. Rather, social movements require an understanding of cultural processes. As Melucci notes, "No process of mobilization begins in a void, and contrary to [collective behavior] theory, it is never the isolated and the uprooted who mobilize. The networks of relationships already present in the social fabric facilitate the processes of involvement and make individual's investment in the collective action less costly" (1988:339). In other words, affective commitment and participation reinforce one another: stronger commitment leads to greater participation, and greater participation leads to yet stronger commitment (Klandermans 1997:31). Thus motivation to participate is not exclusively an individual variable, though it operates at the individual level. Motivation is certainly rooted in individual dispositional differences, but it is constructed and consolidated in interaction (Melucci 1988:340).

Rather than viewing cultural challenges as dependent upon instability in social, political, and economic structures, my study refuses, as Archer (1988) suggests, to reduce structure to culture or vice versa, since doing so may preclude exploration of their interplay. A fuller examination of the ways in which culture and indigenous institutions interact reveals that church and religious affiliated groups contributed to the continuity of civil rights protest in Arkansas by providing meanings that predisposed African-Americans for social action. Polletta (1999) notes that in some ways culture *does* create political opportunities, and not just in the "subjective" perceptions of mobilizers. Movement participants are suspended in a web of meaning (Goodwin 1994), which helps shape their behavior in a way that can create political opportunities through altered cultural perceptions (Polletta 1999:433–34). For example, during the harried era of Jim Crow segregation, a cadre of African-Americans immersed in politicized religious meanings mustered courage to initiate legal challenges to the state of Arkansas's claim that it had enforced the *Plessy v. Ferguson* "separate but equal" clause. At the time that these suits were filed, no southern state seriously entertained complying with the "separate but equal" clause, since maintaining equal facilities for both African and European-Americans induced severe budgetary hardship. Consequently, the African-American initiative in filing these suits made it legally and financially burdensome to maintain de jure segregation in Arkansas, especially after the courts ruled in African-Americans' favor. In this way, cultural challenges destabilized institutional arrangements to create opportunities for social change.

This study bridges the gap between meaning system and structures by demonstrating how religious beliefs, values, and meanings within indigenous institutions are transformed through social interaction in ways that initiate and sustain movement mobilization among African-Americans in Arkansas.

My study suggests that examining the role of culture in movements may shed light on how collective action is generated in oppressive contexts. This study, like Kurzman's (1996) and Rasler's (1996) accounts of Iranian movement emergence in the context of heavy political repression, suggests that theoretical and empirical studies that place culture at the center of movement analysis will provide us with a more complete understanding of movement dynamics. Thus, placing culture at the center of movement analysis promises to further our knowledge of how human interaction and agency mobilize collective action.

APPENDIX

Interview Questions

Age (During Movement):
Educational Level:
Occupation:
Church Affiliation

How did you become involved in the civil rights movement?
Were you engaged in any social protest prior to your involvement in the civil rights movement?
What was your role in the movement?
Were you a member of any movement organizations during the movement?
Did you have any apprehension about participating in the movement?
(Wasn't your participation in the movement discouraging considering the extreme resistance you encountered trying to secure movement goals?)

Where did most of the organizing and strategizing sessions for the movement takes place and why?
Did your religious faith influence your decision to become a movement participant?
Do you think the church has an obligation to work for the African-American advancement?
How involved was your church in the movement?

What roles did women assume in the movement?
How did men relate to women participants?
What were your experiences as a woman activist?
Were there any other women participants in the movement?

Whom do you consider to be the ten most important individual leaders of the movement in Arkansas? And why?

NOTES

Introduction

1. To examine the list of semistructured questions I asked interviewees, see the appendix.

Chapter 1

1. Melucci argues that resource mobilization concepts such as "discretional resources" and "structure of opportunities" do not refer to "objective" realities but imply the capacity of people to define and construct their environment and themselves (1988:342).

2. William Gamson (1992) defines "free spaces" as dense communal social support networks where people construct meaning that may initiate and sustain collective action.

3. As Gamson and Modigliani (1989) and Lincoln and Mamiya (1990) argue, beliefs are always found in a "dynamic tension" that is characterized by multiple conversations contesting, reformulating, defending, and refuting beliefs within as well as between groups. Every argument has a counterargument and can thus create multiple ideational strands.

4. Other theorists who examine the role of culture in the development of social movements include George Rudé (1980); Rick Fantasia (1988); Aldon Morris and Carol Mueller (1992); Steven Buechler (1993); Hank Johnston et al. (1994); Doug McAdam (1994); Sidney Tarrow (1994); Hank Johnston and Bert Klandermans (1995).

5. The 1958 *Bennett law* tried to outlaw the NAACP and other "subversive organizations" by 1) empowering the state attorney general to examine an organization's records and finance if s/he had reason to believe the organization was trying to evade state taxes; 2) defining barratry and making it unlawful to instigate lawsuits over school desegregation; and 3) making it unlawful to solicit or donate money to assist persons to start or maintain court actions over school desegregation.

Chapter 2

1. For further elucidation on this subject, see Jordan (1968); Mencarelli and Servin (1975).

2. See Taylor (1979) for further details on scriptural justifications for slavery in Arkansas.

3. Reverend Garnet, a former bondsman and Presbyterian minister, made this statement in a speech delivered in 1843 before the National Negro Convention.

4. Numbers quoted from Gayraud Wilmore (1994), p. 54.

5. Woodson (1972) lists the Harrison Baptist Church as the first independently organized African-American church in Colonial America while many others, such as McKinney (1971), Sernett (1972), and Sobel (1979), begin with the Yama Craw Baptist Church. Which church came first is of little consequence considering that their establishment dates are separated by only a year.

6. See Aptheker (1966) for further elucidation on Nat Turner's revolt.

7. Unlike Methodists, Presbyterians, and Episcopalians, Baptist structural hierarchy is less extensive. Local Baptist churches are accountable to no one except themselves. Each church instructs its congregation in the manner it deems proper. Consequently, the national Baptist association only has advisory authority over their members. For more information see Haynes (1953).

8. The problem with local autonomy was that the church could not persistently attack slavery as a national body. Carter Godwin Woodson maintained that Baptists reached their most advanced position as an antislavery body in 1789 when they proclaimed "that slavery is a violent depredation of the rights of nature and inconsistent with a republican government, and therefore, recommend it to our brethren, to make use of their local missions to extirpate this horrid evil from the land; and pray Almighty God that our honorable legislature may have it in their power to proclaim the great jubilee consistent with the principles of good policy" (1972:27).

9. The American Baptist Missionary Convention was the first organized convention of freed African-American Baptists. The convention was organized in 1840 at Abyssinian Baptist Church in New York City and led by free African-American migrant and Abyssinian pastor Sampson White. The convention included both Baptist and Methodist churches.

10. This 1850 Fugitive Slave Law replaced the 1793 Slave Act that proved ineffective in halting runaways or suppressing aid given to them. The Fugitive Slave Law of 1850 added U.S. commissioners to courts to issue arrest warrants for fugitives and certificates for their removal from the state. The claimant's affidavit was all that was necessary to establish ownership, making it possible to enslave free African-Americans. Citizens were required to assist in carrying out the law. Anyone harboring, concealing, or rescuing a fugitive was liable to a fine of $1,000, six months imprisonment, and civil damages of $1,000 for each runaway with whom he/she was involved. For a more extensive explanation of the Fugitive Slave Law see Cochran (1972).

11. The building occupied by the Free African Society was rededicated on July 17, 1794, as Saint Thomas's African Episcopal Church, and Absalom Jones, after being ordained the first African-American Protestant Episcopal priest, became the pastor.

12. A decade before the dedication of Bethel, Asbury, one the early bishops of the M.E. church in the United States, had urged the national Methodist conference in Baltimore, Maryland, to adopt a resolution requiring traveling preachers who held slaves to set them free and declare that "slavery is contrary to the laws of God, man, and nature, and hurtful to society; contrary to the dictates of conscience and pure religion, and doing that we would not others should do to us and others" (Blassingame 1979:47).

13. Coker's refusal to be bishop invariably has been blamed on scandal and his light skin color. Speculation was that his fellow ministers considered Coker's fair complexion a strike against him. They believed that darker-complexioned African-Americans would shy away from their church if the bishop's skin resembled European-Americans (George 1973). Moreover, Coker's support for the American Colonization Society, which unsuccessfully tried to convince free African-Americans to return to Africa, may also have been a factor in his refusal to become bishop.

14. According to Walls, the name "Zion" was chosen because "it was the name most frequently used in the Bible to designate the Church of God" (1974:50).

Chapter 3

1. First Colored Baptist Church was the first independent church organized by enslaved African-Americans in Arkansas in 1845.

2. Bethel Institute changed its name in 1892 to Shorter University in honor of Bishop James Alexander Shorter, who on November 19, 1868, organized the African Methodist Episcopal Church in Arkansas (McSwain 1982:81).

3. Rev. Nathan Warren established Bethel A.M.E. Church in 1865 as the first independent African-American Methodist church in the state.

4. Ashley County High School eventually moved to Warren, Arkansas, where it was renamed Walters Institute. While in Warren the Institute merged with Southland College and changed its name to Walters-Southland Institute in 1936. Eventually the new school moved to Lexa, Arkansas, before returning to Warren to close in 1948.

5. For a nice overview of the third party dynamics during Post-Reconstruction see Piven and Cloward, *Why Americans Still Don't Vote*, chapter 3.

6. Arkansas's 1891 General Assembly contained a contingent of eleven African-Americans—ten in the house and one in the Senate. Representatives included John G. Lucas, S. W. Dawson, and Sam L Woolfolk, Jefferson County; John H. Carr and J. N. Donohoo, Phillips County; G. W. Watson, Crittenden County; R. C. Weddington, Desha County; H. N. Williams, Lincoln County; George W. Lowe, Monroe County; and Benjamin. F. Adair, (Democrat) Pulaski County. George W. Bell of the Desha and Chicot district was the lone African-American in the state senate.

7. John Gray Lucas grew up in Pine Bluff, Arkansas, where he later attended the Branch Normal School (now University of Arkansas at Pine Bluff). After graduating from Branch Normal undergraduate school, he attended Boston University Law School, from which he graduated with honors in 1887.

8. Many of these streetcar lines later failed, according to Meier and Rudwick (1976), because of the poor management skills of owners and/or harassment of transportation operators by public authorities.

9. The first bank established was Pine Bluff's Unity Bank and Trust Company in 1902.

10. Mears (1954) and Desmarais (1974) estimated that African-American fatalities during the Elaine Race Riot ranged from twenty to eight hundred. The correct figure is anyone's guess. Undeniably, however the riot devastated Elaine's African-American community.

11. An STFU circular entitled *Slavery, Brutality, Murder in Arkansas* (pamphlet held at the Arkansas History Commission) chronicles the many other oppressive methods employed by landlords to keep sharecroppers from unionizing.

Chapter 4

1. Fabus's progressive stance later changed when he was elected governor. He became a staunch opponent of school integration in Arkansas.

2. Elsewhere, Hot Springs native Edith Irby became the first African-American to be admitted to the University of Arkansas School of Medicine in Little Rock in 1948 (Williams 1986:39).

3. Five undergraduates were admitted: three males and two females. Their names were Kenneth Colby, J. A. Gordon, Lewis Jackson, Vivan T. Hegewood, and Doris Tate.

Chapter 6

1. There is debate in the literature surrounding the authenticity of Sojourner Truth's speech; see Painter (1996).

2. This ideological current was very strong among African-American Baptist women in the 1880s and 1890s. For additional information see Evelyn Brooks (1990).

3. Still other scholars who have examined the role of culture in movement mobilization include Swidler (1986); Lofland (1995); Polletta (1997, 1999); Platt and Fraser (1998).

4. Harris's (1999) recent analysis of Chicago's African-American politico-religious scene also found church involvement cultivates organizational skills that engender political efficacy.

5. Nearly all women's clubs in Arkansas were affiliates of the National Association of Colored Women.

6. For more information on Mary Speight's tenure as president of the ATA, see Thomas E. Patterson, *History of the Arkansas Teachers Association* (1981).

7. Ernest Green was one of the nine original students who integrated Little Rock Central High School in 1957.

8. Little Rock public schools may have been the first school district in the South to offer an African-American history course (Gordon 1987:31). The school board discontinued the course in 1957.

9. Since African-American women were generally denied access to the job market in Arkansas, the only well-paying and respectful employment open to them was teaching. Consequently, the majority of the ATA membership consisted of women.

10. Morris was finally reinstated in 1952.

11. African-American women were also strong participants and organizers of the tenant farmers' Progressive Union at Hoop Spur after World War I.

12. For years Dilworth was an outspoken community leader and Southern Tenant Farmers Union member. African-American women like Dilworth were some of the union's best members and organizers.

BIBLIOGRAPHY

Allen, Richard L., Michael C. Dawson, Ronald E. Brown. 1989. "Schema-Based Approach to
Modeling an African-American Racial Belief System." *The American Political Science
Review* 83:421–41.

Aptheker, Herbert. 1966. *Nat Turner's Slave Rebellion*. New York: Grove Press.

Archer, Margaret S. 1988. *Culture and Agency: The Place of Culture in Social Theory*. New York:
Cambridge University Press.

Arendt, Hannah. 1951. *The Origins of Totalitarianism*. New York: Harcourt, Brace.

Bainbridge, William Sims. 1997. *The Sociology of Religious Movements*. New York: Routledge.

Barnett, Bernice McNair. 1993. "Invisible Southern Black Women Leaders in the Civil Rights
Movement: The Triple Constraints of Gender, Race, and Class." *Gender & Society* 7:162–82.

Bates, Daisy. 1986. *The Long Shadow of Little Rock: A Memoir*. Fayetteville: University of Arkansas Press.

Bell, Howard Holman. 1969. *A Survey of the Negro Convention Movement, 1830–1861*. New York:
Arono Press.

Bernard, Jacqueline. 1967. *Journey Toward Freedom: The Story of Sojourner Truth*. New York:
W. W. Norton.

Berktay, Fatmagül. 1998. *Women and Religion*. Montréal/New York: Black Rose Books.

Biko, Steve. 1972. *I Write What I Like: A Selection of His Writings*. San Francisco: Harper & Row.

Billings, Dwight B. 1990. "Religion as Opposition: A Gramscian Analysis." *American Journal of
Sociology* 96:1–31.

Blassingame, John W. 1979. *The Slave Community: Plantation Life in the Antebellum South*.
New York: Oxford University Press.

Bogin, Ruth. 1983. "'Liberty Further Extended': A 1776 Antislavery Manuscript by Lemuel
Haynes." *William and Mary Quarterly* 40:85–105.

Bontemps, Arna and Jack Conroy. 1966. *Anyplace But Here*. New York Hill & Wang.

Brecher, Jeremy, Tim Costello and Brendan Smith. 2000. *Globalization from Below: The Power of
Solidarity*. Boston: South End Press.

Brooks, Evelyn. 1990. "The Feminist Theology of the Black Baptist Church, 1880–1900."
Pp.167–95 in *Black Women in the United States History, volume 1*, edited by Darlene Hine.
Brooklyn, New York: Carlson Publishing.

Brown, Delindus R. 1979. "Free Blacks' Rhetorical Impact on African Colonization: The Emergence
of Rhetorical Exigence." *Journal of Black Studies* 9:251–65.

Buechler, Steven M. 1990. *Women's Movements in the United States: Woman Suffrage, Equal Rights,
and Beyond*. New Brunswick, New Jersey: Rutgers University Press.

———. 1993. "Beyond Resource Mobilization? Emerging Trends in Social Movement Theory."
Sociological Quarterly 34:217–35.

Burkett, Randall K. 1977. "A. M. E. Zion Clergy and Laity in the Universal Negro Improvement
Association." *The A. M. E. Zion Quarterly Review* 89:4–23.

Carby, Hazel. V. 1987. *Reconstructing Womanhood: The Emergence of the Afro-American Woman
Novelist*. New York: Oxford University Press.

Chafe, William. 1980. *Civilities and Civil Rights: Greensboro, North Carolina, and the Black Struggle
for Freedom*. New York: Oxford University Press.

Chong, Dennis. 1991. *Collective Action and the Civil Rights Movement (American Politics and Political
Economy Series)*. Chicago: University of Chicago Press.

Cochran, William Cox. 1972. *The Western Reserve and the Fugitive Slave Law: A Prelude to the
Civil War*. New York: Da Capo Press.

Cohen, Jean. 1985. "Strategy or Identity: New Theoretical Paradigms and Contemporary Social Movements." *Social Research* 52:663–716.

Cone, James H. 1970. "Black Consciousness and the Black Church: A Historical Theological Interpretation." *Annals of the American Academy of Political Science and Social Science* 387:49–55.

———. 1974. "The Sources and Norm of Black Theology." Pp. 110–22 in *The Black Experience in Religion*, edited by C. Eric Lincoln. Garden City, New York: Anchor Press.

———. 1978. "Sanctification, Liberation and Black Worship." *Theology Today* 35:139–52.

———. 1986. "Martin Luther King, Jr. Black Theology, and The Black Church." *The A.M.E. Zion Quarterly Review* 98:2–17.

———. 1986. "A Dream or A Nightmare: Martin Luther King, Jr. and Malcolm X." *Sojourners* 15:26–30.

———. 1989. *Black Theology and Black Power*. San Francisco: Harper.

———. 1996. *A Black Theology of Liberation*. Maryknoll, New York: Orbis Books.

Cox, Oliver Cromwell. 2000. *Race: A Study in Social Dynamics*. New York: Monthly Review.

Crawford, Vicki, Jacqueline Rouse and Barbara Woods, editors. 1990. *Women in the Civil Rights Movement: Trailblazers and Torchbearers, 1941–1965*. Brooklyn, NY: Carlson.

Cunningham, Floyd T. 1985. "Wandering in the Wilderness: Black Baptist Thought After Emancipation." *American Baptist Quarterly* 4:268–81.

Davies, James C. 1962. "Toward a Theory of Revolution." *American Sociological Review* 27:5–19.

———. 1969. "The J-Curve of Rising and Declining Satisfactions as a Cause of Some Great Revolutions and a Contained Rebellion." Pp. 547–76 in *Violence in America: Historical and Comparative Perspectives*, edited by Hugh Davis Graham and Ted Robert Gurr. Washington, D. C.: U.S. Government Printing Office.

Davis, Angela. 1971. "Black Women's Roles in the Community of Slaves." *Black Scholar* 3:2–16.

Desmarais, Ralph H. 1974. "Military Intelligence Reports on Arkansas Riots, 1919–1920." *Arkansas Historical Quarterly* 33:175–91.

Du Bois, W. E. B. (ed) 1903. *The Negro Church: A Report of a Social Study Made Under the Direction of Atlanta University*. Atlanta, Georgia: Atlanta University Press.

———. 1935. *Black Reconstruction in America, 1860–1880*. New York: A. Saifer.

———. 1971. "History of the Negro Church: Africa to 1890." In *The Seventh Son*, ed. Julius Lester. New York Random House.

Dunning, William Archibald. 1962. *Reconstruction, Political and Economic, 1865–1877*. New York: Harper & Row.

Evans, Sara. 1980. *Personal Politics: The Roots of Women's Liberation in the Civil Rights Movement and the New Left*. New York: Random.

Fantasia, Rick. 1988. *Cultures of Solidarity: Consciousness, Action and Contemporary American Workers*. Berkeley: University of California Press.

Ferree, Myra Marx and Frederick Miller. 1985. "Mobilization and Meaning: Toward an Integration of Social Psychological and Resource Perspectives on Social Movements." *Sociological Inquiry* 55:38–61.

Fireman, Bruce, and William A. Gamson. 1979. "Utilitarian Logic in the Resource Mobilization Perspective." Pp. 9–11 in *The Dynamics of Social Movements: Resource Mobilization, Social Control, and Tactics*, edited by Mayer N. Zald and John D. McCarthy. Cambridge, Massachusetts: Winthrop.

Frazier, E. Franklin. 1964. *The Negro Church in America*. New York: Schocken Books.

Fredrickson, George M. 1981. *White Supremacy: A Comparative Study in American and South African History*. Oxford: Oxford University Press.

Freeman, Jo. 1975. *The Politics of Women's Liberation*. New York: David McKay.

Freyer, Tony A. 1981. "Politics and Law in the Little Rock Crisis, 1954–1957." *Arkansas Historical Quarterly* 40:195–219.

Gamson, William A. 1992. "The Social Psychology of Collective Action." Pp. 53–76 in *Frontiers in Social Movement Theory*, edited by Aldon D. Morris and Carol McClurg Mueller. New Haven: Yale University Press.

Gamson, William A and Andre Modigliani. 1989. "Media Discourse and Public Opinion on Nuclear Power." *American Journal of Sociology* 95:1–37.

Gatewood, Willard B., Jr. 1974. "Arkansas Negroes in the 1890s: Documents." *Arkansas Historical Quarterly* 33:293–325.

Genovese, Eugene E. 1972. *Roll, Jordan, Roll: The World the Slaves Made.* New York: Pantheon.

———. 1979. *From Rebellion to Revolution: Afro-American Slave Revolts in the Making of the Modern World.* Baton Rouge: Louisiana State University Press.

George, Carol V. R. 1973. *Segregated Sabbaths: Richard Allen and the Emergence of Independent Black Churches, 1760–1840.* New York: Oxford University Press.

Giddings, Paula. 1984. *When and Where I Enter: The Impact of Black Women on Race and Sex in America.* New York: Bantam Books.

Gilkes, Cheryl Townsend. 1997. "The Roles of Church and Community Mothers: Ambivalent American Sexism or Fragmented African Familyhood?" Pp. 365–88 in *African-American Religion: Interpretive Essays in History and Culture*, edited by Timothy Fulop and Albert Raboteau. New York: Routledge.

Godelier, Maurice. 1982. "The Ideal in the Real." Pp. 12–38 in *Culture, Ideology and Politics*, edited by Raphael Samuel and Gareth Stedman Jones. London: Routledge and Kegan Paul.

Goodwin, Jeff. 1994. "Toward a New Sociology of Revolutions." *Theory and Society* 23:731–66.

Gordon, Fon L. 1987. "Black Women in Arkansas." *Pulaski County Historical Review* 35:26–37.

———. 1995. *Caste and Class: The Black Experience in Arkansas, 1880–1920.* Athens: University of Georgia Press.

Grant, Jacquelyn. 1986. "Womanist Theology: Black Women's Experience as a Source for Doing Theology, with Special Reference to Christology." *Journal of Interdenominational Theological Center* 13:195–212.

———. 1989. "Black Theology and the Black Woman." Pp. 185–200 in *Black Male-Female Relationships: A Resource Book of Selected Materials*, edited by Delores P. Aldridge. Dubuque, Iowa: Kendall/Hunt.

Graves, John William. 1967. "Negro Disfranchisement In Arkansas. *Arkansas Historical Quarterly* 26:199–225.

———. 1990. *Town and Country: Race Relations in an Urban and Rural Context, Arkansas, 1865–1905.* Fayetteville: University of Arkansas Press.

Griffin, Larry J. 1995. "How Do We Disentangle Race and Class? Or Should We Even Try?" *Work and Occupations* 22:85–93.

Gross, Bella. 1946. "The First Negro Convention." *Journal of Negro History* 31:435–43.

Gurr, Ted Robert. 1970. *Why Men Rebel.* Princeton, New Jersey: Princeton University Press.

Harding, Vincent. 1969. "Religion and Resistance Among Antebellum Negroes, 1800–1860. In *The Making of Black America: Essays in Negro Life and History*, edited by August Meier and Elloit M. Rudwick. New York: Antheneum.

———. 1981. *There is A River: The Black Struggle for Freedom in America.* San Diego: Harcourt Brace & Company.

Harlan, Louis R. 1972. *Booker T. Washington: The Making of a Black Leader, 1856–1901.* New York: Oxford University Press.

Harris, Fredrick C. 1994. "Something Within: Religion as a Mobilizer of African-American Political Activism." *Journal of Politics.* 56:42–68.

————. 1999. *Something Within: Religion in African-American Political Activism*. New York: Oxford University Press.

Hatcher, William. 1908. *John Jasper: The Unmatched Negro Philosopher and Preacher*. New York: Fleming H. Revell.

Haynes, Leonard L. 1953. *The Negro Community Within American Protestantism, 1619–1844*. Boston: Christopher Publishing.

Herskovits, Melville J. 1941. *The Myth of the Negro Past*. New York: Harper & Brothers.

Higginbotham, Evelyn Brooks. 1994. *Righteous Discontent: The Women's Movement in the Black Baptist Church, 1880–1920*. Cambridge, Massachusetts: Harvard University Press.

————. 1997. "The Black Church: A Gender Perspective." Pp. 201–26 in *African-American Religion: Interpretive Essays in History and Culture*, edited by Timothy E. Fulop and Albert J. Raboteau. New York: Routledge.

Hinson, E. Glenn. 1979. *A History of Baptists in Arkansas*. Little Rock, Arkansas: Arkansas State Baptist Convention.

Holloway, Joseph E., ed. 1990. *Africanisms in American Culture*. Bloomington: Indiana University Press.

Hume, Richard L. 1973. "The Arkansas Constitutional Convention of 1868: A Case Study in the Politics of Reconstruction." *The Journal of Southern History* 39:183–206.

Hunt, L. L. and J. G. Hunt. 1977. "Black Religion as Opiate and Inspiration of Civil Rights Militance: Putting Marx's Data to Test." *Social Forces* 56:1–14.

Huntington, Samuel P. 1968. *Political Order in Changing Societies*. New Haven, Connecticut: Yale University Press.

Jacques-Garvey, Amy, ed. 1986. *Philosophy and Opinions of Marcus Garvey*. New York: Atheneum.

Jenkins, J. Craig. 1981. "Sociopolitical Movements." Pp. 81–53 in *Handbook of Political Behavior*, edited by Samuel Long. New York: Plenum Press.

Johnston, Hank, Enrique Laraña, and Joseph R. Gusfield. 1994. "Identities, Grievances, and New Social Movements." Pp. 201–26 in *New Social Movements: From Ideology to Identity*, edited by Enrique Laraña, Hank Johnston, and Joseph R. Gusfield. Philadelphia: Temple University Press.

Johnston, Hank and Bert Klandermans, ed. 1995. *Social Movements and Culture*. Minneapolis: University of Minnesota Press.

Jordan, Winthrop D. 1968. *White Over Black: American Attitudes Toward the Negro, 1550–1812*. Chapel Hill: University of North Carolina Press.

Kennicott, Patrick C. 1970. "Black Persuaders in the Antislavery Movement." *Journal of Black Studies*, 1:5–20.

Kester, Howard. 1936. *Revolt Among the Sharecroppers*. New York: Civic-Friede.

King, Martin Luther, Jr. 1958. *Stride Toward Freedom: The Montgomery Story*. New York: Harper.

Kirk, John A. 2002. *Redefining the Color Line: Black Activism in Little Rock, Arkansas, 1940–1970*. Gainesville: University Press of Florida.

Klandermans, Bert. 1997. *The Social Psychology of Protest*. Oxford: Blackwell Publishers.

————. 1992. "The Social Construction of Protest and Multiorganizational Fields." Pp. 77–103 in *Frontiers in Social Movement Theory*, edited by Aldon D. Morris and Carol McClurg Mueller. New Haven: Yale University Press.

Kornhauser, William. 1959. *The Politics of Mass Society*. Glencoe, Illinois: The Free Press.

Kousser, J. Morgan. 1975. "A Black Protest in the Era of Accommodation: Documents." *Arkansas Historical Quarterly* 34:149–78.

Krass, Peter. 1990. *Sojourner Truth: Antislavery Activist*. Los Angeles, California: Melrose Square.

Kurzman, Charles. 1996. "Structural Opportunity and Perceived Opportunity in Social Movement Theory: The Iranian Revolution of 1979." *American Sociological Review* 61:153–70.

Le Bon, Gustave. 1960. *The Crowd: A Study of the Popular Mind*. New York: Viking.

Levine, Lawrence W. 1977. *Black Culture and Black Consciousness: Afro-American Folk Thought from Slavery to Freedom.* Oxford: Oxford University Press.

Lincoln, C. Eric and Lawrence H. Mamiya. 1990. *The Black Church in the African American Experience.* Durham: Duke University Press.

Littlefield, Daniel and Patricia W. McGraw. 1979. "The Arkansas Freeman, 1869–1870: Birth of the Black Press in Arkansas." *Phylon* 40:75–85.

Lofland, John. 1995. "Charting Degrees of Movement Culture: Tasks of the Cultural Cartographer." Pp. 188–216 in *Social Movements and Culture,* edited by Hank Johnston and Bert Klandermans. Minneapolis: University of Minnesota Press.

McAdam, Doug. 1982. *Political Process and the Development of Black Insurgency, 1930–1970.* Chicago: University of Chicago Press.

———. 1994. "Culture and Social Movements," Pp. 36–57 in *New Social Movements: From Ideology to Identity,* edited by Enrique Laraña, Hank Johnston, and Joseph R. Gusfield. Philadelphia: Temple University Press.

McCall, Emmanuel. 1980. "The Black Church and Social Justice." Pp. 197–212 in *Issues in Christian Ethics,* edited by Paul D. Simmons. Nashville, Tennessee: Broadman Press.

McCarthy, John D. 1973. *The Trends of Social Movements.* Morristown, NJ: General Learning Press.

McCarthy, John D. and Mayer Zald. 1977. "Resource Mobilization and Social Movements: A Partial Theory." *American Journal of Sociology* 82:1212–41.

McDonald, Erwin L. 1974. "A Moral Briar Patch: Religion in Pulaski County." *Pulaski County Historical Review* 22:23–30.

McKinney, Richard I. 1971. "The Black Church: Its Development and Present Impact." *Harvard Theological Review* 64:452–81.

McPhail, Clark. 1991. *The Myth of the Madding Crowd.* New York: Aldine de Gruyter.

McSwain, Bernice L. 1982. "Shorter College: Its Earlier History." *Pulaski County Historical Review* 30:81–84.

Marable, Manning. 2000. *How Capitalism Underdeveloped Black America: Problems in Race, Political Economy, and Society.* Cambridge, MA: Southend Press

Martin, Tony. 1976. *Race First: The Ideological and Organizational Struggles of Marcus Garvey and the Universal Negro Improvement Association.* Dover, Massachusetts: The Majority Press.

Marx, Gary T. 1967. *Protest and Prejudice: A Study of Belief in the Black Community.* New York: Harper & Row.

Mbiti, John S. 1982. "African Views of the Universe." Pp. 193–99 in *African History and Culture,* edited by Richard Olaniyan. Ikeja, Nigeria.

———. 1990. *African Religions and Philosophy.* Oxford: Heineman.

Mears, William C. 1954. "L. S. (Sharpe) Dunaway." *Arkansas Historical Quarterly* 13:77–85.

Meier, August, and Elliot Rudwick. 1976. *Along the Color Line: Explorations in the Black Experience.* Chicago: University of Chicago Press.

Melucci, Alberto. 1985. "The Symbolic Challenge of Contemporary Movements." *Social Research* 52:789–816.

———. 1988. "Getting Involved: Identity and Mobilization in Social Movements." *International Social Movement Research* 1:329–48.

———. 1989. *Nomads of the Present: Social Movements and Individual Needs in Contemporary Society.* London: Hutchinson Radius.

———. 1995. "The Process of Collective Identity." Pp. 41–63 in *Social Movements and Culture,* edited by Hank Johnston and Bert Klandermans. Minneapolis, Minnesota: University of Minnesota Press.

Mencarelli, James and Steve Severin. 1975. *Protest: Red, Black, Brown Experience in America.* Grand Rapid, Michigan: William B. Eerdmans Publishing.

Mills, Kay. 1993. *This Little Light of Mine: The Life of Fannie Lou Hamer*. New York: Dutton.

Mitchell, Henry L. 1973. The Founding and Early History of the Southern Tenants Farmers Union. *Arkansas Historical Quarterly* 32:342–69.

Moneyhon, Carl H. 1985. "Black Politics in Arkansas During the Gilded Age, 1876–1900." *Arkansas Historical Quarterly* 44:222–45.

Morris, Aldon D. 1984. *Origins of the Civil Rights Movement: Black Communities Organizing for Change*. New York: Free Press.

———. 1992. "Political Consciousness and Collective Action." Pp. 351–73 in *Frontiers in Social Movement Theory*, edited by Aldon D. Morris and Carol McClurg Mueller. New Haven: Yale University Press.

———. 1993. "Centuries of Black Protest: Its Significance for America and the World." Pp. 19–69 in *Race in America: The Struggle for Equality*, edited by Herbert Hill and James E. Jones. Madison, Wisconsin: University of Wisconsin Press.

Morris, Aldon D., and Cedric Herring. 1986. "Theory and Research in Social Movements: A Critical Review." In *Annual Review of Political Science*, edited by Samuel Long. Norwood, New Jersey: Ablex.

Morris, Aldon D., and Carol McClurg Mueller, editors. 1992. *Frontiers in Social Movement Theory*. New Haven: Yale University Press.

Muzorewa, Gwinyai H. 1985. *Origins and Development of African Theology*. Maryknoll, New York: Orbis Books.

Myrdal, Gunnar. 1944. *An American Dilemma: The Negro Problem and Modern Democracy*. New York: Harper.

Nelsen, Hart M., Thomas W. Maldron, and Raytha L. Yokley. 1975. "Black Religion's Promethean Motif: Orthodoxy and Militancy." *American Journal of Sociology* 81:139–46.

Nepstad, Sharon Erickson. 1996. "Popular Religion, Protest, and Revolt: The Emergence of Political Insurgency in the Nicaraguan and Salvadoran Churches of the 1960s–80s." Pp. 105–24 in *Disruptive Religion: The Force of Faith in Social Movement Activism*, edited by Christian S. Smith. New York: Routlege.

Oberschall, Anthony. 1973. *Social Conflict and Social Movements*. Englewood Cliffs, New Jersey: Prentice Hall.

Olson, Mancur. 1968. *The Logic of Collective Action: Public Goods and the Theory of Groups*. Cambridge, Massachusetts: Harvard University Press.

Ortiz, Paul. 2000. " 'Like Water Covered the Seas': The African American Freedom Struggle in Florida, 1877–1920." Duke University, Ph.D. Dissertation.

Painter, Nell Irving. 1996. *Sojourner Truth: A Life, A Symbol*. New York: W. W. Norton.

Palmer, Paul C. 1965. "Miscegenation as An Issue in the Arkansas Constitutional Convention of 1868." *Arkansas Historical Quarterly* 24:99–126.

Parrinder, Geoffrey. 1969. *West African Religion: A Study of the Beliefs and Practices of Akan, Ewe, Yoruba, Ibo, and Kindred Peoples*. Westport, Connecticut: Greenwood Press.

Patterson, Thomas E. 1981. *History of the Arkansas Teachers Association*. Washington, D.C.: National Educational Association.

Pattillo-McCoy, Mary. 1998. "Church Culture as a Strategy of Action in the Black Community." *American Sociological Review* 63:767–84.

Patton, Adell. 1992. "The 'Back-to-Africa' Movement in Arkansas." *Arkansas Historical Quarterly* 51:164–77.

Payne, Charles M. 1990. "Men Led, but Women Organized: Movement Participation of Women in the Mississippi Delta." Pp.1–11 in *Black Women in United States History, Volume 13 & 14*, edited by Darlene Hines. Brooklyn, New York: Carlson Publishing.

———. 1995. *I've Got the Light of Freedom: The Organizing Tradition and the Mississippi Freedom Struggle.* Berkeley: University of California Press.

Pearson, Robert W., Michael Ross, and Robyn M. Dawes. 1992. "Personal Recall and the Limits of Retrospective Questions in Surveys." Pp. 65–94 in *Questions about Questions: Inquiries into the Cognitive Bases of Surveys,* edited by Judith M. Tanur. New York: Russell Sage.

Piven, Frances Fox and Richard A. Cloward. 2002. *Why Americans Still Don't Vote: And Why Politicians Want It That Way.* New York: Pantheon.

Platt, Gerald M. and Michael R. Fraser. 1998. "Race and Gender Discourse Strategies: Creating Solidarity and Framing the Civil Rights Movement." *Social Problems* 45:160–79.

Polletta, Francesca. 1997. "Culture and Its Discontents: Recent Theorizing on the Cultural Dimensions of Protest." *Sociological Inquiry* 67:431–50.

———. 1999. "Snarls, Quacks, and Quarrels: Culture and Structure in Political Process Theory." *Sociological Forum* 14:63–70.

Posey, Walter B. 1956. "The Baptists and Slavery in the Lower Mississippi Valley." *Journal of Negro History* 41:117–30.

Raboteau, Albert J. 1978. *Slave Religion: The 'Invisible Institution' in the Antebellum South.* Oxford: Oxford University Press.

———. 1982. "Slave Autonomy and Religion." *The Journal of Religious Thought* 38:51–64.

Raper, Arthur F. and Ira Reid. 1971. *Sharecroppers All.* Chapel Hill: University of North Carolina Press.

Rasler, Karen. 1996. "Concessions, Repression, and Political Protest in the Iranian Revolution." *American Sociological Review* 61:132–52.

Ramphele, Mamphela. 1999. *Across Boundaries: The Journey of a South African Woman Leader.* New York: Feminist Press.

Reed, Adolph L. 1986. *The Jesse Jackson Phenomenon: The Crisis of Purpose in Afro-American Politics.* New Haven: Yale University Press.

Reid, Willie M. 1976. "Changing Attitudes Among Black Women." Pp. 2–12 in *Black Women's Struggle for Equality,* edited by Willie M. Reid. New York: Pathfinder.

Richardson, Harry Van Buren. 1947. *Dark Glory: A Picture of the Church Among Negroes in the Rural South.* New York: Home Missions Council of North America/Friendship Press.

———. 1976. *Dark Salvation.* Garden City, New York: Anchor Press.

Robnett, Belinda. 1996. "African-American Women in the Civil Rights Movement: Gender, Leadership, and Micromobilization." *American Journal of Sociology* 101:1161–93.

———. 1997. *How Long? How Long?: African-American Women in Struggle for Civil Rights.* New York: Oxford University Press.

Rogers, O. A., Jr. 1960. "The Elaine Race Riots of 1919." *Arkansas Historical Quarterly* 19:142–50.

Rudé, George. 1980. *Ideology and Popular Protest.* New York: Pantheon Books.

Rupp, Lelia and Verta Taylor. 1987. *Survival in the Doldrums: The American Women's Rights Movement, 1945 to the 1960s.* New York: Oxford University Press.

Sacks, Karen B. 1988. "Gender and Grassroots Leadership." Pp. 77–94 in *Women and the Politics of Empowerment,* edited by Ann Bookman and Sandra Morgan. Philadelphia: Temple University Press.

Sernett, Milton. 1972. *Black Religion and American Evangelicalism: White Protestants, Plantation Missions and the Independent Negro Church, 1787–1865.* University of Delware, Ph.D. Dissertation.

Smesler, Neil. 1962. *Theory of Collective Behavior.* New York: Free Press.

Smith, C. Calvin. 1982. "The Politics of Evasion: Arkansas' Reaction to Smith v. Allright, 1944." *Journal of Negro History* 67:40–51.

Smith, C. Miflin. 1975. "The Unfinished Task of the Black Church in Higher Education." *A. M. E. Zion Quarterly Review* 87:5–9.

Smith, Christian S. 1996. "Correcting a Curious Neglect, or Bring Religion Back In." Pp. 1–25 in *Disruptive Religion: The Force of Faith in Social Movement Activism*, edited by Christian S. Smith. New York: Routledge.

Smith, Timothy L. 1972. "Slavery and Theology: The Emergence of Black Christian Consciousness in Nineteenth Century America." *Church History* 41:497–512.

Snow, David A., E. Burke Rochford, Jr., Steven K. Worden, and Robert D. Benford. 1986. "Frame Alignment Processes, Micromobilization, and Movement Participation." *American Sociological Review* 51:464–81.

Snow, David A. and Robert D. Benford. 1988. "Ideology, Frame Resonance, and Participant Mobilization." *International Social Movement Research* 1:197–217.

———. 1992. "Master Frames and Cycles of Protest." Pp. 133–55 in *Frontiers in Social Movement Theory*, edited by Aldon D. Morris and Carol McClurg Muller. New Haven, Connecticut: Yale University Press.

Sobel, Mechal. 1979. *Trabelin' On: The Slave Journey to an Afro-Baptist Faith*. Westport, Connecticut: Greenwood Press.

St. Hilaire, Joseph M. 1974. "The Negro Delegates in the Arkansas Constitutional Convention of 1868: A Group Profile." *Arkansas Historical Quarterly* 33:38–69.

Staggenborg, Suzanne. 1998. "Social Movement Communities and Cycles of Protest: The Emergence and Maintenance of a Local Women's Movement." *Social Problems* 45:180–204.

Stampp, Kenneth M. 1965. *The Era of Reconstruction, 1865–1877*. New York: Knopf.

———. 1989. *The Peculiar Institution: Slavery in the Ante-Bellum South*. New York: Knopf.

Staples, Thomas S. 1923. *Reconstruction in Arkansas, 1862–1874*. New York: Columbia University Press.

Stark, Rodney and William S. Bainbridge. 1980. "Networks of Faith." *American Journal of Sociology* 86:1376–95.

Swidler, Ann. 1986. "Culture in Action: Symbols and Strategies." *American Sociological Review* 51:273–86.

Tarrow, Sidney. 1994. *Power in Movement: Social Movements and Contentious Politics*. New York: Cambridge University Press.

Taylor, Orville. 1979. "Baptists and Slavery in Arkansas: Relationships and Attitudes." *Arkansas Historical Quarterly* 38:199–226.

Taylor, Verta, and Nancy E. Whittier. 1992. "Collective Identity in Social Movement Communities: Lesbian Feminist Mobilization." Pp. 104–29 in *Frontiers in Social Movement Theory*, edited by Aldon D. Morris and Carol McClurg Mueller. New Haven: Yale University Press.

———. 1995. "Analytical Approaches to Social Movement Culture: The Culture of the Women's Movement." Pp. 163–87 in *Social Movements and Culture*, edited by Hank Johnston and Bert Klandermans. Minneapolis: University of Minnesota Press.

Tilly, Charles. 1978. *From Mobilization to Revolution*. Reading, Massachusetts: Addison-Wesley.

Tucker, Robert C. 1978. *The Marx-Engels Reader*. New York: Norton.

Turner, Ralph H. and Louis M. Killian. 1972. *Collective Behavior*, 2nd ed. Englewood Cliffs, New Jersey: Prentice Hall.

Turner, William C. 1989. "Black Evangelicalism: Theology, Politics, and Race." *The Journal of Religious Thought* 45:40–56.

Tyms, James D. 1965. *The Rise of Religious Education Among Negro Baptists*. New York: Exposition Press.

Venkataramani, M. S. 1960. "Norman Thomas, Arkansas Sharecroppers, and the Roosevelt Agricultural Policies, 1933–1937." *Mississippi Valley Historical Review* 47:225–46.

Walker, Clarence Earl. 1982. *A Rock in a Weary Land: The African Methodist Episcopal Church during the Civil War and Reconstruction*. Baton Rouge: Louisiana State Press.

————. 1985. "The A. M. E. Church and Reconstruction." *Negro History Bulletin* 48:10–12.

Walker, Wyatt T. 1982. "The Black Church was Born in Response to Slavery." *Crisis* 89:26–27.

Walls, William. 1974. *The African Methodist Episcopal Zion Church: Reality of the Black Church.* Charlotte, North Carolina: A.M.E. Zion Publishing.

Washington, James Melvin. 1986. *Frustrated Fellowship: The Black Baptist Quest for Social Order.* Macon, Georgia: Mercer University Press.

Waskow, Arthur I. 1966. *From Race Riot to Sit-In, 1919 and the 1960s.* Garden City, New York: Doubleday.

Weisenfeld, Judith. 1997. *African American Women and Christian Activism: New York's Black YWCA, 1905–1945.* Cambridge, Massachusetts: Harvard University Press.

West, Cornel. 1982. *Prophesy Deliverance!: An Afro-American Revolutionary Chrisitanity.* Philadelphia: Westminster Press.

Whittier, Nancy. 1995. *Feminist Generations: The Persistence of the Radical Women's Movement.* Philadelphia: Temple University Press.

Williams, C. Fred, S. Charles Bolton, Carl H. Moneyhon, and LeRoy T. Williams editors. 1984. *A Documentary History of Arkansas.* Fayetteville: University of Arkansas Press.

Williams, LeRoy T. 1986. "'Tell'Em We're Risin', 1900–1954." Pp. 28–39 in *Persistence of the Spirit: The Black Experience in Arkansas*, edited by Tom Baskett, Jr. Little Rock: Resource Center, Arkansas Endowment for the Humanities.

Wilmore, Gayraud S. 1994. *Black Religion and Black Radicalism: An Interpretation of the Religious History of African Americans.* Maryknoll, New York: Orbis Books.

Woodson, Carter Godwin. 1972. *The History of the Negro Church.* Washington, D. C.: Associated Publishers.

X, Malcolm. 1964. *The Ballot or The Bullet.* Speech presented at the Shrine of the Black Madonna Church in Detroit, Michigan. Cited from cassette tape.

Yard, Alexander. 1988. " 'They Don't Regard My Rights at All': Arkansas Farm Workers, Economic Modernization, and the Southern Tenant Farmers Union." *Arkansas Historical Quarterly* 47:201–29.

Young, Henry J. 1977. *Major Black Religious Leaders: 1775–1940.* Nashville: Abingdon Press.

Newspaper articles

Allbright, Charles. 1956. "Leaders of NAACP Declare They Want Desegregation Now." *Arkansas Gazette* May 5:1A.

Bosson, Roy. 1953. "Paces Dixie In Drive for Equalizing." *Arkansas Democrat* May 31.

1955. "Broad Rejects Plea for 1955 Integration." *Arkansas Gazette* Aug. 5.

Cather, Effa Laura. 1949. "U.S. Court Rules in De Witt Suit." *Arkansas Gazette* Jul. 8.

1954. "Cherry Says Arkansas To Meet Requirements." *Arkansas Democrat* May 18:1A-2A.

Childress, Carl. 1956. "Negroes Try to Enroll In City Schools; Rebuffed." *Arkansas Democrat* Jan. 23:1A.

1919. "Condemned Negroes Are Victims of Ignorance." *Arkansas Gazette* Nov. 23:1.

Craig, Ted. 1956. "Little Rock Negroes File Suit to Compel Prompt Integration." *Arkansas Gazette* Feb. 9:1A.

1949. "De Witt Ordered to Put Negro Schools on Par With Those for Whites." *Arkansas Gazette* Jul. 9.

Douthit, George. 1956. "State Will Resist Sudden, Complete Integration." *Arkansas Democrat*. Feb. 26:1A.

Editorial. 1949. "Sobering School Decision." *Arkansas Gazette* Jul. 10.

1952. "First Negro at U of A Starts Steady Influx." *Arkansas Democrat* Aug. 26.

Frick, Margaret. 1956. "U.S. court Asked to End School Desegregation Here." *Arkansas Democrat* Feb. 8:1A.

———. 1956. "Little Rock's 'Gradual' Integration Approved." *Arkansas Democrat* Aug. 28:1A.

1965. "Gould Negroes Demonstrate in Little Rock to Protest School Desegregation Plan." *Arkansas Gazette* Sep. 14.

Harris, Sam G. 1955. "Schools Told to Act Promptly In 'Spirit' of Court Ruling." *Arkansas Gazette* Aug. 4.

1955. "Hoxie Decides to Integrate All Its Schools." *Arkansas Gazette* Jun. 26.

1955. "Hoxie Injunction Defendants File Reply Denying All Charges." *Arkansas Gazette* Nov. 13.

1955. "Hoxie Negroes, Whites to Go Back to School Together Today." *Arkansas Gazette* Oct. 23.

1955. "Hoxie Proves Democracy Can Work in Arkansas." *Arkansas State Press* Jul. 15, (11) 15.

1955. "Integration Decision Applies to Colleges And UA, Gentry Says." *Arkansas Gazette* Aug. 4:1A.

1952. "Inequalities in White, Negro Schools Charged." *Arkansas Democrat* Feb 3.

Judge, A. M. 1958. "Hoodlums Force Negroes Out at Van Buren School." *Arkansas State Press* Sep. 12.

1955. "More School Aid Seen as Brake On Integration." *Arkansas Gazette* Feb. 17.

1949. "Negro Arrives on Campus To Enter U. of A." *Arkansas Gazette* Feb. 3.

1967. "Negro Center at Gould Burns to the Ground." *Arkansas Gazette*, Jan. 3:1B2.

1956. "Negro Hits Segregation Proposal." *Arkansas Democrat* Mar. 23.

1956. "Negroes Ask Faubus to Uphold Law." *Arkansas Democrat* Feb. 24.

1949. "Negroes Ask to Enter Children in White School." *Arkansas Gazette* Mar. 17.

1955. "Negroes Enroll in Colleges." *Arkansas Gazette* Sep. 16:1A.

1956. "New Policy is Pursued by NAACP." *Arkansas Democrat* Jan. 29.

1955. "Pupils Mingle at Hoxie School As Racial Barriers Come Down." *Arkansas Gazette* Jul.12.

Sutton, Ozell. 1955. "State NAACP Sets Fall Goal On Integration." *Arkansas Democrat* Jun. 12:1A.

1955. "Van Buren Integration Suit Filed." *Arkansas Gazette* Oct. 29:7B.

1955. "When Comes Integration? (Answer Next Week)." *Arkansas Gazette* Jul. 29

INDEX